What Every Man Needs

A Young Soldier's Thoughts on Christian Manhood

Ryan Kraeger

Dear Diana,

I was 22 years old when I started writing this, 25 when I finished it. In that time I did a lot of growing ~~up~~ and changing so it is almost as if the earlier chapters were written by a totally different person than the later ones. Some parts of it make me shudder (ツ I wrote that?) but it was the younger Ryan. That me was also necessary and much loved by God.

ISBN: 978-0-9836543-0-8

For my younger brothers, especially Matthew and Brett.
The world isn't ready for you, but I offer you this book in the
hope that it will help you to be ready for the world.

Your brother, Ryan

———

"Holiness is for men too...
For very rugged men."

Fr. Matthew Pawlikowski, LTC(Ch) U. S. Army

CONTENTS

ACKNOWLEDGEMENTS

There are too many people whose wisdom and experience and prayer have gone into the making of this book for me to thank them all. Of course first thanks goes to my parents, to my father for showing me how to be a man, and to my mother for showing me why. I owe an almost equal debt of gratitude to Father Morelle, for teaching me to think and shaping everything I've learned about God. He truly is the answer to anyone who doesn't understand why priests are called Father.

More immediately connected with this book, I need to thank all those who helped proofread early editions: Bernie and Joel, who are responsible between them for about fifty percent of the scriptures quoted; Marianna and Caiti, for sharing the point of view of Godly women on what I was writing; and my brother Adam, for his encouragement and praise.

There are others to be thanked, but I will do that elsewhere; if not here, then, God willing, in Heaven, where all manhood will be made complete.

1

PART I

1. To Be A Man

As I sit here at my desk, I am thinking of what it means to be a man. It is a Sunday afternoon and I've been to church. I was going to go to the firing range and shoot, but the Super Bowl is today so they closed the range. So now I am sitting and thinking. I'm not sure what I intend to get out of writing this book. Some of these chapters are mostly written already and were originally posted on my blog. Of course I'll have to modify them to fit in with the rest of the chapters, but that won't change them significantly. What of the ones that I haven't written yet? If they are anything like my blog posts then I will write them for the purpose of better understanding what I've learned in the last few years. All of these contain lessons I wish someone had taught me when I was fifteen, but which I have had to learn since then. Now, just a little on the underside of twenty-five, I'm thinking over these lessons and trying to put them into words. I understand everything better when I can put it into words.

Of course when I was fifteen I was quite well taught and prepared for life. I was raised with great advantages, but I was not yet as old as I am now. Today I am not as old as I will be in ten years. If I had thought of all of this at fifteen, I would have had to learn other things later, and those other lessons would be the ones I would be writing about now. Perhaps I wouldn't even have been able to understand most of these very well at fifteen. So many things in this world we don't learn properly until we learn them the hard way. And after all, what is twenty-five years of age, really? It's not that old at all. I have only begun to learn, and every lesson learned has been the starting point for new lessons. I can only pray that somehow the Holy Spirit will be active in the thinking and praying that go into this book for "I am young in years, and you are old; that is why I was fearful, not daring to tell you what I know. I thought, 'Age should speak; advanced years should teach wisdom.' But it is the spirit in a man, the breath of the Almighty, that gives him understanding." Job 32:6-8. If God speaks through me, if I am His pencil, then no matter how young I am, I will speak wisdom. If He does not, or if I speak only for myself, I shall be speaking nonsense when I'm seventy.

I guess if I could sum up all of the questions in this book, they all come back to one theme: How to be a man. That, all in all, is what I've had to learn in the last ten years, but my learning is not complete. Actually, the most that can be said of the last ten years is that I've learned to ask that question, what does it mean to be a man? Too many men never ask that question. (Incidentally, if you're expecting answers, look somewhere else. All I'm really giving you are the questions.) When I was fifteen it would never have occurred to me. Now I realize that it is almost the point of my existence to answer that question. My whole purpose on earth is to be God's man. Now that I have learned that on some level, I can begin actually to live it, and in living it, I will go deeper, hopefully into experiencing God's Fatherhood.

When I was a teenager I spent most of my time wondering what it meant to be a warrior. I've served in the Army since I was seventeen, and I'm slowly learning the Way of the Warrior and all that it entails. But eventually I realized that warriorhood, like all masculine vocations is built on a foundation of true Godly manhood, so before I could understand what it meant to be a warrior, I first had to ask what it meant to be a man, and now I am asking that. Eventually I will hit bedrock, when I come to understand and live the full implication of God's Fatherhood, and my adopted sonship, of my divine adoption as a son of God Himself. It may seem like a rather long way around, but unfortunately for me there don't seem to be any shortcuts. I just have to take the long way. I don't know whether you will have to take the same long way I took, (it certainly won't be exactly the same in any event). Sometimes you will take shortcuts that I missed; other times you will take the long way that will prove my path to have been a shortcut. I cannot know what your path will entail; I can only describe some of the sights I have seen on my own path. Because I have not reached the goal, I have no advantage over you in any material respect, other than that I started walking a little bit earlier, and I've been taking notes.

"I write to you, young men, because you are strong, and the word of God lives in you, and you have overcome the evil one." 1 John 2:14

2. The Body of a Man

In searching through the world for a definition or model of manhood, I have found that the only model presented is a physical one. Men and manhood are defined in physical terms. It is true that certain elements in society have tried to put forward sensitivity, vulnerability and empathy as "a valid understanding of masculine values," in an effort to de-emphasize the tough guy image, but it is an exercise in futility. Those people have, unfortunately, only sacrificed manhood on the altar of personhood, and have not solved the problem of the tough guy image. For all the sensitive new age attempts at metro-sexuality the world is smarter. People go on much as they always have, admiring warriors, pioneers, workers and macho men. Only now our warriors are UFC (Ultimate Fighting Championship) fighters, not the cops working double overtime to keep the streets safe. Our pioneers are movie makers who push the envelope of immorality in the name of "tolerance" and never give a thought to what they are doing to our society. Our workers are CEO's and Wall Street millionaires making millions of dollars for doing almost nothing worthwhile, not farmers, truckers, fishermen and carpenters, doing a full day's work for little pay. Our macho men are all movie stars, sports icons and gangster rap artists. Instead of manhood being helped by the emphasis on sensitivity and empathy, it has been hurt. People wasted a little time trying to admire the sensitive new-age guys but gave up when they found so little to admire. Half our society is composed of wimpy guys, the other half is made up of jerks, and people are as much impressed by rippling abdominals and biceps with veins standing out on them as ever. Instead of worrying about how to keep people from confusing masculinity with machismo and physique, let's take a moment to see what can be learned from them.

Everything in creation is a symbol of deeper, more spiritual realities. Of course, God created everything physical for our sake, since He really cares about us physical creatures, so much that He became one of us and died for us. However, He also created it to point back to Himself. Both the macro creation and the micro creation, the universe and the amoebas, the galaxies and the atoms, and the deep and all but immutable laws of that universe are all symbols of God. So it is with the body. The male body is a symbol of a masculine soul, which in turn is a symbol of God Himself. The female body, likewise, is a symbol of the feminine soul which animates it, and in turn that soul is also a symbol of other realities that pertain to God. I don't have the time here to go into an overview of Theology of the Body yet (it will come later), but I encourage you to look into it.[1] For now, I'm just interested in presenting a slightly deeper view of the meaning of the male body, and a way of understanding popular stereotypes as to what constitutes the ideal body for a man.

Now, when you think of what the ideal male body would look like, what comes to mind? Broad shoulders, solid muscle, a six pack? Not necessarily hulked out but definitely some biceps and some development in the chest and shoulders? Of course these things are visually appealing to the opposite sex, but the question is not what women like (it is far too varied to be answered) but why they like it. Why do women like to see men who look strong?

It is because strength is the soul of manhood, and the body is the symbol of that strength ("The glory of young men is their strength," Proverbs 20:29). This is the principle which should direct all of your treatment of your body. A man's body is the symbol of manhood, and as such it should be treated with respect and care. However, his body is not his manhood and so it should not be overly glorified. Every man should do some work to keep his body in the condition which best reflects the dignity and strength of true manhood, but should remember that he is not working to make his body look like anything in particular. Looks should never be a consideration. He is working towards the reality of which ripped abs are only a transient symbol. It is even better if you work at a job that keeps you in shape. My father is probably one of the most muscular men of his age and size that I've ever known, but he never lifted weights. He worked. He split wood, dug ditches, threw and stacked bales of hay, pounded posts, and did things that needed to be done, things which benefited his wife and children. That's why my dad is in many ways my model of true physical strength at its finest. He never worked for physique. He worked to serve and the physique came from that. Even though he is in his fifties, he is still 150 pounds of tough, wiry, well-defined muscle.

I think that is the ideal, to be so concerned about service that you forget about developing strength in your anxiety to serve. Strength would develop on its own because it would be needed. Physique would follow and the outside look would accurately reflect the inner reality of true, loving service. The body would be speaking the language of truth, for that is what the body of a powerfully built man proclaims. "I am strong enough to serve, and to love with all my heart, because God has made me so." Unfortunately today we live in a world where real physical work is not as necessary as it once was. Most men go through their whole lives without needing to do anything more strenuous than mow the lawn with a gas-powered push mower. Few of us have any appreciation for the body's value as a symbol of spiritual realities, and so our bodies seldom match our characters. The best-hearted men are so busy living their lives that they seldom take the time to stay in shape. Other men turn to working out because they are obsessed with the shell and forget the heart. The good men often look weak, and too often that physical weakness can cripple us spiritually in ways we do not understand. The men who look strong are often vain and self-centered. I have known too many guys who were beasts at the gym, but who were useless everywhere else. When the time came actually to use that great strength, their muscles were just the cover for weak souls, and they would not serve. Their bodies made a boast their hearts wouldn't keep.

I want to get past all that. I want men to recapture a true appreciation for what the body is and for what it isn't and to treat it as such. As my father showed me, strength has only one purpose and that purpose is service. There is nothing wrong with weight lifting, as long as its purpose is service and not vanity. It is not the means we use to stay in shape, it is the reason why that is important. That is the symbolism of the body of a man, built as it is for strength, mobility, resilience, and damage resistance, relative to a woman's body. And this is the purpose of not only man's body in general, but men's bodies in particular. Are you tall? Reach that top shelf for the people who are short. Are you thick and powerful? Lift for those who are weaker. Are you fast? Speed to the service of those around you. Are your fingers lean and clever? Use them to make good things that people really need, not pointless products that exist only to make their producers rich. Are your hands thick, hard and callused? Carry the burdens that would tear softer hands. The symbolism of the body applies to everything we do to it and everything we do with it. It is a tool to be used in the service of others, even to be used up in the service of others. To do that it must be strong, but it must be strong because the soul that animates it is strong. A strong body with a weak soul is little better than an animal. The strength of a man's body should flow from his soul, as a woman's true beauty flows from the beauty of her soul. I'm sure we've all met women who might not have been considered beauties in the eyes of the world, but who could smile one smile and let forth such a flood of light that the whole world seemed brighter. And I'm sure we've all met the opposite, or at least seen them on TV, the women who look like goddesses but who have empty heads and emptier hearts and make the world seem emptier by their presence.

The philosophy of working out comes from the idea of integrity, which means that everything about you is infused with a single purpose. Mind, body and soul should all exist as one single integrated being, a man, born to care for and protect those around him, born to give of himself, even to lay down his life for the ones around him. Let your body be the true reflection of your soul. If you are blessed with a powerful frame, strengthen your soul to match it and surpass it, in order to take control of that body for God's purposes. If your soul is strong and upright, then let your body reflect that to those around you, to the best of your ability. Then, regardless of whether or not your abs are ever visible from the outside, you will have the body of a man.

Therefore, I urge you, brothers, in view of God's mercy, to offer your bodies as living sacrifices, holy and pleasing to God—this is your spiritual act of worship. Romans 12:1

3. Character and Leg Muscles

I was ruckmarching with a friend once, and as we marched we were talking about the benefits of rucking. Ruckmarching, or rucking, is the art of walking long distances in as short a time as possible with a rucksack or backpack containing a heavy load on your back. I commented that ruckmarching builds character, and then added as an afterthought, "and leg muscles" since it certainly does develop some serious leg muscles. My friend asked, "But which is more important." Of course I answered that character was more important, as it certainly is in life, although others might suggest that it depends on what you want them for. If you want someone who can walk thirty miles with fifty pounds on his back in one day, then you might think that leg muscles would help more than character.

I'm not so sure. I might have thought that way, except that I've seen some of the physically strongest guys simply quitting on ruckmarches. After about twenty miles, nearly everyone's leg muscles are the same, pretty much nothing but blended jello. After that, it's all about character. Once I started seeing that, I began to see that it carries over into pretty much every aspect of physical fitness, and from there it carries over into everything we do in life. The character doesn't just show on the final event when you actually have to walk twenty-five miles, it shows on all the rucking that you do to train up for that event. I read somewhere that a man isn't judged by the intensity of his emotions, but by their duration.[2] Anyone can want to win a race, from the safety of his armchair. Anyone can want to be industrious, as he sits at the computer and plays games. Anyone can want to be a faithful husband, as he surfs the web for porn. Anyone can be in love for a few months, or a year or two, before the thrill wears off, but what about loving constantly and passionately for fifty years? Sometimes even a very weak man might want any one of these things badly enough to try for it, for a little bit, until that streak of emotional fervor burns out. He might even try exceptionally hard. He might try with great energy and vigor, but unless he tries for the long haul, it's worthless. Anyone who is not entirely sedentary can put a rucksack on his back and run 500 yards very quickly, but only those who possess a high degree of discipline and even self-sacrifice can push themselves out for twenty miles or more.

9

This is part of the philosophy that shapes my whole view on physical fitness and working out. Most Americans are somewhat concerned about fitness. In other ages this was almost a non-issue since most people did enough physical work every day to stay in shape, and food in general was healthier. Nowadays, however, most people don't have to do any physical work, and food is plentiful, addictive, and very often not healthy at all. This predisposes a large portion of the population to obesity, while Hollywood continues to place their emphasis on an almost unattainable standard of looks for both men and women. For women this means tall, skinny, almost emaciated, but still with the "right" proportion of curves. For men, think Brad Pitt from "Fight Club" or "Troy", muscular limbs and a lean, shredded torso. Our everyday lives drag us towards laziness and overindulgence, while our fantasy lives, driven by the media, don't do a thing to stop it. They just make us feel inferior when we don't look like the movies say we should.

To me, the whole thing is stupid. Why would you base anything on a standard of looks? The vast majority of Americans value fitness solely for how it makes them look. Someone who is lean and weak seems more fit than someone who is strong but has a bit of a paunch. This obsession with looks-based fitness is clean contrary to all common sense, but if there was a pill available that would make you look like that without ever having to go to the gym or do any kind of exercise, it would fly off the shelves. Most Americans would take it no matter how much it cost or what the side effects were.

I would not. It would completely negate the point of any kind of workout, which is not so much to look a certain way, as to build the ability to do things, and to build character. When it comes to weigt lifting, I am what they call a "slow gainer", meaning my strength level doesn't go up very fast, but after six years of steady, disciplined effort, I am quite strong. I am not built to be a runner, but after running for the past eight years, I've gotten quite fast. I still don't look like a Spartan, and I never will, but I'm good for a full day of manual labor or combat training. I'm good for many full days of manual labor. I'm good for the rest of my life, not simply because I've developed myself physically, but because of the discipline I've developed through forcing myself to train six days a week, usually twice a day for years. That discipline is the biggest benefit, because it has given me the firm belief that whatever I need to do, God will give me the strength to do it. (I work out twice a day because my job requires a higher level of physical fitness than most people need. It is not a standard I recommend to everyone. Once a day is more than sufficient for most people).

So although my ruckmarching friend was probably speaking about the larger sphere of life in general, the principle holds true even in physical endeavors. Muscles are less important than character in life, at least partially because most of the problems we face aren't solved by muscle anymore, but even more so because the spirit determines the use made of those muscles. Muscles are less important than character even in physical endeavors. In building bridges in Afghanistan it wasn't the guys who put up the most weight in the gym who worked the hardest. It was the guys who had grown up working odd jobs to support their families, or who had been given a work ethic by their fathers. In hand to hand combat training it isn't the biggest and strongest guy who wins. It is the one with the drive and attitude who will not give up no matter how tired or outmatched he gets.

I spoke before about physical training as a means to care for the body that God has given each of us, to make it better reflect the spirit that He has given us, but there is another truth here as well. We also build our spirits when we build our bodies, if we do it right. We are not building our spirits to be good for short, intense bursts of activity, and then worthless for everything else. You don't grow strong by three weeks of intense boot camp. You don't become strong in nine weeks of Army Basic Training. You don't get strong in a seminar, or a thirty day results guaranteed fitness program. Thirty minutes a day, three days a week, for six weeks will not get you looking like the guy on the commercial. Thirty minutes a day, five days a week, for six years? Now you might be getting somewhere. Six years is enough time really to get into the habit of training. It is the training mindset that you want. That is the goal, not just the physical fitness. It is the strength of character that determines to be in it for the long haul, to keep doing what needs to be done, every day, no matter what, not because you want to, but because it needs to be done.

Now, I'm using exercise as an example, but exercise is only the beginning, so much so that if this mindset stops after your morning run it will have been worse than useless. Everything ought to be done this way. For instance, there are people in your life that you should pray for every day: your parents, obviously, and your siblings. Your future wife is also on that list. These prayers will not always be a joy, so they must be a discipline. What about the Bible? What good will it do you to read the whole Bible through from cover to cover in a week, and then never open it again for a year? You should read a little every day, come rain or shine, stateside or deployed. I have read the Bible for comfort and encouragement in all the worst places the Army has put me, or remembered passages from it if I couldn't read it, and it has never failed me yet. My only regret is that I haven't read it more. A little bit, a few chapters or even a few verses if read prayerfully, every day is a bare minimum requirement in my book for someone who would call himself a Christian man. In the Old Testament, when God first delivered the Law to Moses He issued this command, "Hear, O Israel: The Lord our God, the Lord is one. Love the Lord your God with all your heart and with all your soul and with all your strength. These commandments that I give you today are to be upon your hearts. Impress them on your children. Talk about them when you sit at home and when you walk along the road, when you lie down and when you get up. Tie them as symbols on your hands and bind them on your foreheads. Write them on the doorframes of your houses and on your gates." Deuteronomy 6:4-9. The command is reiterated in Deuteronomy 11:18-22, warning that if the Word of God is not made the focus of our lives, it is only a matter of time until the world and the devil encroach upon our hearts and steal them from God. Studying scripture is not optional.[3] Four chapters a day will get you through the whole Bible in a little under a year. Read it through, and then start over again the very next day. Whatever you continually study and meditate on, you will know. If you can take a class, or study the Bible in college, so much the better, but never neglect that daily, prayerful Bible reading. Read the Bible, talk to your friends about the Bible, seek out friends who read the Bible, read books about the Bible, but most of all read the Bible every single day that you might be "the man of God... thoroughly equipped for every good work." 2 Timothy 3:17. If you want to be equipped to serve, (I said in the previous chapter that service was the point of manhood), you must be marinated in the Word of God.

What I'm trying to illustrate here is a facet of character that I have been struggling to hone for a few years now, with slow success if any. A warrior never has the luxury of saying "I have arrived. I am now fully trained." There is always more to learn. He can always get a little stronger, or a little smarter, or a little better in some way. A warrior never has the luxury of complacency because that leads to death. The moment you think you know it all Murphy's Law has a way of showing you something new. A warrior never ceases to train throughout his whole life. This illustrates the attitude we need to have. You can't look at yourself in the mirror and say, "Well, if I lose ten more pounds, and put another inch on my biceps, I'll be satisfied." You won't be, because your goal is all wrong. It is an illusion. Instead your goal should be to strengthen your body to be able to serve. You want to get as much done as you can in the short time you have to train every day. You only have twenty or thirty minutes, so put everything you have into those twenty or thirty minutes, and then go on about your day. The next day do it again, and the next day, and the next day, and the next and so on. You need to know the Word of God, but you only have a few minutes a day. So read as deeply as you can in those few minutes, and then go on about your day. Tomorrow you will do it again, and tomorrow, and the next day. Pray today, and then tomorrow pray again and then the next day, and so on. There is no end. It is not something you try, it is something you do, or do not. It is not a goal; it is a way of life, aimed at something beyond this life. We are practicing for the Joy of Heaven, which we are nowhere near strong enough even to imagine yet.

You'd think, having spent the last few years in the Army, that life would be pretty exciting for me? Wrong. There have been exciting moments, and I've done my share of strange and insane jobs, but those are still just exceptions to the daily grind. The truth of the matter is that even in the Army, just like nearly anywhere else, life is best discharged by doing the same things, or the same sort of things, over and over and over again, every day, for years on end. Some changes will come, but the character of the man remains constant, if it is fixed in God as it should be.

"Even youths shall faint and be weary, and young men shall fall exhausted; but they who wait for the Lord shall renew their strength. They shall mount up with wings like eagles, they shall run and not grow weary, they shall march and not grow faint."
Isaiah 41:30-31

4. Teach a Boy to Fight

This was a letter I wrote to my younger brother when he started taking karate last year.

"So Mack, we've agreed on the terms, and you'll be doing karate this year. Just to remind you, the terms were:

1) On non class days, excluding Sunday, you are to spend a minimum of a half hour either working forms or working the heavy bag. I would suggest maxing out your time on the heavy bag, as you do a lot of form work in class, but make sure you know your katas too.

2) Your other schoolwork will remain on par. That shouldn't be a problem, I trust.

However, that really doesn't even scratch the surface, and since you've known me for a while, you probably know by now that I never do anything without a reason. I want you to know my reasons for putting you through karate class. It really has very little to do with physical fitness, self-defense, socialization or any of those other things. I want much more for you than that, and anyway, you can get all three of those in other ways, much more efficiently. I could teach you more real self defense in an hour than you'll probably learn in your first year in karate. I want you to learn something far more important.

There is a saying, "Give a man a fish, you feed him for a day; teach a man to fish, you feed him for life." I adapt that saying to this situation like this: "Win a boy's fight, and you protect him for a day; teach a boy to fight, and you protect him for life." As I said, though, I'm not terribly interested in you winning fights. I am intensely interested in you honing your warrior spirit. Sounds corny? Read on, it gets worse. I'll have you wearing full armor before we're done.

You remember when all the boys were home there was always some form of competition going on? Wooden swords, quarter staves, wrestling, even chess games, you know we were always competing. We are a pretty peaceful lot, we seldom had any conflict, but competition was a constant for us. I'm not sure our mother ever really understood it. You're too young to remember the days when she forbade it. By the time you came along I think she more or less figured out it was an exercise in futility. Anything we picked up became a weapon, every handshake became a "Quiet Man" moment, and every hug became a wrestling match. While I understand her (and every mother's) inherent objection to so much testosterone, stemming as it does from the desire to raise gentle men rather than thugs, I disagree that forbidding physical competition is the way to go. Rather, I think it should be encouraged, taught and mentored by older boys and especially men. Through no fault of my own, I have been thrust into the estate of manhood, so I'm trying to do this for you, and in the process using you as a guinea pig. Don't pretend you aren't a willing test subject.

Testosterone is God's invention. He created it and pronounced it very good. It is a clue to our destiny, yours and mine, as men. We were created to struggle. That competitive reality of our character as men is not deeper than our gentleness (for we were created for that too) but it is the essential road most of us must pass through to achieve real gentleness. So let's start with the purpose for conflict, which is to uphold the right, to protect the weak. Remember that movie "Dragonheart?" "The knight is sworn to valor. His heart knows only virtue. His blade defends the helpless. His might upholds the weak. His word speaks only truth. His wroth undoes the wicked."

These words should be a clarion call to every man, whether he wears armor or not. I happen to wear armor. God only knows what you will wear, but the training is the same, for your vocation is the same. You were created to be strong and to give that strength unstintingly for others. You have to pursue strength, but it has to be true strength, which means it must cost you something. Strength of body might cost you getting up early in the morning to run or do push-ups, situps and pullups before school. Strength of mind costs hours of study. Strength of feeling is especially costly to us men, and you might be too young for it yet. For now, just know that while heartbreak should not be invited, neither should it be feared. Some things are so beautiful that if they don't break your heart then it shows real weakness. If you don't believe me, listen to Samuel Barber's "Agnus Dei." Moral strength, by far the most important, will cost you "not less than everything." I'm afraid that in this world there are only two ultimate choices. Either your heart will know only virtue, or your heart will know only evil. You must surrender completely to Christ, or you will burn in hell. In the end there is no other choice.

What does this have to do with karate? Well, there is another kind of strength that I call Strength of Spirit. (I also call it "Holy Stubbornness"). It is an attitude that must become a part of you, and as much as it is already a part of you, it must be strengthened, honed and disciplined. It is, quite simply, an inability to accept defeat. Defeat is inevitable. If you choose to fight, you will be defeated, which is why Strength of Spirit is so important. When you are beaten, you must not accept it. The moment you get knocked down, you must leap to your feet. If you cannot leap, then just get up. If you can't even do that, then crawl to your feet. When you cannot even do that, then you'll be in a position to learn the most valuable lesson you can ever learn, that when you are at your weakest, God is at His strongest in you, if you'll let Him. Hence karate. I know Shihan's methods, and I know it isn't a combat oriented school. You won't take a punch to the face hard enough to loosen any teeth. You probably won't get choked into unconsciousness. You won't break a bone unless you do something stupid. But there will be evenings when you will think to yourself, "I don't want to train tonight. I don't feel like it." Not fear, just laziness. There will be Saturday nights when you will suddenly realize, "I haven't done my half hour work yet." The temptation will be to let it go, just this once, because it's ten o clock at night. And on sparring nights you might just feel a reluctance to get in there. You won't get physically beaten down, but it can still be intimidating to go up against someone faster and sharper than you, who is going to score on you. The fights that you know you can't win are often the ones that most need to be fought.

I don't think any man can really learn to be strong spiritually unless he learns to be strong physically. To put it another way, we learn spiritual strength in physical ways. Mothers don't understand this. Sisters don't understand this. They are so concerned with wanting us to be gentle that they don't realize that gentleness requires, not just strength, but consummate strength. Asking a man to be gentle when he can't even face a sparring session is a lot like asking him to lift a car when he can't even do a pushup. Don't get it yet, Mack? Don't worry, I will explain.

Gentleness for men involves a lot more than not hurting people. That's a negative thing, virtue is always a positive thing. Gentleness is even more than being nice to people. Gentleness means being good to people and that takes strength. It is nice to hold the door for your sister when you happen to be going the same way. It is good to go out of

16

your way to hold the door for her. It is nice to carry groceries for your mother when you're getting out of the Durango anyway. It is good to pause what you're doing and come in from the shop to do it. Do you see what I am getting at? Any thug can knock someone on the head who looks at his girl in the wrong way. Can you take someone to task for talking to his own girl in an inappropriate manner? A tough man can work all day to support his family, and assume that they will know automatically that he loves them because of it. Only a strong man will make it his mission day after day after day for years on end to tell them so. Do you see now how gentleness requires greater strength? If you can't even discipline yourself to face another student or even a sensei in a point sparring match, then how can you expect yourself to speak the truth in love? (Ephesians 4:14-15). If you can't discipline yourself to stick to an agreement, and train regularly for half an hour every day, rain or shine, fresh or tired, etc. how do you think you'll manage the much harder task of loving troublesome children for hours every day, rain or shine, fresh or tired, sick or healthy, rich or poor, etc.?

So that discipline is the first thing I want you to learn. The second is the fighting spirit. Don't worry about fighting technique. The technique you will learn there isn't really oriented to street fighting, unless you can get very, very good at it. I'll show you some more generally useful street fighting techniques when I'm on leave. But what I do want you to worry about is aggressiveness. I want you to spar aggressively, without sparring stupidly (but it is better to be brave and imprudent than timid and smart. Experience can be learned, spirit not so much.) Don't be afraid of taking hits. Try to fight the best students there, no matter how many belt ranks they have over you. If you find yourself shrinking back, kiai as loudly as you can and throw a technique. Any technique. Crowd them. Attack them. Block in passing only, which means you are blocking only so that you can get in to punch, back fist or kick. Soon you'll be able to pick out the weak sparrers, the ones that you can just overawe and dominate. Don't spar with them, and if you have to, tone it down and allow them to get in their training, but concentrate on fighting only the guys who you know are going to beat you. Do this especially if you don't feel like it. Then after you are done with Karate on sparring nights, see if you can stop at Saint Joe's and make a visit before the Blessed Sacrament. This will teach you two things:

1) You will find that aggression and fighting spirit will often carry the day against cautious technique. You will therefore become prodigal with your body parts.

2) You will learn that aggression can be controlled, and that it must be controlled. Turn it on in class as high as Shihan lets you, and turn it off as you walk out the door. Try deep, slow breaths to bring your heart rate down.

Aggression is a tool that will allow you to protect the weak. Every woman you know, every girl, every child, is under attack right now. At this moment. You haven't been around as much as I have, but I assure you, Satan is viciously attacking women and children. He is more subtle with men, he doesn't want us to wake up and fight, but against women, and especially young girls he is brutal. He attacks with things that you and I either never have to deal with, or see only in a much tamer form: horrible depression, irrational anxieties, crippling loneliness, body image issues, and many other things. He tries to make them believe that they are ugly, just like he tries to trick us into thinking we are weak. Your most important mission as a man is to protect those women that God puts in your life. Physically of course, but physical danger is not nearly as pressing or dangerous as this spiritual danger. Prayer and chivalry are your great weapons, and when you start using them you make yourself a target. You invite attack from the devil for interfering with his plans. This is as it should be. Your fighting spirit that you train in the dojo should tell you that this is precisely what you want. Let him attack you. You are nothing, but Jesus in you is everything, and you can take whatever Satan wants to dish out. Better he attacks us, the sentries, the warriors, the dunedain, rather than those we care about.

This is very much deeper than physical fitness, self-defense and socialization. This is what I want you to learn from karate. If you can keep this in mind in your training, well, you'll meet a lot of spiritual resistance when it's time to train (trust me on that one) but you will come out a better man.

I love you, brother. I'm proud of you. You are becoming a man after God's own heart.

"Everyone who competes in the games goes into strict training.
They do it to get a crown that will not last; but we do it to get a

18

crown that will last forever. Therefore I do not run like a man running aimlessly; I do not fight like a man beating the air. No, I discipline my body and make it my slave so that after I have preached to others, I myself will not be disqualified for the prize."
1 Corinthians 9:25-27

5. Not a Tame Lion

One of the greatest lines in English Literature comes from C. S. Lewis (actually a lot of the greatest lines in English literature come from him) in his children's book The Lion the Witch and the Wardrobe. Mr. Beaver is telling the four children about the Great Lion, Aslan, and one of the girls asks, "I should be afraid meeting a lion. Is he safe?"

"Safe!" cried Mr. Beaver. "...Who said anything about safe? 'Course he isn't safe. But he's good. He's the King, I tell you."

That, right there in a sentence, is the epitome of manhood. Just as the character of Aslan was patterned after the God-Man Jesus the Christ, so our lives should be.

I recently stumbled across the motto, "What Would Tyler Durden do?" which caught my eye because of the obvious mockery of the popular "What Would Jesus Do," slogan. For those who don't know, Tyler Durden was the iconic anti-hero of the book and movie "Fight Club." The movie starring Brad Pitt and Edward Norton was an instant cult classic over a decade ago and to this day ninety percent of men you meet will probably know who Tyler Durden is. You still see teenage boys setting up fight clubs in their basements, and even (so I've heard) men taking legal measures to change their names to Tyler Durden.

"Fight Club" was one of those movies, such as the more recent "300", that appealed very strongly to American men, but which many Christians simply didn't see, and I can't blame them for that. It is a hideous movie, and a lot of Christians assume that its ugliness made it popular. The funny thing is that it wasn't the ugliness, but the underlying reaction against the widespread effeminate stereotype that captured the popular male imagination. Why did the movie and especially the character of Tyler Durden appeal so strongly to so many men? Because he is dangerous. He is a dangerous character. He breaks the rules, he does what he wants, he ignores the social conventions and he forces other men to come to terms with the emptiness in their own lives. He sneers at men who have quietly slipped into the mold of the "nice guy" and just drifted without purpose or direction, "Working jobs we hate to buy (stuff) we don't need," to quote the movie. And unlike most people who live that kind of life, vaguely realizing that spending all their time chasing after success is only emptiness in the end, he does something. He makes something happen, and even though it is something ugly and evil, others follow him.

He is the stereotypical "Bad Boy"; thus his appeal. Instead of looking for fulfillment he chose to look for emptiness and embrace futility. In one way this is more heroic, or at least more thrilling, than his "nice guy" nemesis, but in another way it is even more tragic. He gave men the go ahead to be dangerous, which is what every man should be, but he left it at that. He did not tolerate passivity or weakness, but he did not show honor or courage either. The men in the movie were not sitting in their little worlds and rotting; they were going out into other people's worlds and destroying them.

Tyler Durden appeals to men because every man at some level wants to be dangerous. We all want to be a force to be reckoned with, and when we are not, when we are weak and conscious of our weakness, we are not fully men. If you declaw a cat he is less of a cat. It ruins something vital to his catness. If you geld a stallion you have made a beast good for endless drudgery, docile and safe, but he will never have the strength and fire, and, yes, the danger, that he was meant to possess. He will not be good for fighting or racing because he is not a stallion anymore.

Some time ago America started losing fathers. Some died, most left, a few more were driven out. Boys had no men as role models, and their mothers, listening to those who say that the sexes are not different, raised them. They ended up having to learn how to be men from their mothers. Too often their mothers tried to make them women and the boys ended up with two choices. Either they could follow their mothers and try to fit into a mold that was never meant for them, or rebel against it and find their own path, without direction, guidance or control. The "Bad Boy" was born.

It is a paradox. It really comes back to women, I think. I read somewhere the one thing in the world that women fear most is a man, because a man is infinitely more dangerous than an animal. An animal will kill a human being's body, but men can hurt other people far more deeply and more permanently. If you walk through most large cities after dark, and by some chance see a woman walking by herself, you will probably see fear in her eyes. If a woman has a flat tire and I stop and get out of my car to help her, chances are I will see signs of fear. They are easy to spot if you pay attention. When someone glances around them, maintains distance and at least some semblance of a physical barrier and keeps a potential weapon in easy reach, it is not hard to read her emotions. Fear. A strong man is a threat to women. That is why pepper spray, stun guns, whistles and other forms of non-lethal defense are marketed primarily to women. Guns, knives, and tactical batons, offensive weapons, are marketed to men.

On the other hand, the only real defense against a strong evil man is a strong good man, and so the paradox arises. If you are walking down the street and you meet your hypothetical woman walking alone after dark, she will fear you, but I think most women will fear being alone as well. That is why they travel in gangs. You can see them walking along, just a group of average women in a rough situation, together for mutual support, but they will still all be afraid. Add one man that they all trust to that group, and it changes in nature. If they trust him, the fear generally vanishes but we always have to earn that trust. Wolves and sheepdogs look a lot alike.

This is the breaking point of the Tyler Durden type anti-hero. The nice guy is safe because he is weak. The bad boy is dangerous because he is strong and uncontrolled. A real man goes beyond that and becomes, if not exactly safe, at least reliable again, because he is strong and controlled. In looking for the role model for this type of man we have to come back to the strongest and best man who ever lived: Jesus.

What Would Jesus Do?

The reason men prefer to ask what Tyler Durden would do is because they misunderstand Jesus, and they misunderstand the nature of the question. That, unfortunately, is the fault of Christians. We tend to act as if asking "What Would Jesus Do" is simply asking "What is the nice thing to do?" or "What would Mister Rogers do?" Frankly, that's boring. It's downright lame. Nice is all right for little kids, who are seldom called to be more than nice, but it is not enough for men. We are not supposed to be merely nice, we are supposed to be good. 1 Corinthians 16:13-14 says, "Be on your guard; stand firm in the faith;

be men of courage; be strong. Do everything in love." Do everything in love! This is not a calling for wimps. Love means having the strength to sacrifice everything we are and have for others, grasping nothing for ourselves. It means pouring ourselves out for anyone who needs it, whether we like them or not, whether they can repay us or not, whether they deserve it or not, because our Brother, our Captain, our King, Jesus Christ, did that for us. He died for us who hated Him, who could not repay Him, and who did not deserve Him.

How many of you having heard, "Are you being good," repeated over and over by your mother and father learned from the context that it really meant, "Are you staying out of trouble?" That may be good enough for a two-year-old, but for a man? Are we so degraded that we consider ourselves "being good" merely because we are not being evil? No. We are being good only when we are being good! When we actively pursue goodness, then we are being good. When we go out of our way to help people with no hope of reward, then we are being good. When we do something for someone that costs us nothing then we are being nice. When we pay for that gift in embarrassment or sweat or tears or simply humbling ourselves to serve, then we are being good. When we decide not to be sarcastic with someone who is pushing all our buttons, then we are being nice. When we are firm, polite and charitable, and we go out of our way to show God's love to that person we are being good. When a man gives into his children's demands and lets them see a movie that he knows they should not see he is being nice. When he stands his ground and protects their innocence, he is being good.

Nice is tame. Jesus is not tame. "The Lord is a Warrior! The Lord is His name. Exodus 15:3" Asking what Jesus would do is the most dangerous question in the world because Jesus is the most dangerous man in the world. This is a man who is God! There is nothing He will not dare and do for His people. There is no sacrifice He has not made, no boundary He won't cross, no "there" He won't go. He has no respect whatsoever for anything that comes between us and our best good. He is not nice, and we would do well to fear Him with everything in us that is not already aligned with Him, because all of it is going to go. We fear Him, but we can trust Him. We can even love Him, for He loves us, and perfect love casts out all fear. In His love alone is there any hope of salvation, but there is nothing more terrifying than when you catch a glimpse of the ferocity with which He loves us.

"Behold, the Lord God will come with strong hand, and His arm shall rule for Him: behold, His reward is with Him, and His work before Him. He shall feed his flock like a shepherd: he shall gather the lambs with His arm, and carry them in His bosom, and shall gently lead those that are with young." Isaiah 40:10-11. He is powerful and yet tender; a mighty warrior and a gentle lover. The very image of manhood is contained in those two verses.

The irony is that people switch from Jesus to people like Tyler Durden because they think Jesus isn't strong enough for them. In reality, we are not strong enough for Him.

"Safe? Who said anything about safe? Of course He isn't safe. But He's good. He's the King, I tell you."

"Similarly, encourage the young men to be self-controlled. In everything set them an example by doing what is good. In your teaching show integrity, seriousness and soundness of speech that cannot be condemned, so that those who oppose you may be ashamed because they have nothing bad to say about us." Titus 2:6-8

6. Steel and Velvet

One of the most pivotal books that I read when I was a young teenager was the book Man of Velvet, Man of Steel, by Aubrey Andelin. The odd thing is that I don't remember much of what the book said. I cannot remember any of the specific points that he brought up in most of his chapters. I only remember the very first part of the book where he described the man of steel and velvet and I remember the deep chord that phrase struck. I remember the image I had of a hand of living steel wearing a velvet glove, a hand that could crush or caress, strike a killing blow or wipe away tears, lift mountains or cradle an infant. The rest of the book was an afterthought. I learned from it and there was much good in it, but it was the principle, that great archetype of Biblical masculinity, which caught my imagination and stuck.

This duality of manhood is seen in our society in its fractured form, a world of tough guys and wimpy guys, but no true men. On the one hand we have guys whose hearts are made of rock, on the other hand guys whose hearts are made of mush. A true man embraces both. Stern, grim, unyielding and bold one minute, lighthearted, compassionate and sensitive the next. The ability to be all things to all people as needed is what defines a true man (1 Corinthians 9:19-23).

C. S. Lewis spoke of this in his essay on chivalry[4], remarking that the concept of such a man, who could embrace extremes of both vigor and meekness, was a work of art and not of nature. The man who truly embraces both extremes and everything in between is made not born. Most of us are born with a tendency in one direction rather than the other. Some are mostly aggressive, others are mostly compassionate. Whatever our natural inclination is, that is likely to be the way we are going to go with our lives. I have an aggressive streak in me that has been steering me towards the Way of the Warrior since I was young enough to read King Arthur. Actually, it probably started before that with Disney movies like "Sword in the Stone" and "Sleeping Beauty." However, growing up in the home that I was blessed with, I also developed a strong taste for typically "softer" pursuits like classical music and poetry, and so was trained to live the steel and velvet philosophy before I could even begin to understand it. Every man has to learn some things that will not come naturally to him. The softer guys will have to put some steel in their souls. The harder guys will have to learn control and gentleness, even tenderness. The good news is that no one is completely one sided when they are born. Human beings are too complex for that. Imagine it in the analogy of a piece of music played on a piano. On the right of middle C you have the higher ranges and on the left side you have the lower ranges. Let's say for the analogy that the lighter notes represent the velvet aspects, while the deeper and darker notes represent the steel. Most songs are written more or less around middle C. That's about where every man starts out, some a little to the right, some a little to the left, but we all have some notes on either side. As we grow we can expand our range to include the entire keyboard if we want. We can go from the deepest rumble to the highest ringing if we learn how. The mark of a true master is his ability to play both and bring them together in harmony.

What happens too often, however, is that we stick with what comes most naturally. I am most natural in the bass register, so I stick with that and gradually lose the ability to play anything above a middle C. Others are more comfortable with the higher notes and lose the ability to play below middle C. Then I begin to despise the higher notes, too light, too soft, too tinkling, with none of the depth and grandeur of my bass notes. The higher note artists consider the bass too slow, too ponderous, too heavy and depressing. Neither benefits, and gradually, without the balance that comes from embracing both, both eventually become pointless.

This is not wisdom. Read Isaiah 40:10-11 again and feast your heart on the steel and velvet of the God that we are called to imitate, the God who can be both great and terrible, and yet keep family bonds and mercy with those who love Him (Nehemiah 1:5).

Thank God, no matter how naturally one side may come to us, the other side is not completely unnatural. I don't care how much of a tough guy you think you are, there is a softer side there underneath the shell, and it too needs to be strengthened. Even if there are some things you can't appreciate, for instance classical music if you like rock or country, you must at least respect it. You may never write romantic poetry, but that's no reason to sneer at those who do. You might want to take a leaf from their book if you ever have a wife. As for the less macho crowd, the guys who prefer books and philosophy or piano playing rather than football or hunting, there is still some iron in your soul and you must temper it just as much as the tough guy. You may never be a Navy Seal, but you should at least respect the warriors and be ready to serve as unflinchingly as they do in whatever place you are called.

Expand yourself. Whatever is good, morally, ontologically or aesthetically good, good in whatever way, sample that good if you get the opportunity, even if it is only a recipe for chicken wings. If the good people you know like something, take it for granted they like it for a good reason and look for whatever it is they like. Look for whatever way you can share in that good, no matter how foreign it is to your interests, or at the very least do not sneer at it simply because it doesn't happen to suit your taste. That is a very perilous road to travel. It is only a matter of time before you confuse your taste in the good with the good itself, and then you will begin to despise everything you don't like, fancying that there must be something wrong with it. You must, of course, despise evil wherever you find it. We were created to be the image of Christ in the world, and therefore we must love what God loves and hate what He hates. God's loves and hates are always extreme. He loves all that is good with a love beyond all telling, and hates sin with a wrath we cannot imagine, so I am not for a moment suggesting that we should compromise with sin in order to be doing what everyone else is doing (modern movies are a huge snare in that regard.) You must hate evil, but it is judged as evil on other grounds than whether or not you happen to like it.

So here is what I propose. Look at yourself. A little introspection can go a long way. Ask God to show you your strengths and your weaknesses. Thank Him for all your strengths and then start to work on your weaknesses. They are no less His gift than your strength, and the grace to overcome them is especially His gift. Try this discipline: pick one good thing that goes against your natural inclination and teach yourself to like it. For example, if you are a football player who hates reading and study and wouldn't know a sonnet if it was subliminally imposed in your cerebral cortex, pick up a copy of Shakespeare's sonnets (or E. B. Browning's, if you want my advice) and read one a week. Really put some effort into it. Instead of asking yourself "What do people like in this?" as a rhetorical question, ask it literally, and set yourself to find the answer. Contrariwise, if you happen to be a bookworm, set yourself some hard task to do that will get you good and dirty. Learn to play paintball or set yourself to learn how to fix your car. Don't just learn to do it as a task, but learn to like it. There are people who like that sort of thing. There is something good in it for them to like. Search out and appreciate that good.

Of course what I am talking about here is expanding your horizons. As I said, everyone has some stake in both sides of the coin. If you find yourself to be a well balanced person, then expand in both directions. Write better poetry and up your bench press by twenty pounds. Grow. Continue to grow always.

The reason why I suggest this discipline, which, as lunatic as it sounds, I have actually tried and by doing it learned to enjoy so many things I never used to, is because it sets the stage for an even bigger adjustment. The steel and velvet sides of every man are roughly, but only roughly, analogous to the balance between men and women in general. In general, men are on the tougher, more aggressive, more forceful end of the spectrum, and women are on the softer, more empathic, more relational end of the spectrum. The principle remains the same. You may find that your greatest extreme of tenderness will not even come close to equaling that of most women. Likewise her toughest and most aggressive moments may not compare to the constant drive to succeed in your tasks that you experience and foster as a way of life. Embrace what good you can, and whatever you can't actually practice yourself (it might be a little strange if you started wearing makeup and spending a half hour in front of the mirror every morning) at least learn to appreciate. Make it your constant practice to look for the good in everything and everyone you meet, and to look for ways that that good compliments your own. You will never cease to be amazed at what you can learn to enjoy and appreciate. I have even learned to like country music. (Some of it anyway).

"Finally, brothers, whatever is true, whatever is honorable, whatever is just, whatever is pure, whatever is lovely, whatever is gracious, if there is any excellence and if there is anything worthy of praise, think about these things." Philippians 4:8

7. Worth Fighting For

I wonder if the world has ever really gotten more complicated, or whether we simply start seeing how complicated it really is. There are always more complicated things going on if you are simply willing to dig deeper. For instance, yesterday in anatomy I learned that there are turbinate bones in the nasal cavity. These bones are placed along the inside of the cavity and are basically airfoils that serve to redirect the air you breathe so that it swirls around. The air flows through because it is a fluid, but the heavier particles of debris, such as dust and pollen, get spun out to the edges of the air stream and get stuck on the mucus membranes. Now that is clever. How anyone can possibly say that such a neat trick arose by chance is beyond me, but more than that, it completely shatters the simplistic notion I usually have of the act of breathing. Life is always more complicated if you are willing to dig deeper.

Now, one of the areas where complications arise most readily is in priorities. When we are born we have very simple priorities. We want what we need to survive, and our entire universe is "me" centered. Later on we learn to want other things that we don't actually need and which might not be good for us. Somewhere along the line, we come into conflict with other people and slowly we have to learn how to deal with conflicts. Essentially the question comes down to what is worth fighting for.

Adults quarrel just as much as children, just as childishly and with less excuse. I have seen grown men argue for hours and hours over which sports team is going to win the next game. I have also seen grown men watch their children go into harm's way and not have the guts to fight for them. It seems we are too ready to fight for what doesn't matter and not ready enough to fight for what does. (This is nothing new, see 1 Timothy 1:4-5). Conversely, if you put as much thought into it as I do, deciding where and when to draw lines and how firmly to defend them before you fall back, you inevitably end up being something of an enigma to people around you. At times you have to have no ego at all (easier said than done) and be able to swallow the worst insults to yourself and even to others without batting an eye. At other times you have to argue for hours over forgotten points of ethics, refuse to hang around with friends, and sometimes you even have to say that you are in the right and others are in the wrong. We are all afraid of taking the moral high ground, and rightly so, since that is a terrible temptation. On the other hand, it is strange how many Christians try their best to lead moral, Godly lives, all the while trying to fly under the radar so no one will think they are being "holier than thou." We are almost apologetic about our faith, and especially about our morals. It is as if we are trying to convince the world that we are not over-zealous, we are still trying to maintain some balance by including, if not exactly evil, at least a healthy dose of worldliness in our lives, not realizing that "Anyone who chooses to be a friend of the world becomes an enemy of God." James 4:4.

If you think about where to draw the lines, you will find yourself cooperating with people that the rest of the Christians shun, but absolutely refusing to compromise with them. I don't know why, but it seems that is a hard distinction to understand. I may be committed to walking the whole road. My neighbor is only walking part of the way, and for a different reason than I am, but that doesn't mean we can't share the load for the short distance we'll be walking together. If you think about it, you can be friends with anyone, no matter what kind of life they lead. You can have conversations with them, take interest in them, agree with whatever truth they speak, praise whatever good they do, remembering that we all have our own sins. Who is to say which sin is worse than another, if all lead to Hell? But then you must be prepared to part company even with your closest friend as soon as he comes between you and God for "Bad company corrupts good character." 1 Corinthians 15:33.

Most of the people I know, true to our culture, put niceness ahead of moral abstractions like truth, justice and courage. There are very few left who set their faces like flint and say what needs to be said to those around them. Most are too busy trying to be friendly; they would never let a "dogma" come between them and friendship. This is very unfortunate and wrongheaded, but we can see why it came about. How to change it is the problem. The rest of the people I know seem to tend in the opposite direction. They are so attached to their beliefs that they do not consider the people they crush in their blind pursuit of these beliefs. This is even more tragic and dangerous when those beliefs are true, because then there is even less hope that they can be reached. You can argue all day long and they can always come back to the question, "But isn't what I say true?" They don't seem to understand that just because something is true doesn't mean it needs to be said, or that it is addressed to our condition, or that it is helpful, or charitable. It is perilously easy to get our egos so wrapped around our ideas that we can't tell where one ends and the other begins. The truer and more beautiful the idea, the easier it is to make it an idol. In the end what began as a love of the truth, becomes simply a love of our own opinions about the truth, which is a love of our own ego, which is inevitably hatred of everyone else.

I realize that I seem to have painted myself into a corner here, and really I have. I am trying to walk an impossibly fine line between two alternatives, putting people first or putting ideals first. The easy choice is to embrace neither alternative but that way is not open to me. Instead I have to embrace both; that is, I have to embrace the truth of both. The question is not whether people are more important than ideals, or vice versa. The answer is that people are important, infinitely so, and ideals are also important, infinitely so. People are the children of God on earth, destined for the eternal glory of Heaven by their Father, who sent His only begotten Son to die for them. What could possibly be more important? Ideas are our best attempts to grasp at the truth, which Jesus came to earth to bear witness to and to die for (John 18:37-38). There can never be a choice between the two. It is not either/or but rather both/and. There is no easy way out. In conflict we cannot choose whether to be true to our ideals or to be true to our friends; we must choose to be true to both. There is always a way. If our ideals are ever false to our loved ones, then they are false ideals. I would go so far as to say that if our ideals are ever contrary to the greatest good of any single person on this planet, then they are false. Some ideals are more important than others, but if there is any truth in them then they are important. It is never permissible to tell a lie, but it is not always permissible to tell the truth either. Sometimes we have to say nothing as Jesus did (Isaiah 53:7). Sometimes we have to hurt feelings. So be it. Feelings heal over time. The soul that perishes for lack of the truth will not heal.

Perhaps that is one of the advantages of getting deployed to a warzone. You get into a habit of looking at everything and deciding whether or not it's worth fighting for. If it is, you hold onto it with all your might, protect it at all costs. If not, then you let it go without a second thought. If you evaluate rightly, you will be left with nothing but that which truly matters.

On my desk, beside my laptop, I have an old K-bar fighting knife. It is a fixed blade combat knife with a seven inch blade. The handle, once leather rings on the tang, is now two pieces of wood that I carved for it, wrapped in 550 cord. The cord is dirty brown instead of green, stained by over a year's worth of sweat, dust, mud, grease and oil, but not yet any blood. The blade is dull. You couldn't cut bread with it. You could cut cheese with it, or rope if you were patient enough. There is a light coating of rust, and the tip is rounded with too much digging in solid Afghani roads, looking for IEDs (Improvised Explosive Devices). The back of the blade is dented and chipped from the times I pounded it with a rock to use it as a chisel or wedge. I used to pray over this knife. Taking my cue from Psalm 144:1, I would kneel in the chapel of whatever FOB I was staying on and lay my rifle and my K-bar in front of me and pray over them a prayer I wrote back in Iraq:

"God our Father, I ask you to bless these weapons. Guide my use of them that I may never engage in unjust aggression or killing, and that I may never falter when force is justified. Grant me wisdom to know when and whom to strike, courage to strike without hesitation or fear, and skill to strike with speed and unerring precision. All this I ask in the name of Jesus the Christ by the power of the Holy Spirit, Amen."

I believe that prayer was answered. My rifle was just another rifle, another issue weapon that went back into the arms room after the deployment and was shipped away with the unit when they disbanded. I fired it at a mountain we were taking fire from, but it's a million to one against my having hit anything. My K-bar, however, became a legend in the battalion. It was everything. It was my constant companion, so much so that the guys joked that it was surgically implanted in my hip. It was a chisel, an eating utensil, a crowbar, a trowel, a mine probe, a back scratcher, a pastime (throwing it at hesco baskets) and pretty much anything else that required an edge, or an unbreakable steal bar or wedge. I've pried bolts out of tow shackles under tension with it, and it didn't even chip the edge. It has been everything to me, so far, but a weapon. I've never fought with it. I've threatened with it in crowd control situations, because a big man in body armor with a knife is a lot scarier than a man with a rifle he very obviously isn't allowed to use. I have threatened, but never had to follow through. I dug about a dozen IEDs out of the ground with that knife and never once blew myself up (hence the reason I'm able to write this book).

My prayer was answered. My weapons were exactly what I needed them to be, whenever I needed it. I always had the skill I needed when the time came. Time after time, when it mattered most, the Holy Spirit guided me and I made the right call, despite my own uncertainty. I didn't always know what to do, but God is able to see to it that I do the right thing anyway.

And this is how it is when deciding where to draw our lines. It requires more than human wisdom to love both the Kingdom, and those who oppose the Kingdom (and which of us does not oppose the Kingdom, even on a daily basis?) but more than human wisdom is available to us. Jesus promised that He would be the Way, the Truth and the Life if we would let Him. He told us not to worry about the words to say, for He would give us the words we needed when the time came. Whatever the situation, we are not left to our own devices to figure it out. This tightrope between people and ideas is not a tightrope really. God is holding us the whole way. He will always tell us where to step. The answer is to put Him first. When God is everything, all in all, everything else falls into place. When anything else is first, whether ideas or people, neither one will be in their right relationship and we will never know where to draw the line.

I think it would be fun to have an Alamo. To have one line too sacred to be surrendered at any cost, to be pushed back into that corner, back against the wall, with a K-bar in my hand, and a million enemies in my face. It would be a relief to be in such a transparent situation, I think. No more doubts, no more questions, no more fear, just the one mission, to sell my life as dearly as possible. In a way, that would be an escape. I would have no more responsibilities. I doubt God will ever give me that gift, but hey, you never know. Or maybe He will require me to think until the end. Either way, I'm sure He'll see to it that I will have no choice but to fall back on His grace. I hope He does, because I'm a stubborn guy, and unless He leaves me with nothing but His grace, I doubt I will ever fully be able to rely on it.

Ask yourself this: What is worth fighting for? What is your Alamo, the last place you can fall back to, the last line that must be held at all costs? Don't you think it might be more than a little bit fun to hold that line to the end? Just to say we did it? "Greater love than this hath no man, that he lay down his life for his friend." John 15:12.

(And on an unrelated note, what man in the world doesn't look for that woman who is worth fighting for? The trick, really, is learning to see that all women are worth fighting for. To fight for some of them is a joy, for others it's a chore. That's how you know who is a lady and who isn't. Joy or chore, though, it is always an honor.)

"But avoid foolish controversies and genealogies and arguments and quarrels about the law, because these are unprofitable and useless. Warn a divisive person once, and then warn him a second time. After that, have nothing to do with him. You may be sure that such a man is warped and sinful; he is self-condemned." Titus 3:9-11

8. Playing it Safe

"The Coast Guard's unofficial motto was once, 'You have to go out - but you don't have to come back!' This bravado was a testament to the bravery and commitment to service of Coast Guard men and women. But a more appropriate motto might be, 'You have to go out, and you have to come back, and you have to bring our resources back because we'll need them again tomorrow!' Performing the mission at ANY cost is an unacceptable risk, not only to those immediately involved, but to all those who would have benefited from the efforts of those people and their resources tomorrow, and next week, and next year. Protecting the nation's investment is important and presents a difficult decision when it means failing now in order to succeed tomorrow. Achieving the proper balance is a crucial element of leading."

I found this paragraph on the U. S. Coast guard's webpage on "Leadership Competencies."[5] To me it illustrates the problem with our nation that will eventually shatter us. No, it is not the complete lack of any kind of literary appreciation. That "more appropriate" motto is so dry as to be of absolutely no interest to anyone except a supply clerk.

No, the real problem is the tendency to play it safe. There was a time when that old motto was a recruiting poster. I'm not joking. It was a recruiting slogan for the Life Saving Service, a volunteer organization that manned little huts on the coast and made it their business to rescue people shipwrecked on the coast, and they did it for no pay at all. It was something they did in their spare time. Ridiculous, you say? Perhaps. Certainly we can't imagine their motto attracting mass numbers of eager recruits, "Hey man, you want to join the LSS?"

"What would I do?"

"Well, once every couple of weeks or so you would get to keep watch over the coast, by standing watch in a drafty old hut and staying awake all night. Then, if a ship goes down you get to ring the bell and get all the equipment ready while the rest of us run out to help you. Then you get to row with us in a tiny wooden boat through a raging storm out to a ship that is a hundred times bigger than ours and sinking rapidly. It might not even be there when we get there. Then you get to row around and see if anyone is still alive, and haul them on board, see if we can find any bodies and haul them on board, all in a freezing north Atlantic gale. Fun right? And here's the best part. There's nowhere that says you have to come back."

"Would I get paid?"

"Nope. You would get to do it completely free."

"Sweet! Sign me up. When do I start?"

How are you supposed to pitch that one to your wife? "Hey Honey, you know how you're always telling me I need to get a hobby...?"

The amazing thing is that it worked. The modern day Coast

Guard is descended from that simple idea. How did it work? How could such a dreadful idea possibly attract enough men to make it work? It certainly wouldn't work today, we say, ignoring the fact that many volunteer firemen in small towns across the country risk their lives regularly for no pay.

I'm not so sure that it wouldn't work. I think that it worked then because people lived in a culture that believed in heroism. Nowadays people admire heroism, but we do not believe in it. If you admire something you look at it from afar and think, "That's pretty cool. That's great even. Not really my thing, but good for him." When you believe in something you pursue it and try to make it your own. Belief requires the investment of some part of yourself or even all of yourself. Admiration is much cheaper.

Yet there are many in our society who are sick of such caution. They are tired of living for fun and self-preservation. I think a vast portion of America is sick with the angst of too much ease and comfort, and now they are desperately but quietly looking for something that they can spend themselves on. We keep taking in and taking in, devouring and devouring. We devour food, video games, candy, cars, soda, sex, people, houses, money, nature, adrenaline, drugs, alcohol, gambling, pornography, and on and on. We never make an end of devouring, and we are sometimes full but never satisfied, like a person with a stomach full of ice-cream. We are full, but still mildly nauseous, vaguely uncomfortable, and we are less nourished than we were before. I think there is something about people who live the opposite way that is incredibly attractive. Mother Teresa lived her life emptying herself and that attracted the admiration and bewilderment of millions of people who spent their lives filling themselves. Many admired her but only a few believed in her.

What about the Navy Seal who gave his life to save the lives of his team by diving on a grenade thrown into their position? Many admired him but very few believed in his service. There was not a big rush to be like him. Only a few were inspired to such heroism themselves.

"We few, we happy few, we band of brothers. For he today that sheds his blood with me shall be my brother; Be he ne'er so vile this day shall gentle his condition: and gentlemen in England now abed shall think themselves accurst they were not here, and hold their manhoods cheap whilst any speak that fought with us upon Saint Crispin's Day."

(Ten points if you can tell me where that quote came from.)[6] What will it take to inspire us to die?

Jesus gave everything He had, "He did not count equality with God something to be grasped at, but rather He emptied Himself of everything, taking the form of a slave." Billions admire Him, but very, very few believe in Him. We are all stuck on playing it safe. Jesus' recruiting slogan is as terrible as that of the Life Saving Service and the Coast Guard. He doesn't even have a slogan. He has a cross. Just a single instrument of torture standing on a hill in a storm. A man hangs naked on that cross in agony and tells us, "You can be a part of this!"

"Will I be paid for it?"

"You will suffer poverty."

"Will I be recognized for it?"

"You will be rejected."

"Will I be financially secure?"

"You will have to renounce everything and trust in me alone for your Daily Bread."

"What's in it for me?"

"You will be my brother."

But we are too afraid. We do not want to spend everything. It's nice to believe in Jesus a little bit, but if we really give Him everything, how do we know we will have anything left tomorrow?

The popular churches in America (not the Church herself) make the same mistake the Coast Guard did. The churches try to attract recruits through advertising successful Christians, popular Christians, wealthy Christians, influential Christians, worldly Christians and barely recognizable as Christian at all Christians. 2 Timothy 3:12 says that "In fact, everyone who wants to live a godly life in Christ Jesus will be persecuted." We should be advertising the martyrs. It is the martyrs who will win converts. Tertullian boasted in the early martyrs of the Church, "The more we are mown down, the more in number we grow. The blood of martyrs is the seed of the Church." Those who get rich might be admired, but we can't believe in them. We can believe in those who, in a pop psychology sob fest of boundaries and self-esteem and self-pity, have the courage to dare to die, to the world and to themselves. When everyone is telling us to have a balance, not to give too much, it's all very well to be charitable but you need to take care of yourself first, those few who take care of everyone else, not out of some rescuer complex or need-to-be-needed mentality but out of pure sacrificial love, they are incredibly attractive. Advertising the wealthy, the successful, and the powerful is really false advertising. Amy Carmichal was right; we should be advertising the cross.

But instead, we play it safe.

"Then Jesus said to his disciples, "Whoever wishes to come after me must deny himself, take up his cross, and follow me. For whoever wishes to save his life will lose it, but whoever loses his life for my sake will find it." Matthew 16:24-25

9. Adventuring

I have always been fascinated with adventure. That fascination has been a constant with me since as far back as I can remember, and since then I've had some adventures, and I look forward to more. I will tell you that there is nothing quite like the thrill of uncovering an enemy IED (Improvised Explosive Device) set there for one purpose, namely to kill you. Sitting on top of enough explosives to turn you into a red mist on the breeze, set to go off with the slightest pressure on the homemade pressure plate, well, there is nothing in the world like that thrill. Getting shot at is a thrill as well. It's like a jolt of electricity. You will never feel more alive and more awake than the first time an enemy rocket explodes in the field in front of you.

That is me talking. That is my personal opinion, my personal experience. Other people aren't like that. A lot of men seem to have no desire to test themselves in that way, or at least, no drive to do so visible from the outside. I think all men secretly wonder in their hearts whether they could handle themselves in a life and death crisis, but what I find seriously disturbing is that while all men wonder, so few of us really have a drive to find out.

I was spending a Friday morning walking around the back forty in Fort Riley. One of the other guys at the office and I were walking two of the new candidates on the land navigation course. While we walked I got to talking with the other guy from the office, Luke, about hunting. We saw some deer out there, including one very nice eight or ten point buck quite a ways out. We remarked with some surprise about the number of deer, because they have no natural predators anymore and Luke suggested that maybe the government should re-introduce the predators; some wolves for instance. Then we started talking about big game and predator hunting, wolves, cats, bears and such. It is an exciting concept, hunting an animal that can hunt you. I've read of cats leading hunters out into the woods and then fishhooking around behind and attacking them from the rear. Kodiaks, grizzlies and polar bears will also actively hunt humans in their area, and if they get the chance they will charge you, at which point it comes down to whether or not you have enough gun to stop them. People have died on predator hunts, which sounds like a lot of fun to me. The hunt, that is, not necessarily getting mauled to death by a predator.

Then Luke said, "That's why I really can't wait until the next major conflict, something where we can go in and just really clean house. I know I might die, but at least I would be dying on my feet."

There is something about that statement that, if you are at all like me, resonates inside you so deeply that it sets your blood on fire. Maybe you know what I am talking about or maybe not. Haven't you ever just wanted a righteous battle, one in which you would be proud to receive your death wound? We talked about it for a while longer until I had to get the new guys unlost again which took some time and distracted us. Mostly we lamented the death of adventure. There are too many people, young men especially, wasting their lives away playing video games, sitting on couches, living with their parents, (not because they love their parents, but because they haven't got anything better to do), never challenging themselves, and never realizing what they are missing. They live their lives in fear. It is a common theme among us, the guys who have decided to go even further into the world of arms, into the Spec Ops community, this attitude of pity for the rest of the world. We are still in training, and already we have an unconscious pity for those who are content with the easier road. Soldiers who have been deployed often pity those who have never been deployed, even if they themselves hated it and would never do it again. I suppose it is a bit snobbish, but when you have nearly died a horrible death every day for a year or more, you can't help but feel a little amused at someone who complains because they missed the first ten minutes of their favorite show. Life is a lot more low key for us.

The little things are just too little to worry about, and it seems to us as if that is all that most Americans worry about.

I wonder how it happened. America used to be famous for the quality of its manhood. We were the race who conquered the wilderness, carved out homesteads, explored, settled, fought and died for what we believed in. Men in America preached and worshipped with passion once. Even as recently as World War II, hundreds of thousands of men rose up and saved the world from tyranny. What happened then? What changed that image of a man, full of brains and spirit, vigorous and dedicated, into the kind of guy you see on the streets today living from welfare check to welfare check, or living in his mother's basement, or pursuing nothing nobler than sex and video games? Did it really start out nobly, as I have thought it did? I always thought the popular consciousness rejected the exaggeration and abuse (which was real and terrible) of the typically masculine virtues and started feminizing towards sensitivity, nurturing, sympathy, relationships, talk and feelings. Is that really the case, or as Luke said, is it just a major case of pansy-ness?

Regardless of the route by which we got here, the end result is not pretty. We are a nation of wimpy guys. Carve a civilization out of the wilderness? Please! We're too busy watching other men play sports on TV. Stand up for the innocent? Yeah, right after I get done with this level. I want to beat the game on super-crazy-hardcore mode before the sequel comes out.

Maybe we do have our own values. Maybe the things we value as a society are good things. Those attributes I mentioned above, sensitivity, nurturing, sympathy, relationships, talk, and feelings are all good things, but whatever happened to the other virtues? The hard, uncomfortable, rock solid, iron-like virtues? Are we so far gone we can no longer appreciate strength, courage, honor, discipline, integrity, action and cold, hard reasoning? Have we indeed become a nation of pansies?

The horrible irony of it is that without those harder virtues to shore up and protect the softer ones, the softer ones aren't going to stay virtuous for very long. What starts out as sympathy towards the downtrodden and minorities quickly devolves into a rabid pursuit of absolute and enforced equality for everyone at best, or at worst, an unbalanced compensation for the most vocal minorities by making them more equal than everyone else. We have gone so nice we are a puddle, easily stepped on by the unscrupulous.

Let's face it: the women run America. Turn on the TV and watch any commercial and if someone is the butt of that commercial, it is the man. The hen-pecked husband, or the husband who is so helpless he has to let his wife do his thinking for him. There is no excuse for that. It is partly a symptom, and also part of the problem. If that is how our families respect us, is it any wonder that the men in America have withdrawn from their posts? It is no wonder, but also no excuse. It is useless to argue whether women have ceased to respect men because we are wimpy, or whether we are wimpy because we are no longer respected. Both answers are wrong. Not all are weak, but we all waste our strength on vanity from time to time, and some of us do so habitually. Some have turned into couch potatoes, but even those who long for the strength and fulfillment that should be ours spoil it. We become thrill seekers. Cheap thrills and adrenaline rushes take the place of real work. Whenever the thrill is the goal of the activity instead of a byproduct we are not adventuring, but merely thrill seeking. Is it any wonder? Amid a world full of light, low-fat, non-fat, diet, and sugar-free fluff, is it any wonder that men look for grease, burgers, pizza, wings and beer? We want to be men, even when we don't know how. I think it is better to be a thrill seeker than a couch potato. At least you have some strength to waste, but then again, you are wasting that greater strength.

Adventure isn't dead. Adventure is never dead. Adventurers, however, are at least in a coma. We need to wake up. Walk away from Mom's basement, or from the pizza, or the tube, or the internet, or the X-box. Whatever is holding you, put it in its right place, and live as a man. Do something good and frightening, just to get the stiffness out of your joints. If you have THS (Tiny Heart Syndrome) then do something about it. Start with some pushups if you don't have anything more productive.

I confess, I have a dream, something I've wanted to do since I was thirteen or so, in one form or another. I want to build a school someday, maybe when I am old and retired (or wounded and retired) and I want to train warriors. I wonder will there be anyone to train? Will there be anyone left willing to put themselves through that kind of hardship, the only reward being the honor of laying their lives on the line for others? (Thank God for cops and jarheads). I would like to see more fire in the young men of this nation. My brothers, we have so much strength for good. If each of us were to stoke up that fire, throw some fuel on it, guard it from a world that wants nothing more than to drown it, what good would be beyond us? Where are the men who will worship God with passion enough to take the lead, instead of mumbling along in the prayers because everyone else is? Why are the majority of our political leaders vacillating, cowardly wimps? Why is abortion still legal? Why is there such a thing as pornography, let alone a multi-billion dollar industry that produces and sells it?

Do you say, "Well, that's all very well, but I'm not called to do big things like that. I am called to work a nine to five job, support a wife, raise a family and maybe go on vacation to Disneyland once a year. That's my place in the world."

Most of us are not called to be bright, visible, well-known figures. The temptation of being a great man on a great mission is not ours to endure, thank God. It changes nothing. The fact that a mission is not seen by a million people does not make it any less a mission. Your family is your mission, your adventure. Live that adventure with passion and fury, with dedication and discipline. Do you think anyone can ever aspire to ambition without that base of solid, ordinary responsibility? Really? If you have been given an earth shaking urge for adventure, you are not exempt from the mundane, ordinary responsibilities of the average Joe. You still have the same responsibility to your family that he does, you just have to balance it with other responsibilities.

God does not give us desires without reason. Testosterone is His invention. Everything about you has a purpose, especially that fire in your blood. The strength that is the manhood within you exists for a purpose, to be poured out in service of others, "For we are God's workmanship, created in Christ Jesus to do good works, which God prepared in advance for us to do"(Ephesians 2:10). He may not do what we expect with it, or what we would like, but He gave us that fire for a reason. If you look inside yourself and find a little thrill of restlessness, that urge to conquer, to fight, to resist evil in some form, an edge of ambition even, hold onto it. Don't listen to the worldly who value comfort, or the sanctimonious who fear strength. Refine it, purify it, and watch and wait. "Live self-controlled, upright and godly lives in this present age, while we wait for the blessed hope—the glorious appearing of our great God and Savior, Jesus Christ, who gave Himself for us to redeem us from all wickedness and to purify for himself a people that are his very own, eager to do what is good" (Titus 2:12-14). That longing to excel at any cost is your warning order. Someday God may grab you up to do something about that desire. Be ready. The world will not be right while men shirk their responsibilities, so as a man of God, expect Him to hold you to the fire on that.

How do you get ready? You can start by washing the dishes.

"The Kingdom of Heaven has suffered violence, and violent men take it by force." Matthew 11:12

10. Thrill Seeking vs. Adventure

I spoke in the last chapter about adventure, and mentioned that it differs from mere thrill. Thrill seeking is not the same as adventure, though we sometimes act as if it were. The difference is essential, buried in the very essence of the two different things, informing everything we do in either category, and it is important.

However, before we can decide how they are different, we must know what they have in common. Both adventure and thrill seeking are the refuge of those men who grow tired of mediocrity and seek to live at a higher level of potential. They want to make something of themselves, so they seek out challenges. Challenge is the only thing in the world that will allow us to grow and achieve the full strength of manhood, whether it be mental, physical or spiritual challenge, no strength will come without struggle, and a certain amount of pain. This is what thrill and adventure have in common, that both are challenges, both require us to endure what we thought we couldn't endure, or to do what we didn't want to do. We must face our fears, weakness, laziness, or whatever it is that holds us back and it is that facing that gives us the opportunity to conquer. Both thrill and adventure can liberate us to some extent, but they are not the same thing. They have different outlooks, a different focus imbues each one with a different goal. One is definitely better than the other, because it is more excellent in source, focus and outcome.

There are five differences that I can think of:

1) Thrill seeking is for its own sake, adventure is always for something else. When we seek a thrill, whether it be rock climbing or skydiving, white water rafting or hunting, the motive is everything. It is not necessarily the actual adrenaline rush, the fluttering in the diaphragm and the endorphin high that we are looking for, but the challenge, the opportunity to do something hard. This is not necessarily a bad thing. However, an adventure always has a goal that transcends that activity. There is something that must be done, and the challenge is a by-product, as is the thrill. Those who stormed the beaches at Normandy were definitely not in it for the thrill, for the most part. Most of them, I am sure, devoutly wished themselves a thousand miles away, but they had a job to do and they did it, and so experienced both challenge and thrill. On the other hand, there are a few who really do enjoy that sort of thing, who live for the adrenaline high, and those lucky few, when the battle begins, usually are laughing their heads off to find a job finally that is dangerous enough for them. I've met a few men like that, absolutely crazy, but great to have beside you at the end of the world. They were still on an adventure, because they were doing a job that needed to be done, and even if it had not been fun they would have done it. The focus is on the reason why are we doing this? If it is simply for the sake of a challenge, then we are thrill seeking. If we are doing a job, regardless of how much or little we appreciate the thrill, then we are adventuring. Adventuring requires a task beyond the adventure.

2) Thrill is personal only. Adventure is always for someone else, either in service or obedience. Thrill is about personal improvement only. It is about me facing my fears and so rising above them. It is about me challenging myself or a competitor for my own personal satisfaction. There is nothing wrong with that, but adventure cannot be like that. If you adventure then you seek the good of someone else. There is a difference between climbing a cliff face for the fun of it, and climbing a cliff face to rescue a trapped climber. The two are exactly the same physically, and perhaps mentally if you are a skilled climber, and the same challenge is involved on a personal level, but the reason is different. It is not your own personal achievement that you seek but someone else's good. It can also be in obedience. It is doubtful that any major difference in outcome would have resulted from one soldier refusing to go ashore at Normandy. One person shirking his duty there would not have changed the war, and since he probably would have died anyway,

no one would ever have known. The sacrifice of each individual man who drowned in the surf or was shot dead before he could even set foot on the beach might have affected little objective change in the freedom of his loved ones back home. However the sacrifice was still noble, and it was still an adventure because he was acting in obedience to a lawful authority. The concept of obedience, even to the point of death, is a lost virtue these days, but it is a noble and honest reason for adventure. Adventuring requires a person other than the adventurer.

3) Thrill seeking is freely chosen based on personal preference. Adventure is always given to the adventurer. To reach out and grasp after something so priceless as an adventure is rash pride. It must be given by one who has the authority to give. This can be as simple as a father letting his son swim in the deep end for the first time, or as grand as a general assigning a top secret mission behind enemy lines. Look to the stories of Arthur and his knights; the noble King granted his knights the privilege of riding out to risk their lives. Adventure is a privilege, a gift. For the Christian, adventure comes only from God, though it may come through human authority. This has some surprising consequences, but make no mistake that God alone is the one who has authority to grant us any adventure, and that He has delegated that authority through other humans. Our parents when we are young, our bosses, our officers, our government officials, and especially our clergy have all been placed in authority over us. However, God can also give us missions directly, which is fortunate because all human authority is fallible and therefore any of our superiors to whom we owe allegiance may make mistakes, or may simply do and command what is evil. God's authority always supersedes the authority of humans, and only by His leave may we undertake any adventure. God uses us to do His will. He gives us real tasks that really need to get done. He saddles us with real responsibilities. It is frightening to think about what that means when we shirk His will.

4) One of the surprising consequences of God being the source of our adventure is that while there is no shame or dishonor in stopping a personal challenge if it becomes too dangerous, or we don't feel up to it, there is no way we can refuse one of God's adventures without grave dishonor. This means more than simply saying that if we disobey God we are committing sin. Try to think beyond terms of sin and non-sin, and instead try terms like obligation, allegiance and love. A thousand

opportunities to do good bombard us every day. It may not be strictly a sin to pass any of them up. They are not direct commands, but we are obligated. God has redeemed us, through the death of Jesus. This not only means that He has the authority to grant adventure but also the authority to command it. Not only that, for He has given us the freedom not to follow Him and so He is no longer treating us as slaves, but He has still paid the price for us. We owe Him everything so even if there were some plane on which we could be even remotely equals, we would still owe Him unquestioning allegiance. He has paid our debt, and in so doing put us even more in His debt. It now concerns our honor doubly, we who are adopted as sons when we could justly have been executed as traitors. And beyond even the bonds of honor and allegiance we owe Him love. He has loved us with an infinite love and He is infinitely worthy of our love. Even if by some impossibility we were not beholden to Him we would still be right to obey Him out of love, just as a wife obeys her husband not out of servility but out of love. Once an adventure is offered us and we see that it is from God we cannot shirk it, cannot step aside, and cannot quit. We must see it through or be dishonored, even if it is not technically "a sin". If I am out rock climbing and I get tired or bored with it, I have no obligation to continue climbing. If I accept the call to visit the sick and get tired and give up halfway through, that is great shame. That is the difference between thrill and adventure.

5) The fifth and final difference was the most unexpected to me when I first started thinking about this, because it was a somewhat unforeseen consequence of the authority of God as the source of adventure. If God is the source of adventure, then it follows that adventure can never be wrong and can never conflict with our obligation. If you want to abandon your family to be more active in the mission field, or to fight for the unborn full time, sorry, you can't. The old fashioned, mundane, run-of-the-mill obligations of promises, schedules, bosses, family and vows hold sway over the loftiest and most adventurous ideals. Thus the difference. Thrill is never boring (by definition) while adventure may well be. Think about it. It doesn't make sense at first, I know, but I think it's solid. (I realize that speaking of a "boring adventure" may sound like a contradiction in terms, but due to the poverty of the language I'm stuck without a precise word for the concept of what I mean by "adventure." It includes the ideas of vocation, mis-

sion, calling, challenge, task and quest, so I suppose you can substitute any one of those words if you like.) Thrill, by definition, has to be out of the ordinary. It has to excite some kind of unusual response, some surge of emotion, some extraordinary effort, some "rush," or it fails in its goal. The whole point of thrill is to rise above the everyday, even if it isn't about cheap stomach flutters. Adventure, however, since it is a task, doesn't have to be anything more than 1) given by God and 2) for some goal other than its own sake, (i.e. service or obedience.) That covers pretty much everything in a Christian's life. It doesn't even have to be challenging. Plenty of the gifts God gives us are the delightful, fun sort of adventures, picnics, both literally and figuratively. Even if it is difficult it does not have to be any sort of conventional challenge. Boredom can be an adventure, counter intuitive as it sounds, since that is our challenge. If you are in a situation where God is leading you beside still waters just when you fancied trying a little white water rafting (Thanks to Elizabeth Elliot for that apt analogy), then that boredom is your challenge. When I was at a hardship school for the Army once, the instructors left us for hours at a time with only one command: Don't sleep. In a way that was harder than the actual events themselves. We didn't mind moving, even though it hurt, but sitting around with nothing to do was a million times worse, and that was the point. It was no less a test of our characters than the forced marches and obstacle courses. So it is with our daily duties. Every one of them is an adventure from God, if only we would see it that way for He is the home of all good adventure and nothing is outside His notice.

Of course we tend to draw a line between adventures and the more boring tasks of everyday life. Adventures are the exciting ones. That is how our language is, and I don't foresee it changing so maybe a better way to word it is to say that every task we are given is equally a part of the overall adventure, which is our sonship in Jesus Christ. The truth remains the same, no matter how we put it. Perhaps the boring, day to day grind is not an adventure in the typical sense, but it is no less a mission.

"And whatever you do, in word or in deed, do everything in the name of the Lord Jesus, giving thanks to God the Father through him." Colossians 3:17

11. The Shield Wall

This chapter is going to be something of a departure from the rest of this book. In this chapter I want to explore a concept that has come to mean a great deal to me, but which may sound strange to a lot of other people.

Of course everyone knows that when two or three gather in Jesus' name, He is there with them (Matthew 18:20). That is a given. We also know that when two or three people band together for anything, good, bad or indifferent, they find strength in their mutual support. I read somewhere that when two horses pull together, they can pull harder than the sum of their individual strength. Instead of two horsepower, you find they have two and a quarter horse power because they are working together. When two soldiers are ruckmarching together they will ruck faster because they are pushing each other.

I just completed a six mile ruckmarch (minus a tenth of a mile, apparently, according to someone's GPS). We do these ruckmarches pretty often, since the ability to move at a high rate of speed with a heavy load is a critical skill in SF (Special Forces). The concept is pretty simple. You put an army issue ALICE pack (i.e. a rucksack,) with a prescribed amount of weight, on your back, and you move out as fast as you can. You continue moving as fast as you can until you get to the end of the route. Then you stop. Too easy. I don't mind ruckmarches. I'm blessed with a good blend of size and strength for this particular event, so the weight doesn't bother me, and I have good speed for my size so I can maintain a pretty cracking pace. Today I was only carrying about 50 pounds, and with a ruck that light, unless I'm going up a pretty steep incline, I'm running.

When we were told to go I took off at about an 8.5 - 9 minute mile pace. One guy tried to hang with me at the start, but I left him behind pretty quickly. At about the 2.5 mile point I was running down a hill, and I heard footsteps behind me. A pair of guys were catching up. Well, I wasn't about to have that, but I have one advantage. What goes down must come up, and I don't slow down on uphills as much as other people do. I said a cordial, "Hey, what's up" to the two guys and then pulled away up the next hill.

Now, something I've long been working on spiritually is my habit of competing with other people. I don't like that habit, because it usually involves investing your ego in something that really doesn't matter. You're trying to beat someone else, to prove yourself better than someone else. That doesn't seem like a Christian thing to do. I like running alone because then I'm only competing with myself. When I'm at the front I don't want to look back to see how far ahead I am. I just want to go until I hit the limit, and then run that thin, narrow line where you're almost passing out, but not quite.

However, as I run I'm usually praying, and today I could have sworn God was telling me, almost in words, "If you keep running and do not rest for even a second, you will beat him." When I hit the turnaround point one of those runners was about fifty feet behind me. So I kept running, pushing and pushing, and I moved faster in some places than I probably would have if I hadn't known he was behind me. And all the while I kept feeling that quiet assurance that if I kept going as fast as I could, I would beat him.

I puzzled a little bit about the competitiveness. I don't have much taste for personal competition, all the bragging and smack talking and chest banging that happens when guys compete. But I had forgotten what competition was for. All I saw was the abuse, where physical prowess was measured only against other guys, and the loser is made to appear like less of a man. When I hit the finish line, averaging about a 10.5 minute pace, he was still fifty feet behind me. The next runner was nearly a quarter of a mile back.

I didn't want to care about winning, but it still always feels good to win, and I think God was trying to teach me something. When the next guy came in he complained, "You two took off." And my tail said, "Well, I didn't want to. I was just trying to stay up with him."

I hadn't remembered in a very long time what competition was really for. I did that guy a favor by beating him, because he would never have run as fast without me. He did me a favor by bringing out that competitiveness in me, since I certainly would not have kept the pace for that long without him. Steel on steel, we sharpened each other. It was competition at its finest, used as a means to build each other up. God was not denying that there are abuses, when competition is used as a means to boost ego and break other people down, but He was reminding me, once again, that He knew what He was doing when He invented testosterone.

47

You might think that this episode is out of place. I've already talked about physical fitness etc. at the beginning of the book. Why bring it up again?

This is a symbol. The almost automatic need of testosterone at its finest to rise to the challenge of a competitor, the inborn desire to be a worthy member of worthy fellowship, is a symbol of a spiritual reality that I call the Shield Wall. I think that when two men agree to fight together they are stronger spiritually. I believe further that if we agree to fight together as men, spiritually, we can protect our sisters and the children spiritually, at least to some extent. I literally think that by standing up and facing the devil in combat, we can draw him off the innocents. We can buy them a little breathing space.

I'm going out into left field here. I have no literal scriptures to back this up and I've never read this exact idea in any book. This is entirely a product of my own experience and meditation on that experience, so take it for what it is worth. I believe that the reason why men, and indeed, all humans, work better in teams, in pairs, in groups, is because that is a physical symbol of a metaphysical reality. Metaphysical simply means "beyond the physical." I believe that beyond the physical reality of two young men competing in the gym, the dojo, the basketball court, or in school, in the realm of spirit a real cooperation is taking place. I believe this physical world is a real existence in and of itself. To deny that would be to deny the reality of the incarnation, of Jesus Christ come in the flesh, which we are told is a mark of the Anti-Christ (1 John 4:3). However, to say that the physical reality of being human, of having a body, exists for its own sake is not to deny that it is also a symbol of other spiritual realities. "For since the creation of the world His invisible attributes are clearly seen, being understood by the things that are made, even His eternal power and Godhead." Romans 1:20. I believe that real cooperation, support and mutual strength is possible in spiritual battle. By corollary, real sabotage is also possible. Whenever I hold my ground and win a fight, everyone else is strengthened, particularly those that are consciously fighting with me. Whenever I give in and fail, everyone else is weakened.

The Shield Wall was an ancient battle tactic, and it is exactly what it sounds like. In its most basic form it was a formation of trained fighting men, shield to shield standing in a wall against the enemy, each man covering the man to the left with his shield, while attacking the enemies to his right with his sword or lance. It was used by the Greek city-states, most famously by the Spartans at the Battle of Thermopylae[7], and later by the Roman legions. It was used by many armies and units throughout history, up to and including modern day riot police. The term "right hand man" might originate from the shield wall, since it was the man on your right who covered you with his shield.

In warfare of this type everything revolved around team effort. Exceptionally skillful and powerful individuals were important, but they were important primarily for their ability to shore up or encourage the men in line with them. Since the shields were all worn on the left arm, the right side of the formation was often the most vulnerable, so the practice was often to put the strongest and most experienced men on the right flank. It is probably from this custom that the modern military custom of placing the squad leader on the right of the squad in formation descends. The leader was the one who could safely be trusted to accept more than his share of the danger, while keeping his troops in line and encouraging them to hold the line. The line was everything in this type of warfare. After the initial shock of two shield walls crashing into each other, or of disorganized hordes crashing into a wall, many of the front spears would be broken, and there would be no room for individual heroics. The men in the front line would have to push against the shields of the enemy, with their comrades pushing against their backs. They might be able to stab through the gaps with short swords, while the men behind them would be able to slide lance thrusts over their heads, but the real battle was in the shoving match. The goal was to break the opposing line. Once the line was broken a solid, unified force could march through a disorganized mob, slaying at will. After the enemy's spirit was sufficiently broken, the line could be allowed to break for individual combat. At this point, after the lines had already either been broken or had done their work, individual heroism would become most important, and the single warrior could still carve out a name for himself. Until that point, his only goal was to protect the men to his right and left.

I think this is what is going on in the spiritual realm right now. I really believe that we men were meant to be a shield wall around our society, some in one way, some in another. We were meant to protect our families, our churches, our communities, our nations, both physically and spiritually. The two are not separate realities but different sides of the same reality. It is this responsibility that I think the men of our generation, and the generation before us, are in danger of failing. We will have much to answer for at judgment, much that we left undone.

The line has already broken, and the forces of the Enemy roam through the field, slaying at will. But even if our lines are broken, if we would still fight for all we are worth, we would keep this a battle. Instead it is a rout. Most of the men on the field don't even know they're in a fight to the death. They are busy chasing cheap thrills, or sex, or entertainment, anything but fighting. Because of this, the enemy can penetrate deep into our unprotected sanctuaries and attack those we should be protecting with our lives. Children are falling prey to impurity, drugs, alcohol and foul language at younger and younger ages. Our sisters are being attacked by anxiety, depression, self-abuse, addiction and suicide. These are real spiritual attacks by real spiritual enemies. Our society tries to treat them with drugs and positive self talk, not realizing that the true root is "principalities and powers,… the rulers of the darkness of this age, … spiritual hosts of wickedness in the heavenly places." Ephesians 6:12. This battle cry is sounded right after Ephesians 5, in which St. Paul urges "Husbands, love your wives, just as Christ also loved the church and gave Himself up for her," Ephesians 5:25.

It is time to own up to the truth. It is because of our failure as men that our sisters, our mothers, our children, the old, the weak, the unborn, the infirm, the crippled, the mentally retarded, and every other victim in the world is under to attack. Because we will not fight, they must suffer.

This must not be born. To all those who are playing video games while the world burns, we need to be the trumpet blast in their ears. We need to kick them in the fourth point of contact and tell them to get up and get in the fight already. And we who at least know the truth, we need to band together. We are in danger of going down ourselves because we are isolated. How many men, good men, tough, strong fighters, have been overwhelmed because they were fighting alone? These are not necessarily weaklings, these may well be men of the highest caliber whose strength could have turned the tide of key points in this battle if they had only had someone to stand with them when they needed it most; but we are splintered. It is the strongest men that Satan tries to overwhelm, we who have been given much, because much is expected of us and he fears that strength. Too often the strongest don't cry out for help. We grin, and bear it, and die, and the strength we trusted in is no longer of any use to anyone. This is rank pride.

At this stage in the battle what is needed is leaders, lots of them. Leaders in every church, college, high school or sports team, everywhere men meet, to start bringing them together. When your lines fall apart isolation is ultimately death and our lines have been shattered. The need now is for rallying points, hundreds of them, where little knots of fighting men can come together and stand back to back. A little hillock here, a rock there, a small trench over there, these become our strong points. Too many of us are looking around helplessly, vaguely wondering where we can find a good defensive position, and maybe some sandbags, possibly a wall with overhead cover and maybe even a ready supply of food, water and reinforcements. Idiots. There are no perfect scenarios out here. What we need now is not the perfect solution, but the good enough solution. If there were a perfect defensive location, it would be under siege and the battle would be a lot quieter. No, out here what we need is for men to lead, and men to listen and follow. For someone to say, "Here. Right here. This is where we make our stand." For someone to pick up the standard and wave it above the smoke, dust and cries of the wounded, and collect a little bunch of men. Even if all you can do is find one other man to stand back to back with you, that is a strong point. Shake hands and introduce yourselves. Then fight.

As more and more of these strong points are established, the battle will change shape. Momentum will shift in our favor. Eventually we will be able to connect this strong point with that one, this knot with that knot and form larger defensive formations. Who knows? Maybe, if we got enough men to fight, we might even turn the tide and start reclaiming our society, inch by inch, little by little. Nothing is impossible with God. Right now, though, I think we need to concentrate on halting the damage.

So how do we join the battle?

First, by staying alive ourselves. A team is stronger than individuals, but it is nothing without the individuals that make it up. If you are out in the field, and one man goes down, everyone else has to carry him, and his share of the weight. I've done this literally many times in the Army. It isn't fun. Likewise, in spiritual warfare when one man falls into sin he robs everyone else of his strength. This is true of any and every sin, including my most private and personal sins. Whether anyone knows about it or not, whether it involved a single other soul, if it weakened me, it weakened the shield wall. Whatever I sow, someone has to reap.

Secondly, by banding together. The advantage to spiritual warfare is that two souls can be banded together regardless of physical distance. At the same time we are also physical beings. Our spiritual abilities are tied into the reality of being bodies. What this means is that while it is good, holy and necessary to join yourself in prayer with all the saints in all times and in all places (Catholic Theology calls this the Communion of Saints) it can be more immediately helpful to join together with people that you know physically. When I said to shake hands and introduce yourselves I wasn't being figurative. The ability to connect on the level of physical presence is not a limitation as much as it is a glory of being human. We are stronger when we pray side by side. The Letter to the Hebrews speaks of this, "Let us consider how to stir one another up to love and good works, not neglecting to meet together as is the habit of some, but encouraging one another, and all the more as you see the Day draw near." Hebrew 10:24-25. When we can hear an actual voice and look someone in the eye we are strengthened. When we pray side by side we are strengthened.

Thirdly, by agreeing to fight. Talk about the need to protect each other and to hold each other's lives more dearly than your own. Make it explicit. In battle there is no room for false humility. In a tight knit unit everyone knows everyone else's weaknesses. We know who is going to be sucking wind after the first mile. We know who has a bad ankle, we know who can handle himself one on one, and we know who is going to need closer backup. In a shield wall you will know every idiosyncrasy of the men to your right and you left. You will know which attacks he favors, whether he likes to sit and wait for the enemy to hit his shield or lunge into it just a bit. You will know his every weakness, you will know where he lets his guard down. In training you can remind him of problems you saw him having in battle and you need to listen to what he tells you. In the thick of the fight you'll be shouting things like, "Get your shield up, idiot. How many times do I have to tell you?" He will have similar things to say to you. This means that you will have to be accountable to each other. The more honest and forthright you are with each other about your individual struggles, the better the support and strength you can expect from them. This can be done, whether or not you are in the same physical area, in this day and age. When you come under attack, send a text message to your brothers, and ask for their prayers and support. Technology is a two edged sword; let's not be afraid to use it.

Fourth, agree not to sit still. There is too much work to be done for us simply to band together to protect our own skin. Look for ways to take the fight to the enemy. Put cold steel to him and make him jump back. Teach him caution. Make a list of people close to you and agree to pray for them every day. You don't have to share details about struggles of other people that you may be privy to, but why not attack those troubles together? Memorize scripture together, and challenge each other to search deeper and deeper into the Word of God. Pray outside abortion clinics or "adult" entertainment centers together. Build houses for the homeless together. Look for ways to protect the weak and the helpless, and to protect those given to you to protect, namely your sisters, your younger brothers, etc. Mentor your younger brothers together. Encourage one another to be gentlemen. The list is endless, it goes on and on. That is one of the innumerable benefits of being a good guy. You never run out of work to do. You have job security.

So, Gentlemen, if you are reading this book, and you have gotten this far, you have no excuse left. You have heard the call. What are you going to do?

"Now I beseech you, brethren, by our Lord Jesus Christ, and by the love of the Spirit, that ye strive together with me in your prayers to God for me." Romans 15:30

12. Nomads

This morning my bible reading was Numbers 9-12. In Numbers 9 it tells about how God directed the Israelites during their wandering in the desert. He would let the cloud of His presence settle over the tabernacle whenever they made camp, and then as long as the cloud remained there they would stay in that place, and whenever it was taken up they would move on. Now, for those who have never camped except recreationally it's easy to pass over this without realizing exactly what it means. For starters, it says nothing about God letting people know how long they could plan on staying in any particular campsite. They would make camp with no idea how long they were going to be camping for, whether just a night, or a night and a day, or a week, or a month or a year. Nor does there appear to be any advanced warning for when they would move. No one goes around the night before making sure everyone knows that we're leaving tomorrow morning. Apparently the Lord would just have the cloud up and leave on the mornings they were supposed to depart. If you've never lived like that before, it can be easy to miss how unsettling it can be. We Americans are used to predictability, schedule, and a solid, stable base of operations. Our vacations are planned, our deviations from schedule are planned, our returns are planned, everything is planned out by the hour, days, weeks, months or even years in advance. Moreover we have a tendency to feel ill-used if something interferes with our plans. But think about the Israelites. For one thing they had no home base. There was no dedicated place that they could call home. They couldn't say "Oh, we're going out for three days and then we're coming back, so you can leave most of the heavier stuff behind, just take what you'll need." Instead, every single time they woke up in the morning to find that God had moved the cloud they needed to pick up everything they owned and pack it on the backs of their camels and fall into place in line.

Any experienced team of soldiers can make or break camp pretty quickly. Last night, due to weather delays, I slept in Dulles International Airport. I travel with a pretty heavy carry-on (I always have to check it) so I always have everything I need. I just threw down my poncho liner, rolled up and went to sleep. I kept my shoes on so when I woke up it took me about two minutes to be packed up and moved without a trace. This is a distinctly military skill in our culture. Boy Scouts and Soldiers are used to packing up and moving at a moment's notice, with no idea when they will be coming back. Just as significantly, we are used to making camp quickly and efficiently with no idea of how long we will be staying. I used to see a tendency to spreading out in Afghanistan. (Our platoon was actually called "The Nomads" due to our lack of any fixed home.) We would arrive somewhere without knowing how long we would be staying. For the first few days everyone would pack everything up every morning and unpack everything every night. If we were there for a few more days after that people would start getting careless. They would leave some of their gear in the tent rather than packing it all back in the trucks every morning. I hated that tendency. I prefer to be ready to move at a moment's notice, because I know that when I do move it will likely be at a moment's notice.

So I would imagine it was much the same with the Israelites. I can imagine them grumbling, "So how long are we going to be in camp this time?" "Should I even bother to unpack the plates and cups? Or do you think we'll be leaving in the morning?" "How should I know?" You can imagine the women complaining about never having a chance to get the tent really set up right, the men complaining about constantly having to rush to get the really good tent sites, and never being able to enjoy it when they did get it, the children complaining about driving herds around the desert all day. Knowing the Israelite's proclivity for complaining, I would imagine a lot of it was going on in their everyday lives.

And isn't that really how it is with us? This settled, American dream type existence is not our destiny. It was never promised us by God. He is just allowing us to stay in camp for a while. He hasn't told us to move yet. When the summons does come, it may be all in a hurry, and we may have to leave a good deal of excess weight behind. (See 2 Peter 3:10 and Matthew 24:50). The nomadic lifestyle is a wonderful preparation for death because it virtually forces us to strip away non-essentials. It is wonderfully liberating if you just accept it. The trick is embracing the knowledge that we are not permanent residents. We eat our meals with our loins girt, so to speak. We enjoy our temporary rests, knowing that they are just that. They are temporary. We are all nomads really.

"In this manner you shall eat: with your loins girt, your sandals on your feet, and your staff in hand; and you shall eat it in haste. It is the Lord's Passover." Exodus 12:11

PART II

13. A Follower's Thoughts on Leadership

It is one of the greatest ironies of my life that I have been forced to be a leader. I have never wanted leadership. I have never wanted authority or to be in charge. I don't mind people being in authority over me, if I consider them competent and trustworthy, but the idea of being responsible for other people never appealed to me. This was not so much humility, unfortunately, as it was just plain, ordinary selfishness. I didn't want to be bothered.

God be praised, being bothered is all but inevitable in this world, especially when you make sergeant in the Army, or are put in a leadership position as an E-4 specialist. Then you have no choice but to be bothered. I still think there is something basically wrong about the whole concept of military leadership. I was twenty-one when I made sergeant and most of my guys were either my age or older. I was expected to instill in them, in a few short months, the discipline that their fathers had not instilled in them in the twenty or so years they had been alive. I was also expected to be responsible for all of their mistakes. I remember specifically my battalion commander telling all the NCO's in the battalion that the reason our soldiers were getting in trouble was entirely our fault, because we were not "supervising their spare time." Very properly, I resented that expectation. That's not leadership, that's babysitting. Leadership should never take away the personal responsibility of those led. It ought to free and support that responsibility. So although the army has been the place where I have learned what leadership I possess, I've had to sift through a lot of garbage to get it.

More basically, leadership is an intrinsic part of manhood. No man can ever realize the full depth of his manhood until he learns to be a leader. For those of us who are not natural leaders, this means that we will end up having to do what does not come naturally to us. Of course all males have to do things that don't come naturally in order to become men, it's just that some men have a natural flare for leadership.

I knew one such man in Afghanistan. He was older than I was by about four years but still my junior in rank. I was a staff sergeant when he was still a private first class, and yet he had more leadership ability in one finger than I had in my entire body. He was naturally a conscientious and disciplined guy who seemed to have a flair for going out of his way to look after his peers who were not quite so squared away. We were short of non-commissioned officers so I put him in a team leader position, a job usually occupied by soldiers two pay grades above him. As a PFC (Private First Class), brand new to the army, in a combat zone, he did a finer job of taking care of his soldiers than many seasoned NCO's (Non-Commissioned Officers) I worked with. Better than myself, in many respects for a long time. He was a natural. It came naturally to him to look out for people, to make plans for other people, to think ahead for other people. He had no problem assuming that his way was the right way to do things, but he still had no problem listening to those placed under him and voicing their concerns to me. All in all as fine a soldier as I've ever had the pleasure to lead.

I was precisely the opposite. It comes naturally to me to function as a loner, an individual, responsible for myself and to expect other soldiers to maintain the same level of accountability that I hold myself to. It comes naturally to me to take things one moment at a time, never looking ahead, always prepared for any change at a moment's notice. I had to unlearn every natural habit I possessed, except for my habit of thinking and analyzing, and relearn all new ones. My other team leader, also older than me, and also junior in rank once said to me in a foul mood, after I had once again left something undone that I should have done, "You don't do things like this because you forget, you do them because you're lazy." He was right. There were a million things to be done in the squad, and rather than take responsibility for it myself,

I was delegating to my two team leaders, because they could be trusted to do a good job. It was an easy way out. I stuck to what I was good at, which was basically training my soldiers and doing my personal job well, and left the leading to my subordinates. Now, some soldiers, sergeants and officers, think that is an acceptable mode of leadership. I disagree, and when I finally pulled my head out of my fourth point of contact, I realized how wrong I had been. I had been sticking to what came naturally to me, living with an office style of leadership that isn't true leadership at all. It is management. I was managing my soldiers, not leading them, and looking back, the problem was that I didn't care enough about them. I cared about my job, my responsibilities, and my leadership style, and I was honestly trying from that angle to do the right thing. It was the wrong angle. I think it is safe to say that I learned a thousand times more about leadership from the soldiers I've led than from the sergeants and officers I have followed. I can still remember the month, the week, and almost the day when I finally grasped true leadership without even knowing it. Thanksgiving week, 2007, my senior team leader left for his mid-tour leave and I was finally forced to do actively what I had been delegating thus far. It was this that forced me to come face to face with the one thing needful. Before I had been concerned with getting the job done, not caring who did it. Now I realized that leadership was not about getting a job done, it was about taking responsibility. I had to care for my soldiers. I couldn't care for them simply because it was my job; I had to care for them because I cared for them for their own sake, because each one of them, individually, was important to me. I didn't articulate this for over a year afterward, but I started living the principle. Because the soldiers were now important to me, I could not let things slide. I could not sit back and let other people do things. It was up to me to make sure that my soldiers were taken care of. All responsibility for them stopped with me.

With that change of focus I began to make progress. By the time my team leader came back from leave the entire dynamic of the squad had changed and I was the actual leader, not just the middle man. Now I could figure out what caused soldiers to listen, what earned their respect, and what leadership meant.

I first learned that in order to lead you must be respected, and in order to be respected you have to be believed. This is where integrity comes in. You must be all of one piece, your actions with your words, so that when you give the hard order or make the unpopular decision, they know you aren't just doing it to kiss up to your superior. They know you are doing it because you believe it. If the substance of leadership is service, the form is integrity. To serve others is why you lead. Integrity is how you accomplish this, for it shapes and guides the desire to serve and keeps it on the straight and narrow path. You choose to lead because you have love for those you lead. You lead well because you love something else more.

Does that sound familiar, this theme of not being able to love at all unless you love something more? It does to me. It is no surprise that everything comes back to God, but I fear I have not yet internalized that philosophy, because whenever I think through something like this, I am astounded to find the same themes returning over and over again. Not all men will be soldiers. Not all men will have earthly authority over other men. Most men, however, will be married, and then you will be called upon to lead, more inescapably and with greater consequence than I was. You will be called to lead your wife and your children, with responsibility for them reaching into eternity. Only one thing in the world could cause a thinking man to accept that burden, and that is love. Of course many men take up the role expecting to get all the benefits without accepting any of the responsibilities. These are the men you hear forever trying to convince their wives to be submissive, either by arguing, coercing or other even more evil means. As if your wife simply rolling over and becoming a doormat would make you less of a failure as a man and a leader. Depend upon it, whenever you find someone demanding that others be weaker to accommodate him, he knows nothing about either leadership or following, and certainly nothing about love. It is because they do not love that such men know nothing of leadership. They are seeking their own benefit in a role they have not taken to heart. This way is not open to us. We can only accept the responsibility of leadership out of love; any other reason is flawed. But love is not enough, if by love we mean affection or friendship or erotic love for another person. Love for that person may be the drive that makes us strive to lead, but it is not the guide for how we lead. That must come from something much tougher, and that can ultimately be found only in God.

Leadership is all about example. I said earlier that your actions and words must be all of one piece, and that is true, but it is not enough. I can say and do one thing, while thinking another, and fool people, but that is not leadership. Your words and actions must be of one piece, not only with each other but with the innermost heart of you, your deepest will. Even that is not enough. If everything about you flows from your heart, but your heart is bent, then everything about you is bent. Only if your heart is formed by the Holy Spirit can you live with true integrity, and only by true integrity can you lead.

This means that a leader's first responsibility does not involve those he leads but rather himself. He has to fulfill his own obligations and root out his own vices if he wishes to show others the way. I've learned that the more I harp on other people's problems, and what they need to do to fix them, the less they are inclined to fix them. If I concentrate on myself, and work with all my strength to grow closer to God myself, and in doing so I serve those around me, then people follow. I do not ask them to, they just do. Until I lean on God, I will never be strong enough to support those who lean on me. If I lean on God, the world may lean on me but it will never knock me over. This is the reason why no man can ever be a true leader until he has learned to follow. Unless I submit myself to human authority, I will never learn to submit to God's authority, and unless I submit ultimately to God's authority, God's fatherhood, I will never lead. The mission will fail before it even starts because I would not serve.

So the husband who can't seem to get his wife to practice true biblical submissiveness should probably look to himself to see whether he is practicing true biblical leadership. In the last analysis, no husband has any control over his wife's actions. He can only control what he does himself, and if he took the time I can guarantee he would find plenty of work that needed doing on himself. Unfortunately it's always easier to point to someone else's faults (or perceived faults) and blame them than it is to fix ourselves.

We do not lead people by getting behind them and pushing, we lead them by boldly going wherever God leads us, by going ahead of them. We keep our eyes on Him and only look back once in a while to make sure everyone is still accounted for. We lead by being the point man, the first to take a bullet, the first to step on a mine, the first to wade through the river, the first to hack through the thorny vines, the first to meet any danger. The leader is always the first to get up in the morning, the last to lie down at night, the last to sit down to eat, the first to finish the meal, even if that meal is MRE's (Meal Ready to Eat, the Army's field rations). The leader is the one who prays over an MRE cracker and a half canteen of warm water with as much thankfulness he does over a Thanksgiving dinner. The leader is the one who takes the midnight shift on the gun so that his soldiers can get as much uninterrupted sleep as possible. The leader is the one who can give the dangerous task to another only after he has done it himself many times. Those we lead follow behind us, supporting and strengthening us. We do not get behind and push, we go ahead and inspire. Words are great, especially if you have the gift of using them, but the real coin of true leadership is action. Words gain their strength only if they flow from true depth of soul, true integrity, supported by our actions.

We must go from love of self, to love of others, in order to want to lead. But we must go from love of others to love of God to be able to lead. Only then will we have the wisdom, the strength and the credibility to make unpopular decisions, to require accountability of our followers, and to lay down the law and say, "This must be, because it is right." We earn that credibility by submitting ourselves to the same rule first, which is the Fatherhood of God.

> *"An elder must be blameless, the husband of but one wife, a man whose children believe and are not open to the charge of being wild and disobedient. Since a bishop is entrusted with God's work, he must be blameless—not overbearing, not quick-tempered, not given to drunkenness, not violent, not pursuing dishonest gain."*
> *Titus 1:6-7*

14. To All The World

Most Christians grow up hearing that they need to be witnesses, that they need to share the Good News with everyone they can. In my schooling this training in evangelization was mostly limited to the study of apologetics, which refers to the logical defense of the faith through arguments. This is a very valuable skill, and one sorely needed in today's world, when half the Catholics you talk to don't know what they believe, or why they believe it. Many have never read the Bible even once.

Actually, it's probably more than half. However a problem with typical apologetics is its emphasis on apologetics. It's rather like a self-defense teacher who emphasizes self-defense to the exclusion of self-protection. You can teach someone how to win a fight all day long, but if he never learns how to avoid a fight, it's only a matter of time before he gets beaten. Similarly, you can teach someone how to defend the faith articulately and logically for years, but unless they learn how to open conversations and actually engage people, (as opposed to engaging ideas only) you've taught them for the worst case scenario. As much as we would like to pretend differently sometimes, witness is not about two competing sets of ideas that are impartially weighed in the balance of logic by two objective adults, who then both discard the erroneous one and accept the true one immediately with all the accompanying ramifications for their lives. The real world doesn't work like that, and people don't work like that. The Truth is objective, but we view it through subjective lenses. This doesn't mean that logic is useless, but only that it will never convert people. People are not impartial about religious truths, and those who claim that religion doesn't matter are just as likely to hold their opinions about it as if it did matter very much indeed. As for the Christians, well, if we understand what we believe there can never be any nonsense about it not mattering. It is not to ideas that we reach out, it is to the people who hold them. The ideas they hold are one way that we reach them, and must not be neglected, but it is their hearts that we are trying to reach. Witnessing is about inviting someone into the family of God. You reach out to that person because you want to see him as your brother. You want to spend the rest of eternity with that person in the Kingdom of Heaven. That is why the most effective witnessing I have seen has been built out of a long term relationship between the people, who had many, many things in common besides a willingness to talk about religious questions.

It took me a long time to come to that conclusion, a long time of wrestling argument for argument against many opponents, often many at once, some excessively hostile, some merely curious. I think that when you realize that God desires their minds only as a gateway to their hearts, that He desires to transform them from the inside out, it changes your whole approach to witnessing.

In my opinion actively going out and confronting people verbally about their lack of faith has to be undertaken very carefully if at all.

It is very hard to do so without sounding like you are attacking them personally, and if Jesus would not condemn the woman caught in adultery, we cannot condemn anyone. We must condemn their actions, certainly. We must hate their sins as fiercely and as implacably as we hate our own, but we must love them, as much as, if not more than, we love ourselves. It is because we love them that we hate their sins, for their sins are poisoning them. Loving the sinner and hating the sin is a distinction lost on much of the modern world. If you attack their sins, they will see it as an attack on themselves. While you may know that is not what you mean, it takes great care and tact to get it across effectively, and some people just don't want to hear it.

An easier tactic is to let your life be your only commentary on your attitude to sin. If the guys at work know they can trust you never to lie to them, because you would not lie for them (it happens, believe me) that is the only commentary you need to offer. Remember that action is the coin of leadership, not words? Missionary work, or evangelism, is all about leadership. You cannot push someone into God's arms. If force was all that was needed, our efforts would not be needed or wanted. God would handle it all Himself. Management style of leadership is not an option. Only sacrificial leaders need apply. You cannot push, but you can inspire. Boldly and visibly living day by day the morality that they would never seriously consider is what will shake them up best and get them to consider it. They must respect you as a soldier, student, worker, athlete, musician, or whatever it is that you have in common, before they can respect you as a person. That's just how we men work. Once you earn that respect, they will begin to wonder what makes you tick. How can you be such a good whatever-you-are, and still be one of those Christians?

One of the soldiers I know once accused me of being the guy who is always trying to drag people into working out and staying in shape and things like that. I don't try to drag other people along. I just do what I do and sometimes other people like to tag along. People look for leadership in others who have nothing to recommend them other than that they know what they are trying to do. On finding out that I was going to Mass in the middle of the week another soldier responded with "No, I don't believe it. I can't believe you're a wimpy Christian." There was such a disconnect in his mind between his image of me as a soldier who could stomp him into the ground in nearly any test of strength or skill, and his image of a Christian. In his mind Christians and wimps were nearly synonymous.

In my experience other men will not listen to you unless they respect you. Respect is absolutely the most basic building block for any kind of missionary effort. Inner city missionaries use sports to attract youth, and they are most successful when they are sports players themselves. If you can beat a kid who is good at basketball, then you can get his attention. Guys respect skills, and they respect those who are skilled, and who are skilled at something for its own sake, not merely using it as bait to get people to go to church. In fact, a missionary effort isn't really a goal, because in this environment the moment they suspect you're pushing "religion" they shut you off. In basic training I was the homeschooled, quiet, socially retarded, hyper-religious farm boy until I pulled an amazingly stupid stunt in the field. I hid outside the Drill Sergeant's tent and spied on them until I knew when they were planning on attacking our lines and then warned the guys. Ridiculously stupid. If I had gotten caught the entire platoon would have been in trouble. Since it worked, I earned immense respect not only from my peers but even from the Drill Sergeants once they caught wind of it. No private had ever done that before.

It was the same in every unit I've been in. They found out I was a Christian, a non-smoker, a non-drinker, non-cusser and (Oh horrors!) a virgin, and immediately characterized me as a sap. Then I would earn respect slowly, either by physical strength, skill at combatives or soldiering, or doing jobs so dangerous or dirty that no one else wanted to do them. After that I would start getting a grudging sort of respect: "He's all right. He's strong as an ox but he is one weird dude." "He's smart all right but has no street sense." Eventually even that would die down, and a few guys would start to let their hidden Christian tendencies out of hiding every once in a while, now that it was safe to be affiliated with "religion." Even those hostile to or contemptuous of religion eventually forgive me for it. I'm not sure whether they consider me the one Christian who somehow managed to come out "all right" or whether I'm the high speed soldier who by some fluke turned out to be a Christian.

Either way, when I was new to this and I set out to be a missionary, I made no progress. When I decided to leave them alone and just be the best soldier I could, I earned respect vicariously for the faith. I found it highly ironic that in Afghanistan, while I was making life or death calls for the entire platoon on a daily basis, I had absolutely no confidence in myself sometimes, but every confidence in God. The guys had no confidence in God but every confidence in me. Go figure. I've only known a few times when guys have thought that maybe my faith could be the source or inspiration for my success as a soldier. Usually it is only when they respect me as a soldier that they will then respect the word of God. Once I have earned that respect, I can then preach the gospel wherever I am, because they see that I am trying to practice what I preach.

Both leadership and missionary work involve earning respect, earning respect for things quite unrelated to either leading or talking about Jesus. In fact, missionary work is far more often (in my environment) a matter of leadership than it is a matter of typical speaking or witnessing. The moment you focus on leading or witnessing, you find you can't do it really well. But when you focus on doing what you need to do right now, following God in the moment, opportunities start opening up all around you. People say things in conversation and you suddenly realize you were witnessing to them though you didn't know it at the time. The more I think about it, the more convinced I am that the most important component of evangelism, and the most important thing in the world, is just following God in the moment. He has far more purposes behind every word and action of ours than we can ever know. We can't see all the connections. If we look for the connections, we often miss them. That is why it is so important to concentrate on following. Nothing else matters.

"You are the light of the world. A city on a hill cannot be hidden. Neither do people light a lamp and put it under a bowl. Instead they put it on its stand, and it gives light to everyone in the house. In the same way, let your light shine before men, that they may see your good deeds and praise your Father in heaven."
Matthew 5:14-16

15. Why

One of the questions I have been asked most frequently is, "Why?" Why do I do what I do? Why am I waiting for marriage to have sex? Why do I go to daily Mass every chance I get? Why do I read so much? Why do I not play video games very much? Why do I not have a girlfriend? Why do I not drink, smoke or go out to bars? Why?

Now there are two distinctly different ways that people ask this question. Sometimes they ask it in a way that makes it an accusation, almost an insult; "So why don't you have a girlfriend? Are you gay?" (To which my response is, "No, sorry man. I'm just not into dudes.") They are not seriously asking a question; they are taking a shot. Just as often, though, I hear guys asking for a real reason: "So why don't you have a girlfriend, anyway?" That's a real question, looking for a real answer. I've learned, after long years of beating my head against brick walls, to be cautious about answering the first kind. If I do choose to answer, I answer it in kind, with something unexpected that will shake them up. If I get into an argument and try to provide a real reason, I am only playing into their hands and doing neither of us any good. If I come back with a sharp or clever reply I earn a certain amount of respect and damage their complacency. Until they are willing to listen, that's about the best I can do.

The second kind of inquiry, however, demands a response in kind, as any serious question does, but more so because this is a God given chance to witness. Forcing the issue with people that you meet is usually not good technique for witnessing, but when people ask you about your faith or morals, they are asking you to witness to them. They may not even know it, but God is working through them and through you. You cannot walk away from that or just shrug it off. God sent you that opportunity; He will also give you the words to say.

Why should they not ask, "Why?" You are living a different life than they are. In the college dorm, platoon, or office, you are the one guy, or one of the few guys, who actually believes in these outdated moral codes that most people have abandoned with their belief in Santa Claus. If a knight in full shining plate armor strode into the office and offered to ride out on any quest that anyone might require of him, they would hardly be more amused. It isn't even that they necessarily think you are wrong. Most of the people out there who sneer at Christians have never actually thought about it in terms of right and wrong, in my experience. They think about it in terms of "modern" and "old-fashioned." They don't accept your morality for the same reason they don't accept Frank Sinatra: because he's so old! Once they know that you are different, and it won't take long for them to figure it out, they will want to know why.

So do you know why? If someone asks a real question, looking for a real reason for why you do what you do, do you have a real reason? "Always be prepared to give a reason for the hope that you have. But do this with gentleness and respect, keeping a clear conscience, so that those who speak maliciously against your good behavior in Christ may be ashamed of their slander." 1 Peter 3:15-16.

This is a problem I have seen with too many of my friends, especially the guys that are around my age, that they so rarely have a reason for what they do or for what they don't do. They drift. This is true of Christians and non-Christians alike, that we do not seem to know why we do what we are doing, or why we are not doing what we are not doing. Atheists sneer at Christians for blindly obeying a set of rules laid down by their parents, and they are partially right to do so. We are following traditions without understanding and abandoning traditions without thought. Both are destructive habits, and it is hard to say which is worse.

I try to fight both of these habits. There are certain practices you pick up from your parents that you will carry with you when you leave home and face the world. Some of these habits will draw fire from the people around you, unless you continue among only people who share those habits. In a way it's good to have other people around to challenge your assumptions, in order to force you to sort out what you really believe, and how strongly you really believe it, but be careful how you face it. You are neither discarding your habits because they came from your parents, nor clinging to them because they are what you have always done. There is too much at stake simply to follow your instincts. You need to think, and you need to try to understand where the traditions you have been given came from. Above all you must take responsibility for what you do, and what you don't do. This means deciding, and not drifting, but also, not paying too much attention to those who can't understand why you do what you do. There is only One from Whom all direction must come and that is the Lord. Of course He sends His guidance through fellow humans, through our superiors especially, even that angry old professor who hates your guts or the foul-mouthed platoon sergeant who despises all things religious. Within his sphere of authority God has placed him in authority, and if you wish to lead one day, you must learn to follow now.

However, ultimately you have to make your own decisions. You cannot continue following the same rules your parents made you follow when you were in elementary school without giving them some thought. Your parents probably made you go to church every Sunday. I firmly believe you should continue that practice, but not out of habit or simply because it's expected of you. If you are Catholic, you owe it to yourself and to your God to examine and understand the doctrine of the Eucharist. Once you really accept it, nothing can ever be the same again. Even if you are not Catholic, the decision to seek out other Christians and build Godly relationships with them is a powerful commitment. However, I do not want you to do it just because it is what your parents would expect. You must continue in a path of virtue because you decide to do so, because you make that decision in your heart.

Perhaps your parents had rules about swearing, what words you could bring home from school, and what words were not to be used. Well, they are no longer responsible for you, or they soon won't be. Are you going to keep that practice or get rid of it? Whatever you do, don't drift. This is what happens to too many Christian young men. They leave home and now that their parents aren't around to enforce the rules they start mixing with a set that has different rules. Now, what they should do is critically evaluate the practices they grew up with. If it is a good practice, they should fight for it. If it is bad, they should get rid of it. Most do neither, they never look at it at all, they just go with the flow and lo and behold, they have changed without even knowing it. Bad company corrupts good morals, (see 1 Corinthians 15:33). Most of these guys never really had good morals, they were just imitating those who did, like a parrot in a cage, or a monkey at the zoo. Now they are imitating those who do not, probably with as little thought and understanding. Never once have they really thought or made a decision for themselves. Never once have they really thought to ask, "What does God want me to do?"

I have no problem with change. Change can equal growth, or it can equal death, but one thing it should never be is accidental. You are God's man, you are not a mouse to scurry around wherever your little mouse brain happens to want to go at the moment. Decide, do not drift.

You will be challenged for it. You will be challenged by Christians and non-Christians alike. I've already talked about the challenge from non-Christians, but the challenge from Christians can be just as strenuous and often much subtler. If you decide never to watch any movie that has nudity in it, or even if you decide to wait for the DVD so you can forward skip through titillating scenes, you may get the "prudish" or "legalistic" accusation from other Christians. Perhaps they have no problem with such things. For my part, it seems like plain common sense. It is not denying that impurity exists, it is simply refusing to allow it to have any influence over you, no matter how subtle. If that is what God leads you to do, then do it and stand by that decision, even if other Christians don't understand. They don't have to. It is between you and God. Be "convinced in your own mind" (Romans 14:5) and stick to the discipline that God has led you to. Explain it, by all means, but don't get too hung up on it if they never get it. After all, it is really none of their business.

This will occur again, in a much broader form, as you get up into the age to get married. Inevitably, someone will question your decision, whatever it is. In my case, because I choose not to date until I am ready to marry, that is called into question. Non-Christians ask why dating has to be about marriage, and Christians ask why I don't want to get married yet. I can't blame them for that. The world is full of young men who don't marry because they are afraid of the responsibility, or because they are getting everything they want without marriage, or simply because they never gave it any thought but just drifted wherever life took them. No girl ever tripped and fell into his arms, so he's a bachelor. Others are getting married just because girls chased them until it was easier to marry than not to. With that as our society's norm, it's no wonder that our close family and friends can sometimes question our motives. Of course we wish that they would give us the benefit of the doubt, but I would imagine that much of their questioning comes from real concern for our spiritual well being. However, there are other things to remember.

1) It is not their decision.

2) The only one who can tell you when to stay single and when to marry is God.

3) The Christian man should not be the sort of guy who avoids anything out of fear or laziness.

That last point is important, because one of the most universal complaints of Christian women is the apparent dearth of good men, and there is some justice in that. Most women start thinking of marriage and family a good deal sooner than most men do, and, at least among Christians, most women desire these things more strongly and more consistently than most men. It is no wonder she gets impatient when years go by, and she grows older, sometimes into her thirties while her childbearing years slowly tick away, and still the husband she has prayed for doesn't show up. Now I understand that this might simply be because God has other things for her to do, and no doubt that is the case sometimes. I agree that, regardless of whether or not that guy ever shows up, she is still responsible for herself, and for following God's plan for her. I am not here to talk about women or their struggles. I'm here to talk to men about our responsibilities. I want to suggest a way of looking at it from a different point of view. Suppose she has been praying and living in God's grace for years, and God in His good time brings a man into her life and gives him the responsibility for courting and marrying her. Woe to that man if he shirks that responsibility out of fear or laziness. What if I was the one? What if God has me picked out as the proper spouse for one of His daughters? How will I answer to Him (or to her) if I am too lazy or indecisive to do His will?

That having been said, for nearly all of us there are things that need to be accomplished before we can think of marrying. Hardly any men leave home immediately after high school and are ready to marry. Quite apart from the financial concerns, or matters like maturity level, the time alone is crucial for spiritual development. When a man marries a woman he must be ready to support her, which means she must be able to lean on him when she needs to, without fear of him buckling under the pressure. If he has never learned to lean on God, not just in times of more immediate need, but at all times and circumstances, he can never support anyone else. For women, this period of solitude seems to be less crucial, though helpful when it does occur. I don't know why this is so, but I have heard of women who went directly from living with their parents to marrying and living with their husbands and most seemed to have very little trouble with the transition. In other time periods that was actually the norm. I haven't seen any man doing this, and unless he has lived on his own and taken care of himself for at least a couple of years, I would very much doubt any man who claimed to be ready to get married. This is one more reason why I don't think that men should even date until they are at least twenty or twenty-one. Solitude with God will do more to prepare you for marriage than any amount of time spent with the opposite sex.

I would recommend positively seeking out that solitude, especially in service of God. My top three choices for young men would be:

1) The missions, foreign or inner city

2) Evangelization or apologetics, although these will be at least part time responsibilities no matter where you go,

3) The military, which is a mission field in its own right (believe me!)

There are a million other opportunities for service, including youth ministry, soup kitchens, pro-life activism and cleaning up the environment. The point is that you are actively looking for God's guidance and following Him wherever He leads. You are not merely drifting along in your singleness, you are choosing, for a time, to be free from romantic relationships, to allow God to speak to you more closely. Later on, when God gives you the green light, put the same energy and dedication into courtship, and then into marriage, and so on with everything you do in your life.

"...the generation that carried on the war has been set apart by its experience. Through our great good fortune, in our youth our hearts were touched with fire. It was given to us to learn at the outset that life is a profound and passionate thing. While we are permitted to scorn nothing but indifference, and do not pretend to undervalue the worldly rewards of ambition, we have seen with our own eyes, beyond and above the gold fields, the snowy heights of honor, and it is for us to bear the report to those who come after us. But, above all, we have learned that whether a man accepts from Fortune her spade, and will look downward and dig, or from Aspiration her axe and cord, and will scale the ice, the one and only success which it is his to command is to bring to his work a mighty heart." Oliver Wendell Holmes, Jr. - 1884

It is all a question of responsibility. Am I taking responsibility for what I'm doing, or not doing, or am I just drifting?

"But in your hearts set apart Christ as Lord. Always be prepared to give an answer to everyone who asks you to give the reason for the hope that you have. But do this with gentleness and respect, keeping a clear conscience, so that those who speak maliciously against your good behavior in Christ may be ashamed of their slander."
1 Peter 3:15-16

16. Decision

I used to hate making decisions until I read a quote somewhere that said, "The greatest part of making a decision is living with it afterwards." That made a great deal of sense to me. When we agonize for hours, days, weeks, months or even years over some decision, what is it that we are doing? We are weighing pros and cons, trying to predict probable outcomes and comparing them to see which we like best or which we think we can live with. The more I thought about this (Afghanistan 2007, when I was deciding whether or not to reenlist was when it came up) the more I realized that this was based upon two false statements, or rather a false assumption and a false priority. The false assumption is that we can predict likely outcomes. We know some outcomes of our decisions, the others we only guess at. Whatever the future holds, it will be different from what we expected in some ways and the same in others. There will be good days and bad days. We will have to take the good with the bad whatever way we choose, which is why the biggest part of making a decision is living with it afterwards, taking the consequences of that decision. The false priority is in placing so much emphasis on what we would like or what we would enjoy. Rather, we should be worrying about what God wants us to do. Whenever we act in accordance with God's plan we will be able to be happy, or something better. Whenever we are not acting in accordance with God's plan, it won't matter at all whether we are happy or not. We will be miserable.

Of course once I got that realization I ended up with still more to agonize over. How was I supposed to know God's will? Was I supposed to pray over it until I just "felt" the answer? How was I supposed to know whether that was just me feeling what I wanted to, rather than God's guidance? I can't tell the difference. Unable to answer this question, I adopted a slightly lower method. I decided simply to choose the most honorable choice available, and let the chips fall where they may. I was convinced that no matter what I chose, as long as I chose honorably, God would not fail to help me in keeping my obligation. So in April of 2007 I re-enlisted for four more years in the army. Since I was stop-lossed and going to be doing one of those years in Afghanistan anyway, it worked out to only three extra years, and I got a heavy bonus of $22,500 tax free. Given those circumstances you would think I would be cool with that, but exactly as I expected, as soon as I signed the paper, I felt that, "Oh no! What did I just do?" feeling. I have never in my life made a major decision without feeling that, and I've learned something from it. That feeling has nothing to do with the particular choice I made, but with the mere fact that I made a choice. A choice is a limiting thing. In order to choose the Army I had to choose to limit myself from doing everything else that I wanted to do; college, freedom, and even the possibility of marriage for a while. No matter what I choose, I am limiting myself from other possibilities. No wonder my brain was freaking out. I have more than once wished I could have done something else, but never once regretted what I did.

Decisions will come. At some point you will be forced to make a decision based on far less information than you wish you could have. How can you possibly choose without knowing all the details of each possible choice? I ask, how could you choose if you did know all those details? You would be overwhelmed. Only God can weigh that kind of variety. How can you decide among five different college courses? How can you choose whether to go into business for yourself or look for a job? How can you pick one woman to love for the rest of your life without knowing how she will turn out later on? Well, what did you want? Did you seriously want to go around the whole world comparing every woman alive with every other woman until you found the most perfect one imaginable? Only God has the ability to do that. If not one sparrow falls to the ground without His knowledge, if even the hairs on your head are numbered, if we are to trust Him for everything, even our daily bread, I think we can safely trust him with our love lives too. At some point He will indicate which woman you are to commit yourself to for the rest of your life. Don't be afraid to follow His guidance and forsake all others. It's called trust.

Whatever choice you make you will dislike some of the consequences at some point. It's inevitable in our fallen world. Responsibility consists in accepting those consequences and dealing with them. Worrying about whether or not it was "the right decision" is pointless. Worry about whether it was a morally right decision. Did you make it in good conscience? Was there any sin involved? If it was wrong, then you obviously need to go back and fix it, to the best of your ability. However, if it was a righteous choice, even if you don't like it, then keep going. In the absence of clear guidance from the Lord, stay the course, pray about it and do what seems right to you. God doesn't need us to be certain about what we are doing to lead us to the right decision. The important thing is to trust Him. God is always far more anxious to lead His sheep to where we need to be than we ever are to get there. As far as I can tell, the question "Is this God's plan for me?" has much less meaning than we like to give it. Of course God has a plan for us. His will should determine our actions. However we have free will and so we can do what He does not will, but even if we do not do what God wills, His plan is not thwarted. From our point of view, it might look as if we had missed the path God was showing us and caused ourselves no end of grief in doing so. No one knows what it looks like from God's point of view. It is a quandary that we will never solve this side of eternity. Wrestling with that question is a pleasant philosophical speculation but of very little help in making practical decisions. Even if we step outside of God's will, we are never outside of His plan, and in His mercy He can bring us into His will again. We don't know how He does it, but He does it. Stick to the practical truths that have been revealed to us. He will show us enough for obedience, and that is all we need to see. Individual, day to day fulfilling of the obligations we do know will do more to ensure our continuance in God's will than any amount of deliberation, because it trains our heart to love what He loves. The far-reaching life decisions are most often really made in the day-to-day choice of following God's will.

God has told us how to use our free will. Let Him worry about reconciling it with His omnipotence. This does not mean that we should not pray for God's guidance. I have come to recognize four avenues in which He sends such guidance.

1) Scripture. Some years ago, I started out reading four chapters a day in the Bible. I didn't pick and choose, I just started at the beginning

and went on to the end, and then started over again. Recently I started reading two from the Old Testament, two from the Gospels and two from the Epistles and I think I have an easier time thinking about what I read that way. Many times I have received, from God's hands seemingly, scriptures that spoke precisely to what I was thinking through at that time. I have also opened the Bible casually and had a verse jump out at me that applied directly to my current problem. More often I have had verses jump into my head from memory that answered prayers. This is one of the biggest reasons for daily Bible reading, year after year after year. Scripture is the language God uses to speak to us. How can we listen if we do not understand the language or at least have a decently broad vocabulary?

2) Circumstances. Never underestimate God's ability to use the coincidences of our lives to guide us. When things just fall together allowing you to do what you were thinking of doing, unless you have good reason to believe otherwise, and as long as your plan is not an evil or selfish one, I would suggest that it may well be the Will of God.

3) Advice from mentors. When someone much older, wiser and closer to God than I am gives me advice, it is stupid of me not to listen and weigh it carefully. When several such people give me advice, I ought to have very, very strong reasons before I decide to throw it out.

4) Conviction by the Holy Spirit. Sometimes, very, very, very rarely, I have received a strong, secure inner conviction that what I was doing was right. I don't get it very often, and only in the middle of prayer, and it never lasts very long. If I ever did start getting it often I would be incredibly suspicious. When it does come I usually look for some other sign as well, since I don't know what psychological games I am capable of playing with my own mind, but the Holy Spirit is capable of revealing His Will interiorly. The ability to listen interiorly is one of the gifts we must pray for and cultivate on a daily basis.

The more we pray for God's guidance, the more likely we are to recognize it when it comes. Of course we should never underestimate the possibility that He may be speaking to us and we are just not listening, but I think there are times when God deliberately does not reassure us about what we are supposed to do. It's rather like a father watching his son swimming out to the deep end. The boy swims a little way and looks back, not sure if he is doing it right or if he's still safe. The father just watches, doesn't say anything, waiting. At the first sign of his son being in real danger he'll be in the water to save him like a shot, but as long as the boy is going in the right direction and not in danger, he will benefit by going on without obvious help. Of course this is only an analogy. It breaks down because God's help is constant and inescapable. The only reason we can swim is because He supports and strengthens us. Even when we run full speed away from Him, we run with muscles He gave us, using strength that He constantly pours into us. This is worth thinking about when wondering what He wants us to do. If God is the only one who gives us the strength we use to do wrong, how much more will He support us in doing right? Can we really believe He ever abandons us to our own devices?

In September of 2008 I was still wondering whether God wanted me to join the Special Forces or finish out my time and get out and become a priest. Selection for Special Forces was in September, and in October there was a retreat by the Military Archdiocese for soldiers who were discerning vocations to the priesthood. I had already been through Special Forces selection once and not been selected, and after much prayer I decided that I would go through it a second time. I would do my best, and if I made it through and got selected, I would consider that a sign that that was what I was supposed to do. If I didn't get selected, I would go to the retreat. After two weeks of hell I was selected and after that experience I was left with no illusions that I could have done it without God's grace. I didn't go to that retreat. Now bear in mind that this does not mean that He may not someday want me to change careers. After years of prayer and wrestling in my soul I still have no definitive answer, only the certainty that I will have one when I need it (Matt 6:32-34.) All I can do so far is remind myself that it is entirely up to Him. However, I rest in the assurance that He will guide me, no matter what.

This has become my method of making decisions when God's guidance is not obvious enough for me to pick up on. I'm not good with non-verbal communication and I especially don't do hints, so He has to get pretty blatant sometimes. When He doesn't I first look to myself to make sure that I am in His grace, fulfilling my obligations, praying, attending Mass, resisting sin, etc. "Whoever can be trusted with very little can also be trusted with much. And he who is dishonest with very little will be dishonest with much." Luke 16:10. The more I live in grace in the little things, the more confidently I can rely on my decisions in the big things. Conversely, when I am not living obediently, I can never make a major decision with peace. I must stay under the obedience. Living in the little things conforms our hearts to the Will of God. Then we can more safely trust the deepest desires of our hearts in the big things. Then I make my decision and trust in God. If I'm doing what He wants me to do He will give me the grace to see it through, no matter how tough it gets. If not, He will drop a brick wall in my path before I get too far out of line. Incidentally this is the method used by David (1 Chronicles 17, 2 Samuel 7):

"Now when the king dwelt in his house and the Lord had given him rest from all his enemies round about, the king said to Nathan the Prophet, 'See, now I dwell in a house of cedar, but the Ark of God dwells in a tent.' And Nathan said to the king, 'Go do all that is in your heart; for the Lord is with you.' But that same night the word of the Lord came to Nathan, 'Go and tell my servant David, "Thus says the Lord: would you build me a house to dwell in?"'" David had a plan to do a good thing, he sought the counsel of a wise and Godly man, and made the decision to go ahead with it. When God made it clear that it was not His will, David ceased immediately. That is what I trust God to do for me. He's done it before. I have every reason to hope that He will again, whenever I need it. After all, I'd rather run face first into a brick wall in a fog than run off the edge of a cliff in a fog.

"Do not be anxious about anything, but in everything, by prayer and petition, with thanksgiving, present your requests to God. And the peace of God, which transcends all understanding, will guard your hearts and your minds in Christ Jesus." Philippians 4:6-7

17. Engrained

The word I am thinking of this time is "engrained" as in, "This habit is thoroughly engrained in me." I am the sort of person who can take a single word and spend all day thinking about it, and that is what I have done with engrained.

It reminds me of when I was very young, not quite ten, I think, and my Dad was building the benches that we have even now around the dining room table. These benches are massive things, a good eighty pounds apiece, built of hard maple 3x12's bolted together with lag bolts. Not the sort of benches that tip over easily. Every board first had to be cut, and then planed and finally sanded. The sanding was the most time consuming part, even more so with the other slightly gentler pieces we built, like my little sister's doll cradle which was a joint project between my brother and I, overseen by our father. Every piece had to be sanded, first with coarse grit, then with medium grit, and finally with fine and superfine grit. My dad was an exacting teacher. Everything had to be done right before we could move on to the next step, and his patience was considerably greater than that of two very young boys. We were tired long before the project was finished but he ensured we continued to the end and maintained quality control over our work. I remember especially the sanding. We had to go with the grain when we planed the wood, the planer wouldn't cut otherwise, but when we sanded it we created our own grain. We engrained the wood. We went in circles, thousands of tiny bits of grit repetitively grinding away the lumps and bumps and coarseness, creating their own pattern, regardless of the natural grain of the hardwood. I remember marveling at the feel of the finished product, hard and unyielding but soft at the same time. But right now it is the act of going against the grain that concerns me.

One day in Afghanistan we took rocket fire from a mountain overlooking our bridge site. I was with the small group on the far side of the river from the rest of the platoon, and our few trucks had to go the long way around to join the others, because the bridge had already been taken down. On the way, moving out of a little village, a three thousand dollar, one hundred and fifty pound piece of bridging apparatus fell off the truck in front of mine. I called a halt, and my driver and I went to secure it. Obviously it took some effort to get it into our trunk, especially in such a way that we could close the lid. During that time we were stopping traffic on the road. The first hint I got that something was wrong was when I heard my gunner yelling, and then another NCO (Non-Commissioned Officer) from the truck in front yelling as well. A small white four-door had not stopped and was continuing to pass us, slowly and on the far side of the road, but it was still moving after they had told it to stop. I jumped off the back of my truck and started moving towards it. It was going at such a slow speed that I fully intended to smash the driver's window and drag him out by the throat. Maybe he was stopping already, maybe he thought I meant business, maybe he just suddenly realized his mistake, but before I got in range he stopped the car. Then he turned and looked out the window and smiled at me. It was a conciliating smile, common in the Middle East and universally irritating. They smile like that a lot more than Americans do. It irritated me especially then. I didn't have any weapon but my knife but I was still more than capable of killing him. I could have smashed his car, dragged him out and thrown him off the side of the road and as long as I didn't kill him, no one would have said a word. He deliberately drove into our space after we clearly signaled him to stop. Everyone else in the town had the sense to flee for cover once the first explosion went off, and sure, the shooting had paused, but we were all still on edge. It was an idiotic thing for him to do. That's how people get killed. And this old man had the gall to smile at me!

Understand, this is not what I think now. This is what I was thinking, or more accurately, feeling at the time. I raised my fist to the window and glared at him and he submitted visibly. But I didn't do anything to him. I turned around and went back to my work. I couldn't do anything to him. I realized, talking about it later to the other NCO on scene that I couldn't hurt him because I have trained myself to be unable to. Not to be unable to kill, but to be unable to terrorize. The idea of sufficient force is so strong, so engrained in me that even as angry as I was (and had a right to be, by the way) he had stopped, and so I stopped.

That is why virtue is a habit, and that is why training in virtue, deliberately engraining the habit into your sub-conscious is so important. Later I thought of all the reasons why I should not have hurt him. He was an old man, probably too old to be driving anyway. No characteristics of a suicide bomber. He was driving slowly and on the far side of the road. My goal was to get him to stop moving, not to get him to stop smiling. Those were reasons which I was incapable, literally incapable, of thinking through at the time. Instead training kicked in. Through countless training scenarios, visualizations and situations I had trained my mind to use force only to achieve my goal and no more. Every time was like a stroke with the sandpaper, going against the natural grain of the wood, creating a new grain. For instance, driving down the street, cracking windshields with stones when the drivers wouldn't stop, but holding off if they did stop. I've shouted and threatened one second, and then flipped the switch to "Officer Friendly" the next. Each of these habits slowly formed in me an internalized sense of just use of force. Training saved that old man from a broken skull, not any reasoning of my own at the time. We can't always reason at the time, but we still have to make the right decisions. Only habit keeps us from stepping over the line in a fit of rage or any other strong emotion (2 Peter 1:5-8). Then, over time, our habit of acting rightly even when we don't feel like it will become one of the tools God can use to bring our thoughts and feelings more perfectly in line with His will. "We take every thought captive to obey Christ, being ready to punish every disobedience when your obedience is complete." 2 Corinthians 10:5-6

Another example of engraining, something more people will be familiar with, is the idea of hope. Everyone goes through dark times, times when everything goes wrong, God seems far away, the faith seems like it is a lie, and all your best efforts are futile. Vanity of vanities, all is vanity. Everyone knows that feeling. That is where a habit of hope comes in. Not that you can feel an emotional assurance that all will be well and all manner of things will be well, but that you continue to act as if you did. You train your soul to continue to live in hope, even when you can't feel it anymore. "Therefore since we are justified by faith we have peace with God, through our Lord Jesus Christ. Through Him we have obtained access to this grace in which we stand, and we rejoice in our hope of sharing the glory of God. More than that, we rejoice in our sufferings, knowing that suffering produces endurance, and endurance produces character, and character produces hope, and hope does not disappoint, because God's love has been poured into our hearts through the Holy Spirit who has been given to us." Romans 5:1-5

In times of loneliness it is the active remembering of why God allows us to be lonely that redeems the agony. God allows us to be lonely so that we may come to seek Him first and foremost. When that emotion strikes, when I start doubting whether God has led me here, or wondering why I have to go through this hell or if there will ever be anyone for me, it is the habit of seeking out God, carefully engrained into my will over time, that keeps me seeking Him when I least want to speak to Him. And every time I seek Him when I want to run from Him I deepen the habit just a little bit more, scrub one more little bump out of the way. It doesn't make the pain hurt any less, but it makes me stronger to bear it.

It is the discipline of habit that is the difference between the man who does honorable things from time to time and the honorable man. All of us are on the journey from the former to the latter, and it is a rough journey at times, but it is pushing through those rough spots that makes the easy spots so easy. They strengthen us so that we can face trials that would have crushed us earlier and even laugh at them. The more of God's strength we use, the more able we are to use yet more of it. The important thing is to trust in Him and keep going, no matter what.

In Sapper School, a light infantry tactics and leadership course for engineers, we learned to live, to work, to march, to lift, to fight, even when we had been without appreciable sleep or decent food for a week or more. I do it, not by looking ahead to the goal, but by focusing downwards on the piece of dirt in front of me where my boot is going next. The goal is in my heart but not foremost in my mind. Foremost in my mind is the current challenge. We keep going, keep striving, keep believing, and keep fighting the good fight because in better times we engrained that habit into ourselves. Of course things will brighten up eventually, but that is God's problem, not ours. Until then, we have our marching orders.

> *"And you have forgotten that word of encouragement that addresses you as sons:*
>> *'My son, do not make light of the Lord's discipline, and do not lose heart when he rebukes you, because the Lord disciplines those he loves, and he punishes everyone he accepts as a son.'"* 1 Corinthians 12:5-6

18. Doing and Being

One of the reasons I am so glad to be on my way to the world of Special Forces is because of the higher caliber of soldier you meet. Even to be able to apply you have to have an ASVAB (Armed Services Vocational Aptitude Battery, the entrance test for the military) score of 105, unless you can get a waiver. That's not really that hard to achieve if you paid attention in elementary school and the first two years of high school. You could skip the last two years of high school and it would not affect your ASVAB score in the slightest. The basic math, English and vocational skills that it tests are just that, basic. However, to get into certain jobs you need a higher score than you do to get into others, so some jobs have a much lower average IQ than others. In Special Forces, most of the guys are fairly intelligent. They may be dirt bags, they may be lazy, they probably will have massive egos, they may be any number of other things, but they won't be completely ignorant. They will be able to do basic addition, subtraction and multiplication without a calculator, and they will be able to speak in a grammatically recognizable way when they choose. More than that though, in SF they are guaranteed to have some strength of character. You'll find dirt bags there too, there's always a few who slip through the cracks. You'll find a lot of egos especially, but everyone who is there, in that training, has been through selection, which means that they have voluntarily suffered. You can always have better conversations with someone who has voluntarily suffered. Whether it be putting himself through a hardship school, or studying twelve hours a day for four years in college, that voluntary sacrifice vastly increases the depth that he has to put into a conversation. After all, if I've never done anything worthwhile, what do I really have to say that's worth saying?

So as I go into this training I am enjoying hanging out with more mature soldiers than I have been used to. It's really quite a treat. You would not believe some of the conversations we have on a daily basis, early in the morning or right after PT (Physical Training). I love conversations, in much the same way that I like well cooked food. It is one of the greatest pleasures in life, I think, to sit with people who can think and express themselves and just listen to what they have to say, and try to understand how different people view the same things. We share in common that we are soldiers, we have all deployed a few times, we have similar interests ranging from physical fitness to politics, and we have been through the same hardships. The only superior groups I have ever had the pleasure of conversing with have been groups that were specifically and wholeheartedly Christian, but they are few and far between in my life. Someday I would like to have the opportunity to converse with a circle of passionately Christian warriors, God willing.

This morning we were talking about what we would do if we were not in the army. One of the guys had this revelation to share: "You know what? I'm not going to lie, I hate working. I hate getting up early every morning to go to do a job that I don't really love doing. I don't think I should have to spend my whole life working at some dead end job, all day, every week until I die. And it's not just the army; it's the civilian world too. It would be the same in a civilian job. If I had my way, and I didn't have to work for money to live, I would sit in my house and play video games all day." Yes, I know it doesn't sound like it from this excerpt, but he really is quite a good soldier and not a bad guy.

Of course I disagreed that this would be a wise choice, and I tried to make a case for the value of work, even if you don't enjoy that work. What, after all, do video games accomplish? No matter what you do for entertainment in this world, it will all get old eventually. Why would I dedicate my time and effort for something without an end game? There is no future, no growth, no betterment in video games. It was a futile argument. The discussion kept coming back to his insistence that if that was what he wanted to do, then it would be fulfilling for him. I don't believe it would be fulfilling, anymore than eating cake and ice-cream every day for the rest of your life would be fulfilling, no matter how much you liked doing it. Even if it kept him entertained for the rest of his life, he would never be fulfilled, but of course saying that does not prove it. He might be happy, but not with the true happiness of fulfillment that comes from living out the vocation to which God has called you.

Now, thinking about it, I find that I understand better where he is coming from. I've played a few video games too, way more than I should have. They are entertaining, in their way, but also addictive for some people. I had a WOW account twice (that's "World of Warcraft," an online role-playing game), and both times I ended up getting rid of it. The first time it was because I deployed, but the second time it was because, after having the account for only two weeks, it was obvious I was just wasting too much time, and not getting any benefit as a person. I liked playing. I would play all day every day if I could. In fact, I understand all too well. If I did exactly what I wanted I would sit at my computer and eat pizza and play WOW until I weighed three hundred pounds and had not one spark of ambition left. That may be what I would like to do, but that is not what I want to be. I don't want to be the sort of person that does that. In essence, I want to have my cake and eat it too. I want to be able to do all the fun, easy and useless things I want, while still being a tough, dangerous and worthwhile person.

This is where the conflict is, between what I want to do and what I want to become. My old buddy Mike was the same way. We lifted together for years before he got out of the army. We went through Sapper School (the most fun you'll never want to have again) and the EOCA (Explosive Ordinance Clearance Agent) school together, we kept in touch through Afghanistan, even though we rarely met over there, due to our different platoon Areas of Operation in country, and for a time he wanted to go SF with me. We were very much alike in that respect, that we both liked nothing better than sitting around, eating pizza and watching movies. I had more of a taste for books, but we both had a great love of war movies and cheesy 80's action films. One day, in the middle of a workout I asked him, "So why do we do it, man? Why do we put ourselves through this, all this sweat and pain, when we don't really want to?"

His answer was priceless wisdom. "Because you and me, we're really lazy people, in denial." And he was right. At heart we wanted to do the easy thing, but we wanted to be hard men, and by God's grace, what we chose to be was winning out over what we wanted to do. We sacrificed daily the little things that we wanted to do, keeping in mind what we wanted to become. We died daily, (1 Corinthians 15:31) trusting that God would raise good men from the death of little entertainments.

This is the revelation that I have found today, and I think it's a good one. I'll try to remember it next time what I want to do is the opposite of what I want to be, which will probably be, Oh, I don't know, sometime in the next five minutes.

"Do you not know that in a race all the runners compete but only one receives the prize? So run that you may obtain it. Every athlete exercises self-control in all things. They do it for a perishable prize, but we for an imperishable." 1 Corinthians 10:7

19. Integrity

When you talk to people these days, almost no one knows what integrity really is. It is something that only boy scouts and West Point cadets ever hear much about. It is one of the seven "Army Values", but what does the word really mean? When you hear the word used to describe someone e.g. "He's a man of integrity" what does that mean to you?

Most people, I think, would simply mean that he tells the truth and keeps his promises, but then I have to ask, why do we not just say that he is honest, for that is what honesty means? Words are used instead of other words because they have different meanings, or as in this case, because they *had* different meanings, even if the differences in meanings have come to be lost in this age of casual language.

What other words come from the same root? Integral. Integrated. We speak of a building's structural integrity, and surely we don't mean that the building tells the truth all the time or keeps its promises. We mean that it is solid, all of one piece. From the bottom of the foundation to the tip of the highest peak, all the various pieces have been integrated into one coherent whole and all work together doing their proper jobs to make the building strong. And this is precisely what I mean by integrity as a virtue as well. A man of integrity is all of one piece. There are no divisions in him, no internal conflicts, no warring within himself. He is at peace because he is entirely one being, completely seamless from top to bottom. His deepest choices inform all his thoughts, words and actions, and even his feelings. Everything is dictated by one abiding principle, which for a Christian is… what?

Right and wrong? But we can be mistaken about those sometimes.

Compassion? But that can too easily be used as a weapon. People can make us feel sorry for them and use that as a sort of emotional blackmail.

Logic? Too impersonal. Perfect logic might suffice, but our logic is never perfect. We always miss something.

Love? Now we are getting somewhere, but even that is not enough. We love so many different people and things in our lives. We love our parents, siblings, and friends, and someday we will love our wives, but those loves may come into conflict, and what is our compass then? The love that pulls the strongest may not necessarily be the one that is right.

Of course any of these can work, if it is in its perfect state. If you act on perfect morality, that covers all the others. Perfect compassion sees and desires only the truest good, and therefore cannot be guilt tripped. Perfect logic takes persons into account. But we cannot experience any of them in their perfect state because we do not have perfect integrity. We experience each of these only imperfectly, and so we constantly have to shuffle back and forth between them, using each to balance the other out, "For our knowledge is imperfect and our prophecy is imperfect, but when the perfect comes, the imperfect will pass away." 1 Corinthians 13:9-10. Of course what I'm saying is that perfect integrity is humanly impossible.

Why is it important then? It is important because it gives us a direction to travel in. The destination is an infinite distance away, and we can't walk that far, but at least we can be going in the right direction. In fact, I fancy that is really the way with nearly everything we ever undertake as men. Perfection is a direction, not a distance, for all practical purposes. We can only walk the road in the direction we are given, and God will carry us the rest of the way.

So how do we walk towards perfect integrity? We are looking for a single abiding principle that can guide and shape every aspect of our lives. Of course there is only one source of such a principle, and that is God. It is possible, I suppose, to order your entire life around a flawed principle, and since everything you do flows from that principle, you will bear a certain resemblance to a man of true integrity, but it won't get you anywhere. You can build the most solid building you want, but if you build it on sand it will never be stable. To build true integrity God must be our foundation, and He must also provide the materials that we are to build with. (Read Matthew 7:24-27.)

God's will is our perfect principle, but let's take it a bit further. God is our Creator, and as such we owe Him obedience. He is our master. He is also our King. But beyond that reality He is our Father, and it is in His Fatherhood that we find our guidance. We are sons of God, baptized into the life of God in the blood of Jesus. This sonship is the single most important fact of our lives. Everything we do should flow from and towards this fact, meaning that we should act to deepen and strengthen our understanding of our sonship, and that sonship should inspire and inform our every thought and action.

From this we build our integrity, one action at a time, one decision at a time, then one thought at a time, and even one feeling at a time. We take every thought captive in obedience to Christ, who is the Son from whom we all receive our sonship. We are not our own, but we have been purchased, and at a price. Not purchased in the sense of purchased as slaves, but purchased in the sense that we have been ransomed from slavery for adoption, into the family of God, and the price was blood. And now we repay it back to Him in the same coin. He has given everything for us, given His very life (See Leviticus 17:11). Our only repayment is to give back everything to Him, without reservation, without hesitation, and without counting the cost. We pay with our very lives. And yet, God cannot be outdone. He gave us our lives. We destroyed them and sold them into slavery to sin, both personally and collectively. He bought them back and gave them back to us. We can selfishly hold onto them, or we can give them back, but if we keep them we shall lose by it. If we give them back we are sacrificing what was only ours by gift and receiving a greater gift in return. God can never be outdone.

So what does this mean in concrete terms? Integrity is our response to God, in that it describes the quality of that response. It must be complete, total, unflinching and without reservation. We must "not be conformed to this world, but be transformed by the renewal of your mind, that you may prove what is the will of God, what is good, and acceptable and perfect." Romans 12:2 It is this response to God's gift of sonship that can release us from mixed, conflicting and self-contradictory lives, saying one thing, when we really mean something else. We do what is right and wish we wanted to. We live swayed by appetites and emotions, pitting our emotions against our logic to keep it from being too impersonal, and our logic against our emotions to keep them from being too unruly, and setting both in turn against our appetites. But from the beginning it was not so, and praise be to God He has redeemed us from that turmoil. We need no longer live in internal chaos. As sons of God we can possess the peace of God, perfect peace that passes all understanding. We can be mountains, solid, pure and singular, ready to live and work and love, especially love, purely and passionately, with every fiber of our beings, not just the ones that happen to be cooperating at this particular moment. That is true integrity.

"So I find it to be a law that when I want to do right, evil lies close at hand. For I delight in the law of God, in my inmost self, but I see in my members another law at war with the law of my mind and making me captive to the law of sin which dwells in my members. Wretched man that I am! Who will deliver me from this body of death? Thanks be to God through Jesus Christ our Lord!"
Romans 7:21-25

20. What's in a Name?

A question I have seen posted several times on the internet has to do with a wife taking her husband's name when she marries him. At one time in our society that was simply a tradition and it didn't occur to many people to question it. Nowadays, however, feminists ask why they should have to change their name, as if they need a man to establish their identity, and non-feminists ask why it really matters. Does it make that much of a difference?

(Of course most women still change their name when they get married. I read once that if you meet a single woman and she likes you right off, five minutes after that first meeting she will have already imagined her first name with your last name, just to see how it sounds. Whether there is any truth to that I of course cannot say).

Like most traditions, however, before we can safely get rid of it or condemn it we have to ask why it exists. All traditions exist for a reason, and if they have existed for a long time it is because they worked. They came about because someone saw a need for them, they caught on because other people recognized them as good ideas, and they lasted because they solved a problem, sometimes so well that we don't even remember that there was a problem. As the case with most traditional methods of courtship that have been around for centuries, they exist to solve problems, but we don't see the problems until we get rid of the traditions, and then we're stuck with a mess that our ancestors had traditions to prevent, but which we, in our rush to reinvent the wheel, have brought down upon our heads. I am not saying that traditions are always good. I am, however, saying that the burden of proof should be on those who challenge those traditions.

"Thus says the Lord, 'Stand by the roads and look, and ask for the ancient paths, where the good way is, and walk in it, and find rest for your souls." Jeremiah 6:16a

In regards to women taking their husbands' names, the idea I'm building on was suggested to me by Jeff Cavins' take on Genesis 2:19. He was speaking of Adam giving names to the animals, and that the giving of names signified authority. This is obviously the case, for "Whatever the man called the animals, that was their name." The parallel is too striking. Feminists object to taking a man's name because they feel instinctively that it signifies his authority, and that is repugnant to them, but Genesis does not allow that kind of relationship between a man and a woman. That master/beast relationship is quite proper to the beasts, but no helper was found fit for Adam among the beasts. They are inferiors, they are not equals. Therefore, God creates another person, a woman, drawn from Adam's rib. When Adam sees her he does three things in a specific order:

1) He recognizes her as an equal, "This at last is bone of my bones and flesh of my flesh." She could be a proper helper for him, because she was equal to him, made in the image and likeness of God, for she was made from him.

2) He named her. "She shall be called Woman, for she was taken out of man." My bible footnotes say that the words were ishah and ish in Hebrew "She shall be called ishah for she was taken out of ish." This is very important, for he gives her a name, a name that comes from his name, just as she came from him. This is a symbol of authority, but authority over an equal.

3) He takes her for his own. "Therefore a man leaves his father and his mother and cleaves to his wife, and they become one flesh." In accepting the authority, by giving her a name, he also accepted responsibility, which he would later shirk and thereby fall into Original Sin.

Bear in mind that this is the prototype, or better yet, the archetype of marriage, as it was meant to be "from the beginning" (See Matthew 19:8). This is how things looked before sin entered the world, and therefore is a pattern of how things should look on the natural level. The man must first recognize the woman as an equal. He must recognize his authority and through that authority his responsibility for leadership.

Of course after Original Sin things got all out of whack and the history of marriage since then has been spotted at best. The woman now desires to possess her man, and he rules over her, and so messed up is our understanding of the way things should be that we sometimes cannot even conceive of leadership that does not involve domination, or submission that does not involve subservience. The woman desires after her husband, seeking to control him and keep him with her. The man strays away or dominates her, and things get very ugly. Even marriages that are not so obviously distorted do not often show forth the plan that was in the beginning. A lot of things we moderns consider merely common sense really show a very serious lack of respect for that natural order. The two shall become one, but so much of the time they are one in name only. They have separate bank accounts, separate friends, separate interests, even separate vacations. We think of marriages as successful when they are not separated, and it never occurs to us that we should be positively pursuing oneness, striving for it with all our hearts (Matthew 19:6, "So they are no longer two, but one flesh. What therefore God has joined together, let no man separate.") We no longer have any natural model for what a marriage should look like.

Saint Paul solves that problem by showing us a supernatural model of marriage, or rather by pointing out that marriage is meant to be a natural model of the supernatural marriage of God to His Church:

"Wives, be subject to your husbands, as to the Lord. For the husband is the head of the wife as Christ is the head of the church, His body, and is Himself its Savior. As the church is subject to Christ, so let wives also be subject in everything to their husbands. Husbands, love your wives, as Christ loved the church and gave Himself up for her, that he might sanctify her, having cleansed her by the washing of water with the word, that He might present the church to himself in splendor, without spot or wrinkle or any such thing, that she might be holy and without blemish. Even so husbands should love their wives as their own bodies. He who loves his wife loves himself. For no man ever hates his own flesh, but nourishes and cherishes it, as Christ does the church, because we are members of His body. 'For this reason a man shall leave his father and mother and be joined to his wife, and the two shall become one flesh.' This mystery is a profound one, and I am saying that it refers to Christ and the church." Ephesians 5:22-32

Let's keep that in mind and go back to the idea of naming. After the flood, the covenant was established between God and Noah. Noah passed the covenant on to his sons, passing on the blessing through his son Shem, because Shem was righteous and "covered his father's nakedness." In Hebrew the word "Shem" means "name" and from the line of Shem would come the messiah. The very next thing we read about is how the people of the earth were seeking to build a tower to "make a name for themselves". Of course God thwarts that plan, but in the beginning of the very next chapter (Genesis 12) He promises to Abram, "I will make your name great." Then in chapter 17:5 He gives

Abram a new name, one that He will make great among the nations, and the blessing of all nations will be through the name of Abraham.

Fast forward almost 2000 years to Jesus. By human reckoning He inherited His name from David the king, but His name was given Him by God, (Luke 1:31). Within the Trinity Jesus is God, and yet scripture says, "In the days of His flesh, Jesus offered up prayers and supplications, with loud cries and tears, to Him who was able to save Him from death, and He was heard for his godly fear. Although He was a Son, He learned obedience through what He suffered; and being made perfect He became the source of eternal salvation to all who obey Him, being designated by God a high priest after the order of Melchizedek." Hebrews 5:7-10 Even though He was God, He emptied Himself of His name as God and became known as a man. And this was the result:

"Though He was in the form of God, [He] did not count equality with God a thing to be grasped, but emptied Himself, taking the form of a servant, being born in the likeness of men. And being found in human form He humbled himself and became obedient unto death, even death on a cross. Therefore God has highly exalted Him and bestowed on Him the name which is above every name, that at the name of Jesus every knee should bow, in heaven and on earth and under the earth, and every tongue confess that Jesus Christ is Lord, to the glory of God the Father." Philippians 2:5-11

So what does this mean to us? Looking back at Ephesians 5, it says that the mystery of husband and wife is a type or image of the mystery of Christ and the Church. What happens when we join the Church? We are baptized "in the Name of the Father and of the Son and of the Holy Spirit" Matthew 28:19. We surrender our previous identity as slave or free, Hebrew or Greek, male or female, all of them superseded by the new identity of Christ. We are named with His name. (See Galatians 3:28-29, Acts 4:12) We are Christ's people because we are named with His name. We are even called Christians by the outside world because we take our identity from Christ. At the end, in the wedding feast of the Lamb, God promises: "To him who conquers I will give some of the hidden manna, and I will give him a white stone, with a new name written on the stone which no one knows except him who receives it." Revelations 2:17 A large part of the book of Revelation is concerned with the battle between those who hold to the name of God and those who hold the name (or number) of the Beast.

Why is a name so important? Because a name indicates family, and family is the whole point of covenant. When God gives us His name He adopts us as sons. Every major covenant in the Bible is a case of God extending His name over His people.

But what does this have to do with a legal matter like whether a wife takes a husband's name or not? Everything. The natural model of marriage has failed, but even in the natural model the wife took the husband's name. Now, under the supernatural model, we know that human marriage is to mirror the eternal Marriage of the Lamb, with His bride, the Church. We represent that drama, we act out its parts on our little stage with our costumes, but the parts we play are assigned to us. In a marriage the husband represents Christ, who is God, the Bridegroom, the lamb who was slain (Revelations 5:6). The woman represents the Church, who is the bride, the one who receives the gift from the bridegroom and responds by giving herself back. The man must initiate the gift, not because he is more likely to want to give, but because that is what God does. Even as I write it I am terribly afraid. I am almost looking over my shoulder, sitting here in front of my laptop, as if God is going to strike me down for typing such presumption, but it is in the Scriptures. It is a terrifying statement, to any man with an ounce of honesty in him, for what man can look at himself and say, "So I have to represent God? Sure, no problem. Anything else?" Who could possibly think that? Who could have the arrogance to grasp at that role? And most men do not grasp after it, in my experience. Most men I know would rather do anything than take up leadership for their family. We practically have to be backed into a corner and forced to step up before we will act out this vocation. But this reluctance, containing at least a hint of humility for all its laziness and selfishness, is still better than the arrogance that would clutch at leadership, or that would think leadership was earned, rather than given by God. The sooner we start realizing that this is a gift we are given, not a reward we earn, a responsibility more than a privilege, and a privilege only because it is a responsibility, the safer we will be from all of the dangers that such a truth entails. In a marriage the wife represents the Church, the nurturing, loving, mothering Church. The woman who raises her children, answers their questions, wipes their noses, washes their laundry, cooks their food and shows them how to love God is doing in miniature what the Church has been doing for two thousand years. I am not trying to say, as feminists will no doubt accuse me of saying, that these things constitute the sum of a woman's vocation, but only pointing out that in all the humdrum daily grind of repeated menial service there is a great and noble mission that can never be replaced. In her response to her husband she represents the entire human race in our response to God, with the complication that while God can never be unfaithful to us, a human husband can never perfectly represent God. I am convinced, though, that the happiness of the marriage depends on how hard he tries.

Now mind, I am not arguing from this that the wife absolutely must take her husband's name. That is one of the ways in which our culture has embodied the Biblical principle, and it is a good way. I'm not sure when the practice of the bride changing her name developed, although it is mentioned as far back as Isaiah 4:1. Our tradition is a good way to acknowledge that principle. Depending on the culture you come from, it may not be the only way. Other cultures, for instance some Hispanic cultures, hyphenate the last names. There have not been very many matrilineal societies in the world, and they were exclusively non-Christian societies so I don't know whether that would ever work. I would be suspicious of any attempts to deny this tradition within our own culture, and I would want to know why the couple isn't keeping such a symbolic tradition, but the mere fact of not following this tradition is not going to condemn a marriage, anymore than keeping it will guarantee its success. Too many people keep traditions without thought, so it is no wonder that so many break them without thought. The important thing to keep in mind is this: The name change is a symbol. It is a symbol of Christ and the Church. The man must love the woman and pursue her, and he must have a name worthy to give her, as Jesus had a name from the Father. A man cannot "make a name for himself" if he means to do so apart from God. His name must come from God. Only then will it be worthy to give to his wife. She takes the name in love and trust, surrendering the name she received from her parents, and together they forge a covenant before God, and in so doing, they create a new family, all united under one name.

"Husbands, love your wives, just as Christ loved the church and gave himself up for her." Ephesians 5:25

21. A Male Without Blemish

Yesterday was Holy Thursday, and for those who don't know, it is a Catholic tradition during the Holy Thursday Mass for twelve men to have their feet washed by the priest in commemoration of Jesus' act of service at the Last Supper. Last night the lady who was coordinating the ceremony couldn't find twelve volunteers for the life of her. It was, of course, an oversight to leave it to the last possible minute, but that's beside the point. In a military parish there were not twelve men willing to volunteer. After all was said and done, there were only four males, and I was the only one out of high school. It got me thinking about the tradition itself. I don't think that it is necessarily wrong to have women play the part. It isn't a task or a ministry, and there is no question of roles to be answered. It is, however, a symbol of something. Those who get their feet washed symbolize the apostles, who were the leaders of the Church. It does signify leadership, to a certain extent, and I dislike it when symbols are ignored or diluted. It seems to me a step taken in the wrong direction without a good reason, simply because the guys are too embarrassed.

It is no secret by this point, of course, that I believe in male leadership both in the Church and in the Home. As St. Paul said, "I want you to understand that the head of every man is Christ, the head of a woman is the man, and the head of Christ is God." 1 Corinthians 11:3. I believe in a Biblical model of leadership, in which leadership is viewed as self-sacrifice. This is not surprising, since as Christians our King is a man who washed the feet of His followers one night and died for them the next night. This is reflected in Saint Paul's dictum for male leadership. "For the husband is head of his wife just as Christ is head of the church, He Himself the Savior of the body. As the church is subordinate to Christ, so wives should be subordinate to their husbands in everything. Husbands, love your wives, even as Christ loved the Church and handed Himself over for her." Ephesians 5:22 I'm not really interested in defending that position at the moment, I am on a different track. My question is why it should be the men that lead. Of course because that is what the Bible says, but why did God choose the males as the leaders and those called to lay down their lives and a host of other uncomfortable things? At first glance at our society, you would think women would be better at that Christian model of leadership. C. S. Lewis pointed out in the Screwtape Letters that a man has to be very far advanced in the service of God before he will spontaneously undertake as much trouble on behalf of others as quite an ordinary woman will. Most men, including myself, regard leaving people alone as one of the best things you can do for them. Women do not seem to share that view. Most women are naturally doing things for other people. So right there, self-sacrifice and consideration, natural prerequisites for Biblical leadership. Further, women naturally form deep emotional bonds with the people close to them, which makes them more ready to love than men. Leadership is all about love, so again, women seem to have a head start. Women are intuitive and a lot of leadership involves trusting your instincts. If you can believe our society, women seem to be more naturally religious, and a leader should always place top priority in his Faith, so it looks like women have us beaten there. Women are more relational, more concerned with people, which makes them tend more naturally to a relationship with Jesus, while men are more naturally concerned with facts and problems. We tend to be academic about Jesus, which isn't wrong, by the way, but it isn't enough. Leadership requires relationship, both with God who leads us, and with the people led, and this is true especially of Biblical, covenantal leadership. Why then, in the face of all of these facts, is it that God keeps choosing men to lead? Every covenant in the Bible was established through a man. Every single one was led by men. The early Church was led by men, and although Jesus revolutionized the place of women in society, by insisting they be treated with respect and honor rather than as mere possessions, He never gave any woman leadership, and neither did His Apostles, nor did the Church ever give leadership to women to this day (I'm speaking of the Catholic Church in this context. Other denominations do have female clergy, but they are historically the exception rather than the rule.) It seems that women would be the natural shoe in for leadership positions, given what God expects leadership to look like, but He keeps choosing the men.

So I was thinking about this as the lector read from Exodus that the Hebrews should choose a lamb, "A year old male without blemish," for their sacrifice. Why male? They were to splash the blood on their doorposts, the blood of the covenant, and oddly enough, it was the blood that got me thinking on a different track. Every covenant was ratified in blood. God shed the blood of animals to make clothes for Adam and Eve, covering what they had made shameful. Noah sacrificed animals after he left the Ark. God had Abraham cut a heifer in half to ratify his covenant, and He had him circumcise himself and all the males in his household. Again, with the males. It is the males of the line who have the sign of the covenant literally carved into their flesh. So we have two questions:

1) Why is bloodshed necessary for the forgiveness of sin?
2) Why is it the male who is supposed to make that sacrifice?

The blood is the life, the Bible tells us in Leviticus 17:11, which was why God gave us the animals for sacrifice. Only life makes atonement for life. Blood is the tie that binds a family together, and covenant is family. When God made His covenants with man He was extending His family through those covenants re-establishing the family that we had torn apart. He was sharing His life, literally, little by little until Jesus came along to give it to us in the fullest measure, and that is why we (I am speaking of Catholics again) receive the blood of Jesus in the Eucharist, because by so doing we receive His life.

But why the males? Women often seem more naturally ready to lay down their lives and shed blood for their children and loved ones, but that might well be the point. It is because men are not as naturally willing to sacrifice that sacrifice is required of us. If you have ever had to teach anything, whether it was sewing or hand to hand combat, you know that whatever comes least naturally to the student is what you have to spend the most time on. There is something to be said for that. Also, I think there is more to leadership than the obvious I went through above, and that something more makes it more natural for men to be leaders. For instance, the same structural differences in the brain which allow women to be more relational and intuitive than men also decrease their ability to specialize, abstract and compartmentalize. This is perhaps why men are more efficient at things like battlefield triage and other hard decisions because we can more easily separate the logical from the emotional, while women process both simultaneously. Leadership does require typically masculine qualities, and men are designed for that challenge. That's a topic for another day, however.

I think the answer is in 1 Timothy 2:15, where Saint Paul writes saying that women will be saved through childbirth. While I don't think he meant that unless women have children they are going to hell, every passage in the Bible is worth studying, especially the ones that seem most wrong at first glance. For instance, what did God say, right at the very beginning after Adam and Eve had sinned? "To the woman He said, "I will greatly increase your pains in childbearing; with pain you will give birth to children. Your desire will be for your husband, and he will rule over you." Gen 3:16

I think it's interesting that He said He would increase pain, not create pain. Perhaps this indicates that pain was going to be part of the process from the start, but that is just a speculation. What is true is that all women from then until now have shed their blood both in order to conceive and later to bear children. I think, as with all of God's punishments, that punishment was a gift. He was speaking to Eve, and her daughters, in ways that they could not escape. He was whispering something of the price of redemption and giving them a share in it. We all have to share in that price somehow, but women are given the gift of sharing in it in a way that men will never understand. In order for a woman to have a child she must literally offer up her life.

Men have it easier, in that regard. We don't have any particular biological need to be involved in children, beyond the obvious. Sacrifice and love are harder lessons for us, but I think like most subjects, it is those who have to put in the most work to learn who stand the best chance of excelling. Men are ordered in the Bible to offer up their lives, symbolized by blood, for the ones they are responsible for. Women are not so ordered, because they don't have to be. They can hardly avoid it. It is a gospel of sacrifice preached directly through their bodies and a woman's soul, I believe, is suited to that gospel. For men the sacrifice is less a part of our biological makeup and more a matter of sheer decision. We have to offer ourselves up, actively and voluntarily, sometimes against all our "better judgment." "If anyone would come after me, he must deny himself and take up his cross daily and follow me. For whoever wants to save his life will lose it, but whoever loses his life for me will save it. What good is it for a man to gain the whole world, and yet forfeit his soul?" Luke 9:23-25. We have to make ourselves worthy to be sacrificed, which is a chore in and of itself for we ultimately have to be without blemish. Fortunately for us we don't have to be without blemish before we can start sacrificing or none of us would ever get to the sacrificing part. We would be too busy removing blemishes. The Male without blemish has already taken all our blemishes upon Himself and offered Himself. Now we can be cleaned, so all we need to do is offer ourselves up. Easier said than done, of course, but at least we have a pattern to follow.

"For you know that it was not with perishable things such as silver or gold that you were redeemed from the empty way of life handed down to you from your forefathers, but with the precious blood of Christ, a lamb without blemish or defect. He was chosen before the creation of the world, but was revealed in these last times for your sake." 1 Peter 1:18-20

22. I'm Important

I think that no one can ever be really complete as a human being without changing a dirty diaper at least once in his life. I know you can't tell, because you can't see my face as I write this, but I am not joking. I have my serious face on. Not only do I think that diaper changing is necessary, I would especially recommend a really messy one, you know, where the fecal matter is so plentiful you wonder how so much could possibly come out of one single tiny individual, where it is leaking out both legs and drifting up the back. I'm still not joking.

Why, you ask? Because I have discovered no better way to learn service. Caring for lepers or AIDs patients might surpass diapering, but they are either in short supply, or in need of specially trained care that most of us are not qualified to render. Dirty diapers are fairly common occurrences and almost everyone is qualified. There is just something about cleaning up another human being's, even a very small one's, poop (or vomit for that matter) that brings you closer to them. It creates a special bond. More importantly, it makes it harder to take yourself seriously. Of course it is still possible. Anyone can continue to think themselves a big deal, even while wondering how poop gets in socks, if they are just willing to put in the effort, but it's a fragile effort. At any moment the truth might break through and the unending internal mantra of "I'm important, I'm important, I'm important," might start to echo a little hollow. If the humor of the situation ceases to escape you, it's only a matter of time before truth comes tiptoeing in with all the delicate grace of a herd of galloping elephants.

I write of that which I know. I have no children of my own, of course, but I grew up with four younger siblings, and literally dozens of infants that my family took in for short term foster care. Babies were considered a delight and a gift from God in my family, as was the privilege of taking care of them, so I write this with the memory of many infant foster siblings rising before my eyes as I type.

I discovered the fact about myself a long time ago, that I can do nearly anything for anyone as long as it is hard enough. If it is hard and challenging enough I'll do it just for the fun of it, never mind anyone else. All that this demonstrates is a rather backwards set of priorities. It isn't that that mantra I mentioned above is wrong. I'm not saying that I'm not important. I am important. I am infinitely important, but that's not really what I say when I tell myself that is it? When I have to remind myself that I am important, isn't that a good indication that I am feeling unimportant? If I were really convinced that I mattered, would I have to say it to myself? And even though I do matter, why is that? Why is it that I have the infinite importance that I claim to have? I certainly didn't earn it. All of my brains, muscles and accomplishments cannot earn me infinite importance, only relative importance and precious little of that.

I have this importance, this worth, this value, because it was given to me. Someone else made me valuable. All of my qualities are gifts; I can lay claim to none of those. My use of those qualities, such as have been good uses, are all of grace. I can lay claim to none of those either. I can claim nothing in this whole world that could possibly make me important. I am important because Someone has claimed me. God has claimed me as His own, and Jesus has paid that claim in blood. C. S. Lewis wrote in The Silver Chair, "Even the Lion wept: great Lion tears, each tear more precious than the Earth would be if it was a single solid diamond." Jesus wept over me, He sweat blood over me, and He paid the last drop of His blood for me. If every drop of that blood is more valuable than the entire universe, how valuable does that make me?

This is importance that builds up rather than puffing up. Because it rests on someone else, I do not have to sustain this importance through my own actions, which are not always the best. I don't have to rely on my muscles which will grow old and weak, even if they don't get damaged beyond repair first. I don't have to rely on my brain, which misses things. I don't have to rely on my looks (thank God for that!) I can rely on God to hold me and build me up, and in His strength I will have such strength that I will not have enough ways to burn it, so I will have strength to spare. I can be prodigal with it.

But that's not really all that the "I'm important mantra" has to say, is it? It really says, "I'm more important." It doesn't matter what or whom I think I'm more important than, it is the "more" that is the problem. With that one word I start comparing myself, basing my importance on something other than my adoption as a son of God. That is competition, and competition with what? When a diaper needs to be changed, could I actually think that thought out loud? "I'm more important." More important than whom? A baby? Am I actually competing with an infant? Am I as insecure as that that I can't serve an infant?

Jesus washed feet; not cute little baby feet, mind you, ugly, hairy, dirty man-feet, in an era before pedicures and wart removers and showers were invented. "When He had washed their feet, and taken His garments and resumed His place he said to them, 'Do you know what I have done for you? You call me Teacher and Lord; and you are right for so I am. If I, your Teacher and Lord have washed your feet, you also ought to wash one another's feet. For I have given you an example that you should also do as I have done to you." John 13:12-15

Can we do less? If we are so important, why do we make a big deal over such a small thing? After all, what could be smaller than a baby's butt?

"Have this mind among yourselves, which was in Christ Jesus, who, though He was in the form of God, did not count equality with God a thing to be grasped, but emptied Himself, taking the form of a slave, being born in the likeness of men. And being found in human form He humbled himself and became obedient unto death, even death on a cross. Therefore God has highly exalted Him and bestowed upon Him the name which is above every other name." Philippians 2:5-9

PART III

23. The Point of Chivalry

Nothing gets a reaction out of women faster than chivalry. If you don't believe me, hold the door for a woman today, make sure you make eye-contact with her, and watch what she does. Usually it is a favorable reaction, but not always. Most are just pleased to see a man behaving like a gentleman, after the initial shock, but a few are filled with holy horror at such a display of "chauvinism". One way or the other it is rare enough that it almost always startles. Those who appreciate it and thank you with a smile make the world seem a little more worthwhile, but what about the anti-gentlemen crowd? Do they have a point? Are we demeaning women every time we hold the door for them?

Does anyone seriously believe that the proponents of chivalry actually think that women are incapable of opening doors, or even that they don't like opening doors, or that men are better at opening doors? If it happens to be a solid steel high security door with a bad hinge you might need the extra muscle for it, but other than that, I am sure men and women are quite equal in their door opening abilities. Perhaps we should hold a door opening competition just to find out... but I digress.

The problem is that the anti-gentlemen crowd has no concept of love, which is what chivalry is all about. Chivalry is not about equality or inequality. It ignores such things entirely. It is not even really about kindness. True chivalry goes far beyond mere kindness. It is courtesy which is far deeper and more noble a thing than most people realize. Chivalry is symbolic of sacrificial love, the love that offers whatever strength, energy and time I have to the service of another. This is not at all the same thing as wanting to woo someone, although if you try to woo someone without it, you're going to end up deceiving yourself and possibly other people as well. You can and should have this love for everyone. Chivalry is symbolic of a man's willingness to use his (usually superior) strength to serve others instead of to dominate them. (If you doubt that men are usually physically stronger than women then we could always have an arm wrestling competition, men vs. women. Or maybe you would prefer a crossfit competition. Or a wood splitting competition). Superior physical strength is one of the realities of being male. Most men are stronger than most women, and too often men have used that strength to dominate women. Women then resent men (and rightly so) and use their charm and wiles to get advantage over the men (wrongly so). To combat this, chivalry was developed (actually it was developed and pushed into the mainstream by certain influential women of the middle ages and renaissance).[8] In its present form its symbolism is two-fold. Men do little things that they do not have to do, symbolizing that they are using their strength to serve, rather than to dominate. Women accept these small courtesies that they could just as easily do themselves, symbolizing that they are choosing to trust these men and allow them to do things for them, rather than insisting on being constantly in charge. Perhaps that is why so many women are made uncomfortable by chivalry, because secretly they are not secure enough in their own worth to surrender even the slightest amount of control over their own lives, like Peter who said, "Lord, you shall never wash my feet." John 13:8. We, as men, are called to image Christ to the world. "Husbands, love your wives, just as Christ loved the church and gave himself up for her." Ephesians 5:25. Jesus humbled Himself to serve by washing the feet of His Church. Holding the door for those who are to image the Church to us (Ephesians 5:24) is not an chore but an honor and privilege.

Chivalry, with all its abuses, is better than the alternative that our modern society has come up with. Since the feminist movement the sexes have become less equal, not more equal. Men are not taught to be chivalrous, and so we have a generation of men who will not serve. The latter part of this generation is leaning towards the older and more dangerous pre-chivalrous model of men whose sole outlook on women is expressed in the phrase, "Go get me a beer, b---h." Is this the equality the feminists were looking for? Men have not been taught to be chivalrous for the last few decades, and now for some reason we are surprised to find more men than ever who will not think twice of hitting a woman. Some equality. Okay, now you have it, enjoy it. Since women can do anything men can do, grow some cahones and fight back. Punch him. Get in a fistfight. That will solve all of our problems. Society will be equal and at each other's throats.

But this does not only make men more self-centered and unwilling to help, it also hurts women. Because women are not taught to accept chivalry (which is just as important as teaching men to be chivalrous) we have an entire generation of women who are jaded, cynical, discontented and unable to accept favors without suspecting everyone of an ulterior motive. We have an entire generation of women who cannot trust men. These are the women who complain about how hard it is to find a decent man and then complain about the decent men wanting to protect and care for them. These are the women who are constantly and loudly insisting "I'm just as good as you are!" The odd thing is that it rings hollow. If you really are just as good as someone, and you really know you are, then there is no need to keep saying it.

So we have a society of men who are untrustworthy because they live in a society of women who will not trust, and the women will not trust because the men have proven themselves untrustworthy. When one man tries to break the mold and speak the old sacrificial language of chivalry, whether he knows what that language is saying or not, he risks bringing down upon his head a shrill, vocal and indignant crowd of women who are so caught up in saying, "I'm just as good as you, I can hold that door for myself!" that they have never even considered that maybe he already knows that. They can't trust him. Somewhere, somehow, those who are caught up in this cycle have to find a way to get out of it, to learn to trust and be trustworthy again. Otherwise I'm afraid there is no hope for the future of male/female relationships in America.

This is an extreme version, of course. I hold doors habitually and even allow women to go first at buffet lines, and I have rarely had one object too strongly, after the initial surprise. I think most women have the good sense to welcome chivalry. They recognize it for what it is.

"They came to Capernaum. When he was in the house, he asked them, "What were you arguing about on the road?" But they kept quiet because on the way they had argued about who was the greatest. Sitting down, Jesus called the Twelve and said, "If anyone wants to be first, he must be the very last, and the servant of all."
Mark 9:33-35

24. Serve and Protect

I read a blog article once which was entitled, "Men, protect the women in your life." I have to say, it was pretty good for the most part, although to be honest I did not really click on it to read the post itself but to read the comments. I was sure they would be pretty well divided between the "Awww, that's so sweet" crowd and the "Back off, jerk, I don't need protection," crowd. Always a fun dialectic to watch. The funniest comment was by a woman, to the effect, "I don't need a man to protect me, a swift kick to the nuts will bring any man to his knees."

It is hard to imagine anything more irrelevant than that comment to the actual point of protecting. First of all, it is a gross overestimation of the effectiveness of that technique. I could write a whole book just on the topic of female self-defense myths and stereotypes. It is a topic I take very seriously and have researched pretty thoroughly, believe it or not. However for the moment I will just say that a kick in the groin is not a guaranteed fight stopper and never has been. Sure, it hurts like the devil, but if a man really wants to, he can fight through it. I have done so many times in combatives matches, and they weren't even life or death situations.

But that really is a distraction from the real point of the blog. Sure women can fight if they have to. Most aren't much good at it, because they haven't been trained, but they can (and in some parts of the country probably should) develop the ability to defend themselves effectively. That's not the issue. If you think getting into fistfights all the time is what it means to protect someone you have watched too much TV. Even in the very narrow area of physical protection and even narrower area of self-defense, the point is not that women cannot defend themselves, but rather that they should not have to as long as I am around. Even if I knew that some woman was a champion martial artist and more than capable of taking care of herself, I would still consider myself honor bound to step in first. Not because I am a better fighter, but because it is my responsibility as a man. Not only that, but it is my responsibility to prevent danger when possible, rather than waiting to confront it after it arises. Getting into fights over petty things is a young man's game (and by young man I mean teenage hot-head). It's fun if you're by yourself and you can avoid getting damaged, but no matter how impressive you think it might be it is plain contrary to good common sense if you have a responsibility to look after some-one else. Protecting people means preventing trouble more often than it means fighting it, being constantly on the lookout, pre-empting the bad guys before they get the chance to strike. If you are a sheepdog in a world full of predators, a little paranoia is normal.

It is the same with other types of protection. Verbal abuse is much more common than physical abuse and definitely also calls for protec-tion. Anyone who has ever argued with a smart and determined wom-an knows that they can be verbally sharper than the sharpest men out there. When women are sarcastic, they are nasty. In fact, some might even complain that men should need protection from them! Still, miss-ing the point. Of course women can learn to take verbal abuse and dish it back out again, but they should not have to. (Neither should we, by the way: "Do not scold, like a kitchen-girl. No warrior scolds. Courte-ous words, or else hard knocks are his only language.") It should never reach them because that is our service, our place, our responsibility. If I can't get there, or I get beaten down, then she can defend herself to her heart's content. Until then, I'm going to be doing most of the fight-ing. Yes, I do consider physical response to verbal abuse justified under certain circumstances. Justified, but not necessarily prudent. Better if we can create an atmosphere around those we care about such that that kind of abuser doesn't enter. Forestall the trouble if you can (Proverbs 15:1). You will find you have to fight less. In a society of mainly gentle-men and ladies, the sort of people who abuse others verbally will find themselves in the minority and outmatched by the strong and good men around them. There should be order and harmony among the men and women in a society of believers, "For where you have envy and selfish ambition, there you find disorder and every evil practice. But the wisdom that comes from heaven is first of all pure; then peace-loving, considerate, submissive, full of mercy and good fruit, impartial and sincere. Peacemakers who sow in peace raise a harvest of righteousness." James 3:16-18.

What about spiritual protection? Or don't we believe in that? Of course we all believe in temptation, but what about other subtler attacks that we generally consider to be normal, just parts of life to be treated with drugs or therapy? Depression? Discouragement? Anxiety? Fear? I would consider all of these as attacks of the devil one way or another, unless there was some other known cause. Of course you cannot fight principalities and powers with fists or guns (more's the pity) but that does not one iota reduce the obligation of protection. If God has given you a battle to fight, He has also given you the weapons, particularly prayer, and most especially the prayer that is the Word of God. Unfamiliarity with scripture is like going into battle without your sword. In the military, one of the more technical terms for someone without a weapon is "Bullet Stopper."

Don't just stand there, get on your knees and fight. Again, build and maintain an atmosphere in your home that will be toxic to the enemy, but know that this enemy is different. He will not walk away from a hard target like a human threat would, because this enemy is well and truly full of hate. When you start locking him out it enrages rather than scares him. The more successful you are in this, the more he will attack. The more often you can take the fight to him the better off you will be. Do not be on the defensive, just sitting around taking his assaults as if you were helpless. "For you did not receive a spirit that makes you a slave again to fear, but you received the Spirit of sonship. And by Him we cry, 'Abba, Father'." Romans 8:15. As soon as the devil attacks you or someone you love, counterattack with every ounce of strength you have. God has made you a warrior to protect others, especially your sisters and your younger brothers.

"Be strong in the Lord and in His mighty power. Put on the full armor of God so that you can take your stand against the devil's schemes. For our struggle is not against flesh and blood, but against principalities and powers, against the rulers of this dark world and against the spiritual forces of evil in the heavenly realms. Therefore put on the full armor of God, so that when the day of evil comes, you may be able to stand your ground, and after you have done everything, to stand. Stand firm then, and gird your loins with the truth, with the breastplate of righteousness in place, and with your feet fitted with the readiness that comes from the gospel of peace. In addition to all this, take up the shield of faith, with which you can extinguish all the flaming arrows of the evil one. Take the helmet of salvation and the sword of the Spirit, which is the word of God. And pray in the Spirit on all occasions with all kinds of prayers and requests. With this in mind, be alert and always keep on praying for all the saints." Ephesians 6:10-18. This is a battle, Brothers, and we are the fighters. God has chosen us. If we do not fight, then I ask you, who will?

Of course women should be able to speak, pray and even fight for themselves. And they should definitely exercise all of these at need without hesitation. That does not in any way reduce our responsibility as men to pray, speak and fight on their behalf. The irony of it is that even our own inability does not reduce that responsibility. We have not been made men because we were good at it (think about that for a second) we are made men so that we can become good at it. Whatever doesn't come naturally does not show us where we can slack off, but rather where we need to concentrate our training. I've heard stories of boys getting into fights in school and getting bailed out by their older sisters. In my opinion she probably would have done better to let him lose rather than humiliate him like that, as long as he wasn't in any serious danger. (Although, the way schools are these days, he may well have been in serious danger.) He would have learned more by losing than by getting bailed out. Some men are weaker than many women, but as long as women refuse to let men take their place, and even more, as long as women don't expect men to take responsibility and don't hold them to that standard, then men will remain weak. A lot of women neuter men in this regard. After a few times realizing that every time he steps up to do something he will be doing it wrong, or she can do it faster and better, or that she will have gotten to it already, or that she will be insulted by it, don't be surprised if he stops stepping up.

My theory is that chivalry and etiquette were invented or developed as a sort of purgatory. Each gender has to learn to do what comes least naturally to it. Men have to learn to live for others, to notice things that need doing and do them, and women have to learn to let other people do things, rather than trying to do it all themselves. The men must do something, the women must stop doing things. The symmetry is perfectly uncomfortable. It is no more permissible for a man to say, "I'm not naturally an assertive person, I can't be the leader," than it is for a woman to say, "I am not naturally a submissive person so I cannot follow." Try that in the military and see how far it gets you. Rank has nothing to do with personality. Of course it doesn't come naturally. God never said it would, only that He would guide us.

The issue of protection, in the final analysis, really has nothing whatsoever to do with which individual is better able to handle themselves in a fight. Of course we can rightly generalize that men are better suited for it, but there remain exceptions, and the more spiritual the realm, the more exceptions we will find. It is not important. The question is who has been given what responsibility? Ours is set. Our post has been logged in, so to speak, we cannot leave it. So if you find yourself in the company of a woman stronger than yourself that is no excuse to let her be the man. Nor does it mean that you should demand she be weaker in the name of "submission". It is actually God telling you that you need to be stronger than you are. She should not abandon her strength, you must find yours. You've got work to do.

On another note, doesn't the phrase "Serve and Protect" make you think it would be a great thing to be a cop? Where else can you get the opportunity to do so much for so little, and be so universally hated for it?

"Likewise, you husbands should live with your wives in understanding, showing honor to the weaker female sex, since we are joint heirs of the gift of life, so that your prayers may not be hindered." 1 Peter 3:7[10]

25. Nothing but a Sister

In case you haven't noticed from the table of contents, the next few chapters are going to be talking about girls, and how I think a Christian gentleman should relate to them. By girls, I mean the kind of girls you might want to have as a girlfriend, the sort that you might one day want to get married to. Be warned, it is not going to be a fun few chapters. I am far more concerned with disciplining emotion than I am with feeling it. Feelings happen to good, bad and indifferent men, but it is what we do with those feelings that determines which category we fall into.

110

So I enter into the most interesting part of the book with a mood spoiler. Instead of talking about girlfriends and how to treat them, I will talk about sisters and how to treat them.

I never do anything without a reason. In this case, I have two reasons:

1) I have never had a girlfriend. More on that in a later chapter, but for now you need to know that me talking about how to treat a girlfriend would be something like a private fresh out of basic training trying to tell a raw untrained recruit about combat. He may have been in the army longer, but he still knows nothing about combat. So if you're looking for romantic ideas, find another book.

2) I believe with all my heart that unless you have learned to treat your sister properly, you have no business having a girlfriend. That's my principal. Take it or leave it, but if you leave it, you may as well not even finish this book. It would be a waste of your time.

Now, you'll notice that in the last two chapters I have already talked about chivalry and the need for men to protect women, long before I'm getting to the girlfriend type relationships. This is by design. Chivalry has absolutely nothing to do with romance in this regard. It is far more basic than that. Chivalry is an expression of love, sacrificial love, whereby we give of ourselves to and for those we love. That is the basic meaning of being a man. Of course it is expressed most completely and accurately in the married relationship. In the marriage covenant the man and the woman become one in a sense somehow analogous to the way in which Jesus unites to the Church. "'For this reason a man shall leave his father and mother and be joined to his wife, and the two shall become one flesh.' This is a great mystery, and I speak concerning Christ and the church." Ephesians 5:31:32.

This relationship between man and woman is established by the one flesh union, the joining of their hearts and bodies in sexual union. However, notice why the joining of the bodies is possible:

"'This is now bone of my bones
And flesh of my flesh;
She shall be called Woman,
Because she was taken out of Man.'
Therefore a man shall leave his father and mother and be joined to his wife, and they shall become one flesh." Genesis 2:23-24.

The one flesh union of marriage is established based on the prior relationship of the man and woman as Brother and Sister. This is echoed in the Song of Songs, when the Bridegroom calls his beloved, "My Sister, My Bride" (Song of Songs 4:9, 4:10, 4:12, 5:1, and 5:2).

This is important for two reasons:

1) Unless we learn how to love our sisters, we will never be able to love our brides properly.

2) In order to love our brides properly, they must also be our sisters in some sense.

The first one is the focus of this chapter. I intend to touch on the other one only very briefly here.

A movie I really liked when I was very young, Disney's "The Aristocats," illustrated for me the exact place in the universe which sisters were created to occupy. In the movie, the three young kittens were all running for their little cat door, and the girl, Marie, called out "Me first, me first." When one of her brothers asked why she should go first she replied with great self-importance, "Because I'm a lady, that's why."

To which her brothers very memorably replied, "You're not a lady, you're nothing but a sister."

Of course my views on sisters and their roles have matured somewhat since I first saw that movie, but I do think it illustrates a common distrust of the whole gentleman/lady dynamic. Girls who are raised in families where that norm is instilled and enforced sometimes expect to reap all the benefits of ladyhood, without accepting any of the responsibility, and brothers very properly resent that. Even women who have no use at all for real femininity will still ape ladylike qualities to get what they want. I am not denying that women can be sly and manipulative.

However, that is really not our concern, is it? We are not women. This is not a book about how to be ladylike. Let them manage their own concerns for a while without us, while we take a deep honest look at our own failures.

We are gentlemen, and gentlemen treat women based on who their Father is, not on how they act. And honestly, doesn't it seem as if that resentment and blame throwing is a rather flimsy excuse for the fact that most guys just don't want to treat their sisters with chivalry? How many times have you seen a guy, who never had a kind word for his sister, suddenly turn into the sweetest and most chivalrous "gentleman" imaginable as soon as a non-sister type of girl of about his own age showed up? I have seen it many times. And if we're honest, we have not only seen it, we've done it.

Loving a woman whom you have a crush on is pretty easy. It comes naturally. Loving your sister is very different and not as easy. You don't have the strength of hormones to do the work for you, you have to do it yourself, love her because you have chosen to based on a relationship that was given to you without your consent. You have to accept the reality that she is your sister, and hence your responsibility is to love her. Beyond that, even for married couples, especially for married couples, love is a lot of work. It requires effort and self-sacrifice. Is it worth it? Judging by all the old married couples and happy families I know, I would assume that it is. But contrary to what our society tells us, the happiest marriages are not the ones where everything is done for them. The happiest marriages are the ones in which the couple put in the most effort, and in which everything is surrendered to God.

No one has to learn how to "fall in love." That happens by itself, and rather too easily to some people, it would seem. We do have to learn to love, though, and that takes practice. It takes a lot of practice. In fact, that is the whole point of being on this earth, to practice loving, since that will be our full time occupation in Heaven. For a boy to become a man he has to learn to love women. If he does not, he will learn to use them for his own amusement. He has to learn, and in order to learn he has to practice. It is not enough to read books about it, you actually have to get out and practice on a real live girl, or several real live girls, but here we run into a problem. You can't just go around being sweet and loving to every girl you know, at least, not at the level I am talking about. They would almost certainly get the idea that you were pursuing a romantic relationship. That's a sure recipe for broken hearts and compromised integrity.

But God, in His infinite wisdom, has provided most men with plenty of women to practice on. Every man has a mother. Most men have sisters or cousins. There are definitely a lot of women that you know who are much, much older than you, from your friends' mothers to the little old ladies at church. All of these are worthy recipients of your chivalry. However, with sisters it goes a little beyond that. Not only do you get to practice being chivalrous, you get to practice being affectionate too.

Seriously, if you have a sister, or a female cousin, when was the last time you told her you loved her? Can you even remember? If you can't, or it wasn't within at least a week, you should probably fix that as soon as possible.

I know it doesn't sound like much fun. I know that we all love our sisters dearly, and we would do anything for them, but for some reason, we just can't bring ourselves to say it. I understand that. Better still, I think I understand why that is. We are reluctant to be chivalrous to our sisters because the devil is actively discouraging it. He is subtly driving a wedge between sisters and brothers in our society, and he has done a frighteningly efficient job of it.

Why do you think I put the "Serve and Protect" chapter right next to the "Point of Chivalry" chapter? It was not accidental. The two are inextricably linked. Chivalry, or what we know today as chivalry, grew up out of a warrior culture. It was embraced by the elite armored knights of Europe, and encouraged by women, and the two, chivalry and protection, are very similar on a profound level. In fact, with the benefit of a few hundred more years of history, we can see a wisdom in the practice of chivalry that the knights and their ladies probably couldn't see.

Chivalry is a language of love. The body of a man is designed in all its parts to enable us to give of ourselves for other people, whether by carrying things for them, fighting for them, or in the marital love of a husband and wife. The man is designed to give, the woman is designed to receive, and then to give back a greater blessing still. This language of the body,[11] far from being concerned only with the physical body, instead informs and determines the rightness of our entire being and everything we do for it. As our bodies are designed to give, our souls are designed to give also.

As a woman's body is designed to receive, so her soul is designed to receive also. Women have an unbelievable hunger to be loved. They want to be loved and to know that they are loved. They want to be cherished and know that they are cherished. I have met some women who were very wounded by what life had done to them, but this still held true in some deep, perhaps forgotten corner of their hearts. They still desired to be loved. So I say with complete confidence that your sister desires your love, especially if she is your younger sister. Whether she knows it or not, she desires you to love her.

Hundreds of books have been written on the wonderful effect of a father's love on his daughter, and the horrible effect of his hatred, abuse or neglect. Young girls who grow up not knowing the love of a father grow up with a horrible void in their hearts. They desire the love and affirmation that he was supposed to give her, and so they often end up seeking it in destructive and evil ways. They give themselves body, heart and soul to the first loser who sweet talks them into believing he really cares. They might end up hating men entirely. They might end up with any one of a number of eating disorders or self abusing behaviors. The lack of love cripples and wounds women on a level we men cannot really understand.

It is in the face of this hatred of women by the devil that chivalry expresses itself as protection. This is where chivalry and protection become so fused that they are really one thing, or different parts of the same thing. The devil attacks women who are not loved with terrible effectiveness because they are vulnerable. The more loved a woman is, the easier it is for her to tell the difference between the truth of God and the lies of the devil. When the men in her life, father and brothers, love her and let her know that she is loved, this becomes a layer of defense around her that negates the effectiveness of some of the devil's attacks, and make no mistake, he is attacking her. When God said, "I will place enmity between you and the woman, between your seed and hers," (Genesis 3:15) the serpent took it literally. To this day he has been attacking women and children venomously. He doesn't attack us men quite so directly, usually. He usually tries to distract and disorient us, keep us busy with other things, discourage us, slowly building off of wounds received in childhood. He doesn't want to push too hard, or we might wake up and start fighting. He has less concern with women. He wants to crush them. He hates women with a vengeance. You need only take a look at the way women have been treated throughout history to grasp something of how vulnerable they are.

This is why God has given you to your sisters, and your female cousins. By visibly and openly loving them you create an extra barrier between them and the attacks of the devil and greatly increase the ease with which they can grow to be able to trust and love freely, as God created them to do.

So how do you do this? Well, I can think of a number of ways. They are not going to be easy, especially at first, but they are all doable.

1) Tell her so. A quick hug and "I love you, Sis" is a pretty cheap gift, and isn't likely to throw the world too far off its axis. Sure, it might

embarrass you if you're not used to showing affection to a mere sister, but that's good. It only makes that little gift more valuable.

2) Take an interest in her life. Ask her what's going on with her, and listen, no matter how trivial or insignificant the details are. You don't have to comment on it, and in fact, it might not be a good idea unless you can comment without criticizing. Just get to know her. Listen, store up all this information. Learn what makes your sister tick, no matter how weird it is. You may not think pink ponies are all that riveting, but make sure she knows that you love her no matter how many pink ponies she has. In this way, later on if she develops interests that might not be so innocent, for instance in a music group that pushes un-Godly ideas, you will have the freedom to speak out honestly, knowing that she trusts you to speak out of love. Whether she agrees with you or not, or listens to you or not, is not your concern. Your only concern is to listen and speak the truth with love.

3) Protect her. When someone says something bad about your sister, especially in front of her, punch him in the nose. Yes, I do advocate physical force in defense of your sister, if the situation calls for it. It is not because we are so nice and loving that most men won't protect their sisters. It's because we're too wimpy.

4) Tell her the truth. The truth is, no matter what your sister looks like to you, God created her to be beautiful. He gave her a beauty that is all her own. Tell her that. We all know that there are certain things that can reduce or obscure that beauty, like ugly behavior, immodest clothing or a lack of concern for the health of the body. The world encourages all of these, explicitly and implicitly. Be the one voice that does not encourage them. Make sure she knows that what you value is real beauty, depth of beauty, beauty of soul. Be very, very careful what kind of woman she hears you praising. If you're praising swimsuit models and immodestly dressed girls at your school, don't be surprised if that's what she wants to be. Don't even look approvingly at a woman, unless you would look approvingly at your sister dressed the same way. She has enough people telling her that beauty is a supermodel body with a flawless complexion and next to no clothes. You need to tell her the truth. Beauty is a healthy, happy woman who is passionately in love with God and who is constantly giving of herself to those around her. However, in order to tell her the truth, you have to possess the truth in your heart. Do not just pretend you like that kind of girl when she is

around. She will see through it eventually. You cannot lie to a woman forever. Instead, mold your own heart after the truth. Learn to value those women with all your heart, and value that in her, and encourage that beauty every time you see her displaying it. If she does something loving for a younger sibling, praise her for it. If she does something nice for you, thank her for it. If she dresses modestly and beautifully, tell her so. Learn to appreciate her particular beauty. Ask God to teach you how, for He created your sister and delights in her. Ask Him and allow Him to let you enter into that delight.

5) Live up to her expectations. Most sisters, especially younger ones, have a tendency to think their brothers a lot better than we really are. This gives you a mark to shoot for. If you are tempted to do anything, but you would be ashamed to do it if your sister were present, then you probably need to run away, far and fast.

6) Pray for her. Every single day, every night. Pray for her in every way you can think of, and as you are led by the Holy Spirit. Pray for her protectively.

This idea of praying protectively needs to be addressed a little more here. I don't mean that you ought merely to ask God to be nice to her before you go to bed every night. It ought to cost more than that. Prayer should be an act of sacrifice. In praying for others we should be offering ourselves, body and soul, in the service of that person's greatest good. We should be surrendering entirely to God's love. There are certain people I pray for protectively every day, including my sister and several of my cousins, meaning that I pray that they may be guarded from spiritual and other forms of attack. I do not think that this is merely a question of me asking a favor of the Lord. Rather, I think real, personal sacrifice does need to occur on some level. At some level I have to die, if I am really to offer my body up as a living sacrifice. (Romans 12:1) If my sufferings can really make up what is lacking in Christ's sufferings (Col 1:24), what does that mean? There is nothing lacking in Christ's suffering except application. They must be applied, accepted, positively embraced, in order for them to be effective. "Take up your cross and follow," is not a bit of optional advice.

I am not asking God to do me a favor and keep an eye on my sister. That would imply that God is not already doing so, or that I could get God to do things, or even that I love more deeply than God does. God is already protecting all the people I care about far more effectively and lovingly than I ever could. So what is the point of my prayer? God is allowing me, as a favor, to desire something that He desires. I am entering, cautiously, fearfully and with unending prevarication, into the blazing torrent of God's fierce love for His little ones. When I pray protectively I am not asking that He do anything He is not already doing. Rather, I am humbly asking the privilege of being joined to it. God is already standing with His arms around all the innocents of the world, tenderly and protectively. His angels are shields to them. The people I care most about in the world are already surrounded by a wall of light. The devil can do nothing to them that God does not allow. I cannot ask better protection, but I can ask to be a part of it. I can offer myself up to this service.

This is why I say that on some level some real sacrifice of self has to take place, whether it be a black eye, sleepless nights, or some embarrassment or whatever. In order to be joined to the sacrifice of Christ, we must sacrifice. I think it works in ways we could never have dreamed. I ask to be included in God's labor of love as a privilege. That fact that I can ask at all is a privilege. I am my sisters' keeper, and there is hardly a greater honor imaginable.

By now it should be obvious that I am not talking about an easy or convenient thing. What I am talking about is real sacrifice and it will cost you, not the least in embarrassment for a while, until you get used to it. But remember the language of the body. God created you to give of yourself, and He will give you the strength to do so. Beyond that, He also created women to receive that gift of self and transform it into a greater blessing and to give it back. In the natural order of marriage, this is what we call a child. The husband gives himself to his wife, she receives that gift, and in her it is transformed into a new life, and she gives a child to her husband. Between them, they have the glory and honor of giving a new human soul to God, one that will last into all eternity as a member of the family of God.

This happens in different ways on every level when men and women interact as they were meant to. The women who are loved by their fathers and brothers become ladies, as opposed to just being women. They can love their brothers with an intensity and loyalty that is incredible. The love of a sister who is a true lady, in the deepest sense of the word, can literally save your soul, when you are assaulted by the lies of the world, the flesh and the devil. I know. That's why I am able to write this, because my sister and my cousins have loved me and prayed for me when I needed it most and deserved it least. They saved my soul.

This means that part of your job as a brother, is to help your sister become a lady. You do not do this by teaching her how to be one (you probably wouldn't be very good at it yourself) but rather by treating her as if she already was one. If she is a lady, this will be easy. If not, well, you'll have an opportunity to give a real, costly gift of love. A lady is not some prim and proper girl who can't get dirty, who sits around all the time with her nose in the air. A real lady is dangerous. She can inspire you and shame you, she can pray for you in times of trouble, she can humble you, she can strengthen you. A lady may be soft, gentle, gracious and elegant, but she is never tame. God put her in this world with a real job to do, just as much as He put you here to do a job. So when your sister offers to do something for you, accept it, no matter how much your pride wants to refuse. So she doesn't realize she is embarrassing you? So what? You are helping her to live out her vocation, just as she helps you to live out yours by accepting your well meaning but sometimes clumsy efforts.

Another way to put this is to say that you ought to treat your sister like a princess. Now, in my terminology "Princess" is not a euphemism for spoiled brat. It is a literal and objective description of a woman who is a daughter of a king, in this case, The King of Kings, God Himself. It is both a wonderful privilege and a terrible responsibility. A Princess deserves respect, but she also has a responsibility to live out her vocation and to serve those around her. So I am not talking about treating your sister like some sort of china doll, as if she were too fragile to be of any use. Rather, I mean that a brother should protect his sister's very real vulnerability, while at the same time encouraging her peculiarly feminine strengths. Yes, that will require you to allow her to serve you from time to time. It will not unman you. It is a very high and noble courtesy that can be humbled equally by both serving and being served.

This is enough work to keep you busy for many years until you are ready to think about getting married, and by that time you will be the kind of man who can love out of your heart, and not just out of your hormones. So yes, the gift that you give your sister now is also a gift you are giving your future wife, and she doesn't even know it yet!

"We should no longer be children, tossed to and fro and carried about with every wind of doctrine, by the trickery of men, in the cunning craftiness of deceitful plotting, but, speaking the truth in love, may grow up in all things into Him who is the head— Christ" Ephesians 4:14-15

26. The Modesty Battle

Modesty is one issue that the Christian community in general seems to consider a women's problem. Women don't dress modestly in this day and age, (in case you hadn't noticed) and, being the visually oriented creatures that we are, men suffer because of it. I have written elsewhere about it, from the point of view of what I would like to see women doing to fix the problem, but that doesn't concern us here. What concerns us here is a much more troubling trend I've noticed a lot in discussing this with Christians of various backgrounds. Many women, I find, are angry at men over this issue. They have three main points:

1) Why can't men learn to control themselves?

2) Why should they have to change what they wear for men?

3) Why is it that whenever men have a problem with this they say, "She tempted me," and it immediately becomes her fault?

The answers to these are:

1) We can and should.

2) Many reasons, including self respect and Christian charity, if they are causing their brothers to stumble by what they wear, or more importantly, by how they act.

3) Very good question:

The issue with modesty has two parts. On the one hand, generally speaking you have us men who are set up to be visually oriented. We are attracted to good looking women. Now some will protest that women are attracted to good looking men, but this is something far beyond that. To put it succinctly without being vulgar about it, men are quite capable of desiring sexual activity immediately and with no other stimulus than seeing a sexually attractive woman in a sexually attractive pose (dress and behavior). We see a woman walking along in a suggestive outfit, and instantly she becomes the whole universe and sex with her is the point of that universe. Women, for the most part, are not like that. Women tend to be more focused on personality and personal relationships so while they may admire a man that they think is good looking, images of his body, or specific portions of that body, aren't going to try to dominate their thoughts for the rest of the day.

I'm not concerned with female responsibility in this subject. Yes, they have a responsibility, but this book is not for them, so let's focus on ours, shall we?

This is the main problem here. Some women simply don't understand the problem. Other women do understand and use it to their advantage. The ones who simply don't grasp how much of a snare immodesty can be to us, usually end up thinking that since they cannot understand that kind of obsession it must be wrong or perverted. It isn't, necessarily, any more than any other part of our nature so twisted by original sin is wrong. We are fallen humans. Obviously it isn't normal in the sense that Adam didn't have that problem before he sinned, but normal in the sense that this is how male sexual drive works in a fallen world, it definitely is. It isn't the visual attraction that is the problem either. If we were not attracted visually we would not be equipped as well to seek out and pursue women, which is what God has designed us to do. The problem is that the visual orientation has deteriorated until only that which can be seen visually is considered. We now are tempted to look upon the beauty of a woman, without seeing a person, but merely an object to be used for our own pleasure. It is not the fact that we look that is so perverse, but the way we look, when we look with lust upon a body, rather than with love upon a person. A friend once expressed this by saying that an active, lustful fantasy is nothing more than pornography internalized. Lusting after women we see on the street, to any degree, is no less perverted than pornography is.

Even in a world of perfect modesty in women's fashions, we would still be visually oriented in our sexual drives. We would just have less skin and more imagination to go on and less fantasy from the media to lie to that imagination. The point of this is that no matter how modestly or immodestly the women around us act, we are still the masters of our own minds. It is our responsibility. The buck stops here. When a woman dresses in a tiny two piece swimsuit to go to a pool and then acts offended when guys leer at her, she is a complete and total idiot, and also a stumbling block to those of us who don't want to leer. But her behavior, in the last analysis, is her responsibility and not ours. Just so, if we fall and allow ourselves to stare or fantasize it is our fault and not hers, and if we have gone to a pool or a beach where women are dressing like that we are equally fools. 2 Timothy 2:22 warns us to flee youthful lust. The very fact of not fleeing can be sin.

Perhaps this is why I tend to speak about this to women as if they could solve the problem, for they could solve the immodesty problem by dressing modestly. However, I talk to men as if it never will be solved, because it won't. We will always be fallen men. We live in a worst case scenario as a society, and instead of worrying about whose fault it is, it's time to get down to business on how to deal with it.

I have heard from many people involved in ministry that something like a hundred percent of young men struggle with sexual temptation, but I don't think that this is so. Only the good men struggle with sexual temptation. The rest just kind of go with it. It is a struggle, make no mistake about that, and we often pray that God would give us rest from it, but it sometimes seems as if He doesn't. After years of thinking and praying about this I have come to the conclusion that God does not give us relief because He prefers to give us victory, and the only road to that kind of rest is the hard one of crucifixion and death of the man of sin. God will give us rest. Not the rest that we ask for, but the perfect rest of being victorious and fully redeemed in everything, even our troublesome sexuality. This rest comes to us, however, only by fighting, and by fighting one battle at a time. Do not look ahead at the years of struggle that await you. You cannot fight them, because they do not exist. You are just beating the air to try to accept them. Instead look at this battle right here, right now, and fight it for all you are worth.

Job boasted that he had made a covenant with his eyes, not to look at a maiden. Jesus said that any man who looks at a woman to lust after her has already committed adultery in his heart. But how can we not look? How can we not desire? Well, Job didn't say he wouldn't see, only that he wouldn't look. Seeing is something that sort of happens to us whether we like it or not, sometimes. Looking is something that we do.

I don't think we can ever not desire, in some way, shape or form. At least, I haven't figured out how not to desire. However, I can avoid looking because I can desire something else more. This is the root of sexual purity for both men and women. It is neither possible (in most cases) nor desirable to desire sex less. Absence of desire for sex would spell the death of the human race and of every marriage and family in the world in very short order. Therefore, since we can't desire sex less, we must desire something else more. We must set up a hierarchy of desires.

On the bottom, the most basic level, we desire sex, plain and simple, physical release. Nothing more. This is wrong. In order to have this by itself, we have to use other people as objects, either as fantasies or as living sex toys. We can't do that.

On the next level we want a personal connection, with the one that we have sex with. We want to feel close to her, even to love her in some sense. If we get this, we will have the most basic level, the physical release, but we will also have something better, so we learn to give up searching for the physical release and search for a personal connection instead.

But that is not enough. A personal connection can die and leave us more alone than we were before. We might fall out of love with her and be left with the misery of guilt and shame. She might fall out of love with me and leave me rejected. On the next level I want permanency. I want to love this person, really and truly, all my life. I want her to love me. So I stop looking for mere connected feelings and try to look for the reality, common interests, common beliefs, common values and the same goal of permanent love. If I can find that, then I will have the other two, the connection and the release, but unless I can have trust, those two are worthless anyway.

But even that is not enough. I may want to love her forever, but unless my love is more than feelings, it will not sustain me for the long haul. I need to desire something more than that relationship, if that relationship is to last. I have to want to be true, to be a man of my word. So I practice honesty and strive for integrity. Instead of searching for the answer in the people around me, and the girls I hang out with, I look for that answer in myself, trying to develop true honor that will fortify my resolve when the feelings are gone. "I could not love thee, dear, so much, loved I not honor more." If I can achieve that honor, then I can have her with trust, and then I will have that connection, and then at last I can have that physical release.

But even now there is still one more step. I find that I cannot be honorable on my own strength. I fail. Only God can make a man out of me, and as long as I'm still in love only with honor, I am willing to let

God in so He can help me with the honor issue. But it won't do. I have to make a crucial switch. Instead of wanting God for the sake of my honor, I must love my honor for the sake of God. It is when I love Him first and foremost of all that I can finally truly enjoy everything else I love. I know honor for what it is, my response to my King, my trust, my faith, my love for He who shed His blood for me. Then, because my honor is secure, I can securely love my wife for a lifetime. Because I can love her for a lifetime, I can allow myself to open up and be vulnerable with her and experience that connection to the fullest, and at long last that simple physical release I was after from the start will finally be mine. It will be greater for having been conquered, more truly itself because it is where it belongs, on the bottom of the totem pole.

Do you see how I progressed? That isn't my actual history. In the actual development of this philosophy I started somewhere in the middle and reasoned my way in both directions from there. I'm afraid my living leaves somewhat to be desired. The principle is sound though. Now we just have to relate it to our dealings with immodesty.

When a bikini clad body catches my eye that is level one, the basic level of attraction, no different from an animal. I can't desire it less, but I can desire something else more. I can think of the fact that I don't want just a living sex doll, but a person that I can talk to, share with, know and be known by, and that is more important. Then I realize that even a person I can talk to and have sex with isn't enough unless I can share more than that, everything, my whole life with her. I don't just want to care about someone intensely for a night, week or month (if that were even possible). I certainly don't want to love for a year or two and then lose that love. I want to love someone constantly for a lifetime. Then I remember that to do that I have to be worthy, I have to keep my covenant with her, for her alone and no one else, and so I think about the honorable thing to do. But the honorable thing to do is so hard, and I will fail unless God helps me, and now I remember God, and how much He has done for me, and that in Him alone is there any refuge. I flee to Him, and in so doing I rediscover my relationship with Him, and dive into it headfirst in holy terror.

Of course that's backward. If I were really God's man I would be in that level all the time and never be tempted. That is how we will be in Heaven, fully liberated from lust, fully free to love with the love for which sexuality is a mere symbol. "The world is passing away and all its lusts, but He who does the will of God lives forever." 1 John 2:17. Even in this world, if I were really honorable, the very idea of breaking my word would be repugnant to me, and I would never dare to lust. If I were really in love with my future wife, I wouldn't even want to look at another woman lustfully, and so I would turn away as quickly as I could. I have heard some men who said that they were so concerned about the people they were meeting that the body on display barely even registered. These men were very far advanced in their walk with God. We can only fight at the level we are at right now. That is where the line is drawn, and that is where we make our stand. If we have to start right at the bottom of the pyramid in order to control our desires, then so be it, just so long as we don't stop there. We cannot stop until we reach the very top. There is no security short of God. The Church has typically seen the purity of heart spoken in the beatitudes as sexual purity, but as a wise priest once pointed out to me, there is a wider definition. The pure in heart are single-minded in their pursuit of God. God is the one and only desire of their hearts. Deep, interior sexual purity of the kind that I talked about in this chapter, is the result of the purity of heart that truly loves God above all else.

On one obstacle course I did in an Army school I attended there was an obstacle consisting of two logs set up to form an up ramp and a down ramp. The angle was fairly steep and the logs were worn smooth by countless boots running up and down them but other than that it looked deceptively simple. The idea was to run up one log and down the other one, but what usually happened was that we would walk up to the obstacles and start walking up the log, get about halfway, slip, slide, lose our balance and fall off. A couple of guys twisted ankles on that one and were dropped from the course. The only safe way to do it, the only possible way to do it, was to hit the bottom at a dead run and power up it without a backward glance. If you stopped or slowed down you were going to fall, but if you kept going until you got to the top, then you were secure. You had it made. So it is with purity. It is all a battle of the mind, not the body. The mind has to run from the temptation, sprint all out for the refuge of God, all the way at the top of the pyramid with no questions and no backward glances, not stopping until we are secure with Him. Only then will we be able truly to enjoy everything below us, when it truly is below us. When God is in the right place, or rather when we are in the right place in relation to Him, everything falls into place. Grasp at anything lower and you will lose it and taste only ashes. Reach for God, and He will give you everything lower. He will give you the world.

> *"Your heavenly Father knows that you need these things. But seek ye first the kingdom of God and his righteousness, and all these things will be given you besides." Matthew 6:32-33*

27. The Meaning of Virginity

As you move around in the world you'll run into one of the biggest, oldest and ugliest double standards in existence, the stigma against male virginity. For women, remaining virgin until marriage is, if not exactly normal, at least understandable. People think of that as just something that some women do, because they believe in true love and things like that. If you are a man, though, and you choose to remain virgin until marriage, be prepared to be ridiculed for it. Conversely, women who have sex with many different men are called hard and ugly names, like "whore" and "slut" while men who have sex with many different women are rather admired more often than otherwise. They are called names like "pimp" and "lady's man." For the record I consider both pimps and "lady's men" to be the scum of the earth.

To this day I don't know why it should be so, but there you have it. It just makes no sense. I suppose you have to take into account that these men, and women too, have been brought up in a culture that is so deluged in sex that everything revolves around it, but no one understands it. No one knows what sex means, so obviously no one knows what virginity means.

If you were to ask the average Joe on the street what sex means, he would think you were asking him what the word meant, and he would think you were either crazy or naïve. But we know what the word means. What we actually want to know is what the reality means? What is the meaning of this division of the human race into masculine and feminine, male and female, and what is the meaning of the joining of the two in one flesh? Does it have no more significance than merely physical pleasure, a stirring of the hormonal cocktail and the possibility of creating another human? (As if the ability to cooperate in the creation of an immortal human soul was a trivial affair!)

If it means nothing more than that then what are we to make of half the world's greatest poetry, and about ninety-five percent of the second rate poetry? Who can count the number of songs, movies, poems and books celebrating the relationship between the sexes and ascribing some transcendent meaning to the whole mess? Is it all an illusion?

I don't think so. The world hates the Church because the Church stands for that greater meaning, and this is the irony of it, that the world accuses us of thinking so little of sexuality that we must always be hiding it and circumscribing it with rules and laws. The truth is that the Church alone out of this whole world right now truly values sexuality, because only the Church really understands it. Although when you think about it, deep down in our hearts we really do expect what the Church commands. When we fall in love we really can't believe that it won't last for all eternity. Why should we be surprised if the Church commands us to do what we wished for? I believe it was G. K. Chesterton who once said, "The common man has always promised that love should be permanent. The Church just paid him the courtesy of taking him at his word." It is because the Church values sex that she guards it so fiercely. We do not build walls around trash. We do not hide our plastic party jewels under lock and key. We do not put monopoly money in a bank vault. Only real treasure warrants such protection, and this is indeed a treasure.

The meaning of sex can be seen in Saint Paul's take on Genesis 2:24, "Do you not know that he who joins himself with a prostitute becomes one body with her?" 1 Corinthians 6:16. The two shall become one. Even the most casual and degraded joining of the flesh still retains that power that was given to the true model at the beginning of the human race. St. Paul tells us why this should be so:

"Be subordinate to one another out of reverence for Christ. Wives should be subordinate to their husbands as to the Lord. For the husband is head of his wife just as Christ is head of the Church, He Himself the Savior of the body. As the Church is subordinate to Christ, so wives should be subordinate to their husbands in everything. Husbands, love your wives, even as Christ loved the Church and handed Himself over for her to sanctify her, cleansing her by the bath of water with the word, that He might present to Himself the Church in

127

splendor, without spot or wrinkle or any such thing, that she might be holy and without blemish. So husbands should love their wives as their own bodies. He who loves his wife loves himself. For no one hates his own flesh but rather nourishes and cherishes it, even as Christ does the Church, because we are members of His body. 'For this reason a man shall leave his father and his mother and be joined to his wife, and the two shall become one flesh.' This is a great mystery, and I speak in reference to Christ and the Church." Ephesians 5:21-33

St. Paul begins by saying that we should be subordinate to one another, and then details how that subordination should go and most importantly, why. We are a living allegory, a living sacrament of the divine romance, and this sacrament achieves its highest natural parallel in the supernatural sacrament of matrimony. Sex is a mirroring of the relationship between God and us. Think about this for a little bit. That means that a husband and wife, in the marriage bed, enacting a physical act, are really representatives of a greater spiritual reality that is the point of the whole universe. God created us to be His bride, the Church, spiritually, both individually and collectively, and then created sexuality in us to mirror that great mystery. Do you begin to see why this is so important? Why divorce is such an evil? From the beginning it was not so! (Read Matthew 19:3-9) Do you begin to see the power we tamper with when we play around with this great mystery so casually? The world says, "You need to lighten up; it's a natural part of human life." They are right, it is natural, and yes, we should lighten up. But we can be light hearted without being empty-headed, jovial without being vulgar. We can laugh with delight, wonder and joy, without cheapening ourselves through flippancy and cynicism, for though it is natural it is also supernatural. Greater things than we realize are going on when human beings enact this mystery in their bodies.

With this in mind, let's re-examine the meaning of virginity. I am not talking about physical virginity here, necessarily. That can be forcibly taken by rape. I am talking about something a little more complex. As I've said before, the body mirrors the soul, and for those who have never had sex this mirroring is critical. Plenty of people have not had sex because they were afraid or because they couldn't find anyone to sleep with them. That is obviously not what I am talking about. I am talking about reasoned and freely chosen virginity (whether temporary or permanent). The physical virginity is, or should be, the result of spiritual virginity, an intimate and perfect integrity between the body and the soul, so that it becomes impossible to act out the language of love with the body unless it is chosen in the heart. Because of this spiritual virginity, the heart cannot choose to grasp after passing affection, the outward trappings of inter-personal relationships, unless the will has freely chosen to accept the responsibilities that go with it.

Virginity is the gift of looking on a body and seeing a person. Without that distinction virginity means whatever you want it to mean, everything or nothing, and this is not an option for a Christian. "Male and Female He created them." God has created us male and female, masculine and feminine, through and through, from the inmost recess of our souls to the outermost parts of our bodies. Sexuality is not a superficial matter of plumbing arrangements, but it is the core of who we are as human beings.

Established from the beginning as the prototypical sacrament, the very first covenant, it is also an image of Christ and the Church (Ephesians 5:21-33) and infidelity to that image is literally sacrilege. The union formed is formed whether we desire it or not, as even the most casual sexual union causes the two to become one flesh (1 Corinthians 6:16). This meaning of the body and of sex is inherent in the reality and in the act, for "God created man in His own image. In the image of God He created them. Male and female He created them. And God blessed them and God said to them, 'Be fruitful and multiply'." Genesis 1:27-28. We are created in the image and likeness of God, in our individuality of course, but especially in our union as male and female, which was why Saint Paul referenced Genesis 2:24 in Ephesians 5:31. Hebrew 13:4 echoes the theme, saying that the marriage bed must be kept pure. The marriage bed is the place where this great sacrament is enacted, but it is enacted in and through our very bodies. If the bed must be kept pure, how much more so must our bodies be kept pure, and this applies before marriage as firmly and as bindingly as after marriage.

Proverbs 5 has an interesting thought on fidelity to one's wife. "Keep your way far from her (a loose woman) and do not go near the door of her house; lest you give your honor to others, and your years to the merciless; lest strangers take their fill of your strength." Proverbs 5:8-10. And again "An adulteress stalks a man's very life." Proverbs 6:26b

Male sexuality traditionally has been associated with the source of strength and vitality, and this continues even today. The men who can have lots of sex every day are cultural icons. They are even considered the ultimate in machismo by many deluded individuals. There is a physiological basis for this. After sexual intercourse male testosterone levels drop, along with other hormonal shifts, which causes a corresponding drop in energy levels. He is hormonally spent. Of course the Old Testament writers knew this as well as we do, minus the hormonal cause, but unlike us, they expected it to mean something. They expected it to have a deeper significance, and so it does. When a man gives himself to a woman sexually, he gives his self to her. All his strength and vitality is given in love for her. That is the meaning of the male body, whether we like it or not.

Nowadays we assume that whatever you value most you will spend your strength on, but what we often ignore is the truer principle that whatever you spend your strength on most freely you will value most. With every act spent on someone who is not his wife a man values her more and his wife less, and so perverts the mystery. Beyond that, with every thought spent on someone other than his wife he perverts the mystery.

Now, I am not writing to give guys a bunch of reasons why they should not have sex. I am assuming we are already striving for purity, and if not then we need to get back on course as quickly as possible. I am writing this for those who are preserving themselves but who don't know why. What I want to do is focus less on the "thou shalt nots" and learn to enjoy the "thou shalls". Just because sex is not one of those "thou shalls" yet is no reason to enjoy it less. We are enjoying it differently. We are preserving our strength for it is not our own (Corinthians 6:20). We are not avoiding something bad, we are actively pursuing something most admirable. The discipline now is part of the joy then. I am spending my strength on what is truly valuable and letting all the rest pass by, for I am spending my strength on my wife. Every sacrifice you make now to keep yourself pure is a sacrifice you make for the wife you may not even have met yet. You can be in love with her, whether you know her or not, for whatever you spend your strength on you will value. Make no mistake, virginity is a costly gift, but it is a priceless gift for all that. It is paid for in humiliation, in sweat, in loneliness and frustration, and even in blood. This is the price of a gift that is truly priceless. For that is what virginity is. It is a gift. A gift that can be given only once, not because it is given and then spent, but because once given it must either continue to be given or it must die. Do you think that a man and woman who save themselves for each other until their wedding night then cease giving of themselves the next night? Nonsense. If the body is integrated with the deepest reality of the soul, then the body given on the wedding night is the same reality, not merely a sign, but a sacrament of the giving of the heart and soul. The gift of virginity is the gift of your self, you, the full and complete person, the gift that you can give only once, and after that must never cease to give.

> *"The body is not meant for sexual immorality, but for the Lord, and the Lord for the body. By his power God raised the Lord from the dead, and he will raise us also. Do you not know that your bodies are members of Christ himself? Shall I then take the members of Christ and unite them with a prostitute? Never! Do you not know that he who unites himself with a prostitute is one with her in body? For it is said, 'The two will become one flesh.'"* 1 Corinthians 6:13-16

28. When Should I Start Dating?

This is a question every guy is going to have to face, either squarely and reasonably, or by default. Either he will think it through and make a decision, or he will have it answered for him by his circumstances. My perspective on this question is rather unique, I think. When I was fifteen I decided that I would not date until I was older. Later on the magic number I settled on was 25 years of age. Why I picked 25, I don't know, but as I get nearer to that age, it seems more and more like a good call on my part. Perhaps even a bit short, but it is obvious to me now that in giving me that resolution God was looking out for me, and I didn't even know it. The catalyst for this decision was a summer camp I went to at Magdalen College, a small Catholic Liberal Arts college in Warner, New Hampshire. Through the classes, the thinking, the community, the prayer life, and the overall atmosphere of holiness in that place, I came to the decision that I was not mature enough to date, and that I probably wouldn't be for a number of years. I would certainly not be ready to marry until I was in my twenties, most likely out of college, which was my plan at the time, and therefore I saw no point in dating when I had no intention of getting married. Other ideas and practices followed from this logic and that decision which don't really concern this topic, but on the whole, I think my idea was right, though not perfect, and I have stuck with it thus far. If nothing else the discipline of remaining alone with God has proven well worth it.

However, that was my choice; I cannot recommend it for everyone. It is simply my way of answering the question for myself. What about for everyone else?

In order to answer that I have to ask, what is dating? What are we talking about when we use the word? Although the word has a lot of different shades of meaning, connotations and whatnot, I will narrowly define it as two people of opposite genders making arrangements to do things alone with each other in the context of a romantic relationship, or at least a potential romantic relationship. It is the aloneness that is the goal, along with the romantic feelings. This arrangement is usually exclusive. In fact as practiced in America it often resembles what used to be called "going steady," although it can be more casual, especially in the very beginning of a relationship. To narrow it down further I ask, what is the point of dating? Is it companionship? Is it emotional bonding? Is it to get to know another person? Is it to determine 'compatibility?' Is it to find a potential spouse? In order to decide whether or not we are to do something we must take a serious look at why we are doing it.

I believe that dating is usually done initially as a means to get to know someone or to deepen a relationship with a prior acquaintance. After that relationship has been formed to some extent then companionship and the pleasure of company come into the equation. Then the question, "could this be the one?" may show up and then the two begin starting to determine whether or not they want to be married.

This is the assumption I am going to work with for now, realizing that it is certainly not all inclusive and may not even be very typical. I am basing it on observation rather than experience so it is definitely open to criticism. Also, I completely left out the whole question of sexual relations since I believe that for a Christian there is only one answer to that question.

First of all, we must ask whether these aims are best suited by dating? Do you really get to know someone when you spend time with them alone? Yes and no. You will know one side of them very well, but most likely it will be the side that I would call "best behavior." What of the cranky side? The relaxed, familiar side? The group setting side? The adversity side? The family side? There are so many sides that one person alone can never bring out in anyone, no matter how close they are. When friends are together they rejoice in a large group because each and every friend brings out something a little different in every individual around him. The entire group is lessened when one leaves. This is all valuable intel on a person that you cannot get from one on one communication. I would say that getting to know someone first in a group setting is generally a better way to start things off. This can carry over into the letter writing and blogging world, for again, only one side is shown, not the whole person. This has a great deal of application to the modern world, but not much to my topic. A further disadvantage of one on one relationships is the crush. I use that word for lack of a better one. Infatuation might work also. By crush I mean an emotional and predominately romantic preoccupation with a particular member of the opposite sex. People tend to regard it as something that happens to you without your permission, which you cannot control. They are partially right. It may suddenly happen that for some reason you find yourself thinking of one girl more and more without even knowing her beyond the most superficial way. Five minutes of seeing her at home with her family might be enough to cure you of that feeling, but you never get that opportunity. Often enough this sort of thing arises from ignorance, i.e. you don't know her that well, and therefore, yes, I grant you, sometimes it happens whether you will or no. This does not mean it is entirely unpredictable. If you put two young people in the same place at the same time, with no one else around, often enough and for long enough, they will either come to hate each other very much, or they will come to like each other very much. Since we don't date people we have an initial dislike to, this very much increases the odds that over time a casual dating thing might turn into a very serious romantic attachment. And this is the part where I will be most at odds with most people. I have never been able to understand why this feeling alone should be considered a goal in and of itself. If I have no intention of marrying, why would I be looking to go steady? If I have chosen not to go steady, why would I want to put myself in a position to feel an emotion for which I have no honorable outlet? In a word, why would I want to date? Yeah, sure, sometimes you just like someone and you don't know why, but I would tend to disagree that it means you have to do anything about it, especially for a teenager. It may be very helpful to get to know someone, but not in such a setting that will only encourage the feelings and make them harder to deal with. You guessed it; stay in group settings. Have friends around to bleed off a little of that excess tension, or at least to give you someone to talk to when you are too tongue tied to talk to her! I would further argue that when floating in a dizzying sea of her-ness you are probably not in the best position to notice what would otherwise be red flags. This is another reason why a more distanced and balanced view is best, especially initially. Honest and trustworthy friends are great spotters of red flags that we might miss, which is yet another advantage to group settings. Further, once emotionally invested in someone, most people experience a strong reluctance to break things off, even when it is clearly better to do so. A little foresight goes a long way.

Am I coming down on alone time? Not at all. I am pointing out what I would perceive to be its risks and disadvantages and suggesting that alone time not be the primary method of getting to know someone. Seriously, I see no point in anyone putting himself through avoidable and unbeneficial grief.

I don't consider romantic feelings of intimacy to be the main goal of a relationship. They are the icing on the cake. They are the desert of a multi-course banquet. When you reach for that emotional intimacy first, without considering anything else, you are going against the whole ethos of being a man. You are grasping a privilege without accepting the responsibility. You are looking for connection without commitment, and this defrauds the woman you are dating. Unless you are willing to consider seriously the possibility of marriage to this person, you have no business stirring up feelings in her, or in yourself, for which marriage is the only outlet. If such feelings do arise, keep them to yourself until you are ready to act on them with honor. I do not say that you have to be ready to get married tomorrow in order to start dating, only that you should know what you are asking of the young woman, and that you should be pursuing this relationship for the purpose of determining God's will, not simply because you're lonely and you need a shoulder to cry on for now until you can find something more permanent. No man should ever treat a woman as merely a stand-by, just a between meal snack to keep him satisfied for now, until he can get to the main course. No woman is disposable. If marriage is not your ultimate goal, or you have no reasonable plan or expectation of being ready for marriage any time soon, then have the common decency not to waste the lady's time.

I guess, from my point of view, I see too many guys getting the cart before the horse. They are out chasing after women, even with completely innocent intentions, but without first ensuring that they have something worthwhile to offer her. Even if no sexual sin is involved, how is it even remotely honorable to tie up a woman's time and affections for months or even years, without any intention of commitment? And if I have nothing to offer a woman yet, then why would I waste my time with a superficial relationship that I have no realistic expectations for? I have more important things to do. I have this limited time, as a single man, to concentrate on building my relationship with God, on training virtue into my mind and will, on excelling in my field of work. If I waste this limited training time on transitory dating relationships, am I not defrauding my wife?

So my answer to the question: I think that dating one on one should be discouraged for teenagers, especially teenage guys. Most of us aren't anywhere near date-worthy until we're well past nineteen anyway, so Ladies, you're not missing much. Further, when dating is begun, a clear idea of the point of it all is absolutely necessary. Not just individually, but as a pair. Both should be honest enough to communicate that at least. Until a person is old enough to be honest about what he is looking for both with himself and with his date, he is not old enough to date. If he is not old enough prayerfully and honorably to consider marriage to this woman, then he is not old enough to make any claim on her time or emotions. Period.

Beyond the question of age, there is also the question of availability. Someone with commitments to college and work, or to the military, needs to take those into consideration. Someone who has never been able to hold down a job is going to have trouble supporting a family. It's a bit thick asking someone to trust herself to you for everything when you have nothing but the clothes on your back and no prospect of anything else. There is a lot to be said for developing and perfecting yourself as much as you can before you take on responsibility for another.

On the flip side of the coin there are problems with waiting too long. Waiting until you make a hundred grand a year is not necessary. I am not really talking about material readiness, I am talking about character, the ability to work. You should either have the means to support your wife, or the wherewithal to procure those means. I don't think it hurts to start out modestly. If you haven't the maturity to work together with a little, it won't much matter whether you start out as a millionaire, because you certainly won't have the maturity to deal with that. Further, people who have been living alone for a long time consulting no one's wishes but their own will have to work extra hard to integrate into a community again. There was one line from the movie "Mrs. Arris goes to Paris" that stuck in my head from when I was a kid. An older widow was giving a young girl this advice, "Men, they're such slobs, all the really nice ones anyway. Never marry a tidy bachelor." My voice coach from back in the day, who was an untidy bachelor, mused that it was probably because someone who was neat and ordered would be set in his ways and would like things done all his way. He followed that up with, "So I must be a pretty nice guy." This makes sense to me. The longer I live in the barracks or in my own apartment, consulting only myself on what I want to do, the more set in that way I get. Of course it can be circumvented simply by being aware of that and preparing to make adjustments, just as the whole money thing can be circumvented by a willingness to work. My point is that these are considerations for which a timeline cannot be laid down arbitrarily. I would say it is probably not smart for teenagers to date, certainly not seriously. Not necessarily a sin, but not smart or prudent to my way of thinking. After that the timeline must be God's and no one else's. We're pretty much guaranteed to mess it up.

When you do start, my idea is that dating should be somewhat cautious and sparing before marriage, and as intimate and frequent as possible after marriage.

> *"I would like you to be free from concern. An unmarried man is concerned about the Lord's affairs how he can please the Lord. But a married man is concerned about the affairs of this world how he can please his wife and his interests are divided." 1 Corinthians 7:32-34*

29. My Type

One time when I was in an internet café in Afghanistan, a fellow soldier was on the computer next to me on his facebook account. Every so often, while I was typing he would get my attention and point to a picture on the screen and say, "Hey, what do you think about her?" They were all pictures of his ex-girlfriends that he still keeps in touch with, and he wasn't mocking, he was seriously asking, "Do you think she was pretty." I was busy, and, to my discredit, not very interested so I answered in one of two ways, either, "Yes" or, "She's not my type." I wasn't really thinking about it, and I paid for that later on.

One of the girls in particular I remember, and he remembered her as well, or rather my response to her, because the next day, after mission when we were chilling in the hut, he interrupted my reading to ask, "Hey, you remember that girl I showed you yesterday, the blond one in the skimpy little outfit, you said she wasn't your type."

"Yeah," I answered. When you interrupt a reader and he looks at you with the book still in front of his face and with a thumb still in the page, you know he isn't paying attention.

Then he asked the question that I so roundly deserved. "What is your type?"

When a reader turns his head a little more and sets the book on his stomach, you know you've caught his attention. "What is my type?" I repeated, a very bad habit of mine when I can't think of an answer and need to stall for time.

"Yeah, what type of girl do you like? I really want to know." He added the last by way of making sure I knew he wasn't just making fun.

"How can you answer that?" I asked in puzzlement.

"I don't know," he said.

"Neither do I," I returned. To my even greater discredit I turned away from that question and went back to my book.

He said, "You really confuse me," and walked away.

The problem was, I really didn't understand the question. It took me a full five minutes of pretending to read to formulate it in my head in such a way that I could even get a handle on it, and by then it was too late to strike up the conversation again. Not really too late but no longer convenient.

So here I am, several days later, and what with driving halfway across Afghanistan recently I've had plenty of time to mull it over. Now I need to set it down on paper so that it will stay straight and organized until I can get a hold of it.

The first problem was that looking back, when I said "She's not my type," that is not exactly what I meant. What I really mean is, "I don't like the way she looks (or acts or dresses,) but because I don't want to get embroiled in an argument over some woman's looks I am going to make it sound like a casual opinion." The phrase sounds like I actually have a type of look that I prefer, and she just doesn't happen to be it, but what I really mean is that I don't like her and I am not willing to say so right out. The girl in question was wearing a leather mini skirt and leather boots, and she looked, if not exactly like a prostitute, at least like the sort of cheap, sadly pathetic girl you see in some bars. I'm not going to tell a guy "I don't like your ex-girlfriend because she looks like a hooker," and instead of taking the time and effort to think of a more diplomatic way of putting it, I prevaricated. It's easy to do when you are good with words. Serves me right for using a phrase without thinking it through. I got caught.

The second problem was, "What exactly do you mean by 'type'?" He was not talking about personalities, character, talents, likes, dislikes, backgrounds, values, religion, favorite music or anything else of substance. To all of these questions there is an answer, and probably an answer I have given some thought to over the years. At least an answer I could give some thought to because they are all objective questions and I would know where to start. Either they are objective in the sense that they correspond to some degree to moral rightness or wrongness, or because they ask about what I think would fit best with my personality which, though not something I have turned my attention to yet, is at least a real question with a real answer. None of these traits was in question though, because all that was involved was a picture. There was nothing to judge, apart from facial expressions (hers was unpleasant, but who's to say that wasn't just a picture caught at a bad moment?) and choice of outfit. Modesty or lack of modesty is a powerful indication of what the focus of a woman's heart is, but perhaps she was just ignorant, or she just dressed like that for that one night. Maybe she was pressured into it. Whatever the explanation for her complete lack of modesty, there is little in a picture to indicate an answer to any of these important questions, and there definitely is no solid basis for any type of sweeping judgment. The only question he could have been asking was, "What kind of look do you like?"

That is what nonplussed me after I got around to interpreting his question that far. All the other questions I would think about and answer very quickly but this one was a little different. It was asking me to give an opinion it would never have occurred to me to form. How can you form an opinion as to the best "look?" How can you form an opinion as to the best weather? Or the best kind of music? Isn't there some beauty in any one of these examples that is specifically its own and none other's? (Well, the music question is not rhetorical, but the other two are). How can you ask me to cast a vote that 1) is meaningless in any objective sense because it is superficial, 2) is going to exclude something else that is equally worthwhile and 3) in the end will not have any bearing on anyone but me because it is my opinion only.

What is a "type?" Is it defined by build? By style? By ethnicity? That at least would be something I could define, but it wouldn't really be helpful. I thought about all the different countries I've been to. I may not have been actually around the world, but I've been a few places around the world. I've seen women of all ethnic groups in America. I've met Korean and Filipino women when I was stationed in Korea, and I've even seen a few Iraqi and Afghani women who weren't covering their faces. Of all the ethnic groups I have met, each one has had its share of good looks. Not better looks, different. It is the same with individual people, ethnicity notwithstanding. Why else would we have so many words for beauty? There is of course "beautiful" which I take to be either the overall category or the pinnacle of that category. Other words include "cute," "lovely," "pretty," "attractive," "gorgeous," "adorable," "nice," "sweet," and the ubiquitous "hot," and "sexy," both of which are horribly overused. Every single one of these words is a way of saying "beautiful" (in the appropriate context) but every last one of them has a different meaning. Thinking back on my female friends and relatives (the field is limited, thanks to my inveterate loner tendencies) I think every one of them has a tendency towards one or the other. My mother is beautiful, my sister is pretty, one cousin is cute, a friend might look sweet, another lovely. Some girl might just look nice and feel left out. But nice, far from being just a catch-all word to avoid hurting someone's feelings, for me means that she looks satisfying, like

I can look at her and feel assured that she is as she should be, neither trying too much, nor caring too little but simply as she should be. It is a very respectable word and one I don't give out very often. (Come to think of it, I don't give out any of these words very often. Comes of living with a bunch of dudes I suppose.) But those descriptions are just overall tendencies. They are ways of saying that this person tends toward this or that look, much as some people tend to be mechanically minded, or relational or analytical. It does not mean that someone who is usually cute might not suddenly turn out drop-dead gorgeous one evening, and then the next day be back to normal. There is no one so hopelessly analytical than he can't be relational once in a while, and if there were, it would not be a benefit but a crippling disability. It goes even further. I am getting in way over my head here, but I think most married men would agree that their wives have many different looks, that sometimes change with startling and disconcerting rapidity (along with moods, attitudes and other less pleasant things, no doubt.) Are you to take one woman and say, "I like this particular look on her better than any of her others?" What then of the loss of all her other looks? How far are we to take this appetite for comparing and making value judgments on things whose value we assign ourselves?

So I am left with the conclusion that I have no type, as far as looks go. Nor do I want one. How can I say, "I like black hair better than blond, blond better than red, red better than brown, blue eyes better than hazel, this set of features, that sort of figure, on and on ad nauseum?" Enough. Why not just take a magazine full of super models and play cut-and-paste? In the end I don't think I could come up with a favorite type because 1) there is no one in any type who does not also fit into some other type in some way. 2) Every type, however you divide it from all others, has its own attraction that is no other's. 3) The physical is not important enough to warrant such effort. 4) All that work is for nothing because it means nothing to anyone but me. 5) And, I think most importantly, once you have succeeded in closing your mind to all other types of beauty, you will have only limited yourself. If you begin to say you like October better than any other month, well and good. If you begin to think of October in December, that is not good. My policy is to take all things as they come, sure that there is good in every one beyond what I deserve, and therefore it is not for me to make such silly judgments.

I wonder if I should have told him my answer was, "I don't understand the question."

I must be cautious because I am still very young. What husband would not prefer his wife's beauty to every other woman's beauty? And rightly so. Once you commit to your wife you will have agreed to exclude all others, so that you will no longer have the right to be attracted in that way to any other woman's beauty. That I have not yet experienced, so I leave that question open. It wasn't the other soldier's question anyway, but it is related, I think. My Lieutenant once advised some younger soldiers to marry women who look good without makeup, because you'll probably end up seeing her without makeup a lot. I think he had a point. If I get too narrow with my definition of "my type" I'm setting myself up for failure when she gets older and no longer fits that narrow, shallow definition. There are more important things in life than "my type."

Mother Teresa is quoted as saying "I will take any child, any time, night or day. Just let me know and I will come for him."[12] Now that is a beautiful woman.

"Charm is deceitful, and looks are vain, but a woman who fears the Lord is to be praised." Proverbs 31:30

30. Picking Up Chicks

A soldier recently said something that I thought was a bit weird. He said, "You know what sucks about having a wife or steady girlfriend is that you forget how to pick up chicks. You know how when you're single you get that routine down and you get good at it so it works? Well when you get married you forget how to do that." I wanted to laugh because although I admit I don't know much about it, it seems to me it would be the other way around. If you're single it's pretty much hit or miss, sometimes there is a girl to hit on, sometimes there isn't, sometimes she'll listen, and sometimes she'll stomp on you. However with a girlfriend or wife (again I don't know, I've never had either) I should think you'd always have someone there to practice on, for lack of a better term. Even more importantly, you wouldn't be stuck with a general CDI factor anymore; you would be able to move to a particular CDI factor.

CDI stands for "Chicks Dig It," and it is a very complex and contradictory concept. Basically however, things are rated on a one to ten scale with one being indifference and ten being irresistible (and minus ten being "She'll probably never speak to you again.") It is further divided into general and particular CDI's with general being what most girls would like, and particular being what one particular woman would like.

Obviously a particular CDI scale should be easier to work with. If you are picking up a different girl every week you don't have time to get to know her particular likes and dislikes so you're stabbing in the dark, while after a few months or years with a woman you should have most of her broad likes and dislikes pretty well pegged, and then you don't have to waste your time on things that many women might like but she might not. I'm sure there are women out there who don't like mudslinging monster trucks, for instance. If you happen to be into that sort of thing, that is a useful bit of intel to have on a woman. I don't see any reason why after a few years you shouldn't be better at it than ever, and after ten years you should be pretty darn good.

Unless of course he was talking about something a bit different than I am. If by "Picking up Chicks" he meant a sort of superficial relationship in which only the physical is involved then in that case I grant you, you would probably get out of practice being married. One is like going on a very long journey to places unknown with someone, without the possibility of ever changing your travel partner. The other is like walking a hundred meters down the road with someone, going back, getting someone else, walking the same hundred meters of road, going back, and then with another, and another, and another, always walking that same hundred meters of road. Of course you would get good at it. You would walk it blindfolded and avoid every pothole, every puddle, every stick or stone, and the only rut you would hit would be the one you were stuck in. You could make that trip very smooth for anyone who wanted to walk it with you, especially if she has been walking the same stretch of road for a while also and plays by the rules of the game. As long as she knows that she is never under any circumstances to look up at the horizon, or wonder what it might be like to travel further, the two of you can get on admirably in your little strip of road. You would know that stretch of road so well you could take anyone on that trip without thought and never hit the slightest bump. But you would never go any further. If you did start to move past that bend in the road, into unfamiliar territory, you would start to stub your toes again, take wrong turns again and step in puddles again. You would not have trained yourself for real walking, only for walking that one short stretch. It is like when Grandma and Grandpa come over for a visit. Everyone is nice, everyone is on their best behavior, and everything goes smoothly because we only have to be nice for a little while until they go home again. It is a different matter when the aging parents move in with us. After a week or two the artificial wisdom of repeated shallow experience fails us. We cannot be nice all the time, and we are not yet good, so we become nasty.

So this young man got married, and hitting bumps in the road, having to grow and learn and become better than he was, he looked back with longing on a time when things were easier.

There is also some pride there. A lot of my colleagues regard "picking up chicks" as a sport. I have driven them home after a long night at the bar and listened to them talking like hunters comparing their bags. Again, superficial. That is the easy part of the road, moving from my driveway to the end of my street. How anyone ever came to confuse that with manhood I'll never know. I'm a reasonably persuasive person; if I put my mind to it I could probably convince someone to walk to the end of the road with me. A little one mile stroll is nothing. Could I convince someone to walk to the end of the world with me? Difficult question. That is tougher, more of a challenge, if a challenge is what you are looking for. There are other challenges and other tasks, and each one, in its own way is the measure of your manhood, but in dealing with women romantically, being a night's entertainment for a hundred different people one after the other cannot compare to being everything to one person for a lifetime.

That at least is what I think, but I'm in the minority here. What do I know?

> "May your fountain be blessed,
> and may you rejoice in the wife of your youth.
> A loving doe, a graceful deer
> may her breasts satisfy you always,
> may you ever be captivated by her love." Proverbs 5:18-19

31. How to Get Friend Zoned

On the blogging service I use I have heard a lot about a phenomenon known as "friend zoning," usually from guys who are lamenting having been "friend zoned." Upon further investigation, I found that most of these posts ran something like a Rascal Flatt's song: high pitched, effeminate, sappy and hilarious in an utterly pathetic way.

Apparently "friend zoning" occurs when you have a crush on a girl, and finally work up the courage to tell her, only to have her reply with something like, "Oh, I'm sorry. I like you a lot, and you're really (insert insipid compliment here) but I've always thought of you as a really good friend/older brother." It happens a lot in movies and apparently in real life. In the movie the guy always manages to change her mind. In real life the guy blogs about it.

Of course that is just ripe for a full load of satire, but I decided to hold my fire on it, for the simple reason that I may find myself in that same position someday. While I certainly won't blog about it, I will probably find the situation less humorous than I currently do, so I'm going to empathize as much as I am able and not unburden myself of a lot of pointless irony.

However, it occurred to me that while others are busy trying to figure out how to avoid getting friend zoned, there might be something to be said for the ability to get friend zoned when you choose. "Of course," you think, "this might be a good idea for, say, Brad Pitt. He needs to keep women at a distance. The rest of us seem to have the opposite problem."

Let's ignore that statement for a bit, and look at this from a more serious point of view. I don't have Brad Pitt's problem (thanks be to God) but still, there is something to be said for the ability deliberately to keep yourself in that "just friends" territory and to make it so obvious that no one else is going to question it. I can think of at least two good reasons for this:

1) It avoids confusion. I've heard girls complain about how guys are leading them on by doing nice things for them but not saying anything or offering to "take the relationship to the next level." Of course, these might just be really nice guys, or just basic gentlemen who stand out a bit so the women are misinterpreting them as really nice guys.

Unfortunately, the world we live in makes it easy for that to be misinterpreted. What I consider the common level of courtesy (hold the door, remove your hat, be polite), is so far beyond common practice, that many women assume there is only one reason why a guy would go to that kind of trouble, namely, to impress her personally, when that simply may not be the case.

2) Since you're only going to marry one woman, all the rest need to have no illusions. For some reason, a lot of the married guys I know (in the army) get hit on every once in a while by single women, which makes no sense to me, but there you have it. Most will notice the ring, I think, and not give you a second glance (if they even gave you a first one) but the few that aren't scared off by a ring will be sent running by your secret weapon of last resort (more on that later).

3) I know I said two reasons, but I'm busy thinking of more as I go. If you've ever had to give the "just friends" speech, you seriously need to examine your behavior and try to determine whether or not what you did may have given rise to your friends' suspicions. Remember, you may not care what people think about you, but you are absolutely responsible for the young lady's reputation as long as she is in your company. To whatever extent you gave people cause to think anything, no matter how innocent, was going on between you, to that extent you have failed that trust.

4) It keeps you free. You never get pressured by false expectations because you never raise any.

So I put together this list of techniques. Most come naturally to me, which, I think, is why I've had so few entanglements with the fairer sex. I scare them off. A few I had to learn the hard way, and those I have put to good use. The secret weapon was recommended in the book "Every Man's Battle" by Arterburn and Stoecker. I haven't had to use it yet, but it sounds like so much fun I'm almost disappointed about that.

1) Say what you mean, mean what you say. This of course should be a given, but I'll elaborate a little. By "say" I'm not talking about just the words that come out of your mouth. Be aware of what your actions, facial expression and tone of voice are conveying as well, and keep your integrity. Everything about you should be of one piece, through and through. If you are planning one thing and saying another, then you are deceiving. If you cannot say what is on your mind, as often happens when women are involved, then say nothing but keep your actions in

line with your deepest decisions. So if you say, "I am not interested in dating anyone," or "I am your friend and nothing more," she should take you at your word, and there should be no action in your history together that would give her cause to think otherwise.

2) Never pay a direct compliment, if there is any danger whatsoever she will take it the wrong way. If she is a sister, a cousin, or dating your best friend, and maybe if she is fifteen years younger than you, then it is safe. Occasionally you will meet an exceptionally honest and straightforward woman who can be trusted to take a compliment for what it is worth without either denying it or reading more into it. Ironically, if you do meet such a woman, you might want to consider trying for more than friendship if you are able, since such women are few and far between. Otherwise you're going for the annoying big brother vibe. Think about how you compliment your little sister. She means the world to you, but you can't really say it, because she's your sister and that would be weird. So you pay half compliments, with a little friendly insult even (only if she has a sense of humor). Save the real compliments for real relatives, or for those few women who won't let an acquaintance be spoiled by them.

3) Never be alone with her, if you can help it. This may seem a bit over the top, but seriously, that's how rumors start. I've seen too many completely innocent friendships ruined simply because of rumors. When everyone assumes something is going on, it tends to become a self-fulfilling prophecy. Remember, three's company, and company is exactly what you want. Bring a buddy along. Drag him if he doesn't want to come.

4) Do not share your innermost thoughts. In fact, don't share much of anything beyond general interest (a good argument for having a wide range of general interests, so you'll have something to talk about). Keep the conversation light. Remember, little sister. Little Sister. Little Sister! Above all, joke around a lot. Goof off. Make it impossible for her to take you too seriously. If you and a bunch of friends (see point #3 above) get done with a serious conversation about literature, social justice or raising families, make sure you finish off the evening by doing something childish and goofy. You don't have to be obnoxious or rude (no scatological humor, please), just impossible to take seriously. Wear a Santa Claus hat. Quote at length from a kid's movie at every possible opening. Get overly excited about a game of go-fish. Cheat at Phase-10

or Uno. (Make sure you get caught though. If you actually succeed in cheating it defeats the purpose). You are not trying to hide the serious side, you're just trying to make sure that the last thing she remembers about you from the night makes her shake her head in disbelief.

5) Be somewhat thick. This should come naturally. I hear that when women are interested they let on by subtle hints. Too easy. On the off chance you actually pick up on such a hint (or think you do, which is not the same thing at all) pretend you didn't.

6) Do not, under any circumstances, call her up "just to talk" if there is the slightest danger she's interested. If she's not already to the point where she will say "What? You? But you're like my brother. That's too weird," then you don't need to call her just to talk. Talk when you happen to run into her or when there are other people around to eavesdrop on your conversation. If you have to set up an appointment or something, keep it short, not sweet, and to the point. I don't know why, but girls seem to put a lot of stock in phone conversations. Personally I hate talking on the phone.

7) Make sure she knows that she is not personally special to you. If you hold the door for her, make sure you hold the door for every other woman in similar circumstances. Bonus points if you can be polite to the elderly as well. If she knows that courtesy is part of who you are, and not something that you are doing just to impress her, she will be less likely to take it personally.

8) If all else fails, you have a secret weapon. This is what I call, Sheer Boringness. That's right, you want your target to dry up and wither away under your onslaught of sheer boringness! Talk about something. Anything. Pick a subject as long as it is something she has no interest in whatsoever. Then get as technical as you can. Don't just talk about guns. Don't even talk about ballistics. Talk about bullet weights and piston operated vs. gas operated weapons. Talk about the metallurgy of spark plug wires or the website programming you are doing or the aluminum frame of the new bike you're building, anything as long as she can't stand it. The more minute and inconsequential the details, the better. If she is searching around for topics of mutual interest, try searching around for topics that completely disinterest her, and work them like a gold mine. There are two looks you want to cultivate. You can either go for the nerd look, in which case you get extremely excited and monopolize the conversation proclaiming as loudly as you can

about whatever the topic is; or you can go for a more absent minded approach, stare off into space a bit, say "huh?" a lot, and keep a dry tone to your voice. Whatever she is hinting at, it isn't going to work. You are like the rock of Gibraltar and all her wiles roll off your armor of sheer boringness. Now just to be clear, this is a worst case scenario since it is incredibly rude. Even as a joke I'm not sure how it would fare against the, "Would Jesus do that?" test. This is for the girl who asks you out or asks you to dance, and doesn't go off in a huff after you say, "No. Thank-you." Most women, I think, will get the picture if you just stick to the 7 points listed above. If you really are more devoted to God than to any woman alive, any woman who is not likewise devoted is likely to be scared off pretty quickly.

I'm partly joking with this chapter but still partly serious. Sometimes it's hard for people to tell which is which, even for people who know me, so I'll be completely serious right here. I'm not for a second suggesting that single men cannot have serious friendships with single women. I am fortunate to have a few such friendships and, in fact, as I get older I wish I had cultivated more of them. However, there is always a danger and if you, as a man, are to protect the women you care about from getting false impressions you have to be on your guard. Unless you mean to pursue her honorably and openly, then you have no business encouraging her to feel more for you than friendship. Take that responsibility, and watch the messages you are sending. If you fail, and someone gets the wrong idea, take a step back, maintain some more distance, as much as you have to, and if approached about it tell the truth, that you have no romantic intentions towards her. Most of these ideas are geared more towards the casual acquaintances. It gets more important as you get older, into your twenties. A good many women, I think, especially the mid-to-late-twenties-and-I'm-still-single-what's-wrong-with-me set, are always looking. Every man they meet is evaluated based on potential husband material. When you first meet, and you're in that good-impressions phase of an acquaintance, that's the dangerous point when she is still thinking, "Could he be the one?" I'm sure they are quite innocent in this desire, for the most part, but if you have no freedom to get married then you have no freedom to pursue a relationship or even to act as if you did. When dealing with ladies, odds are they are going to be waiting for you to make the first move which places all the advantage on your side. If the advantage is on your side then so is the responsibility. It also means that they will be prone to reading more into things than you mean and so will their families. So when in doubt, say a good deal less than you mean. Telling the truth doesn't necessarily involve saying everything that comes into your head. If you get even a hint that she is starting to think in more-than-friendly terms, cordial but rigidly maintained distance is your best friend. Once she has become convinced that you definitely aren't the one, then you're safely friend zoned and may allow things to warm up just enough to enjoy an open and free friendship.

Hopefully. You never can tell with girls.

One thing more. This is will not work if you have a crush on her. Do not even try it. Do not make the mistake of thinking you can hide any kind of strong attraction from the woman you are attracted to, while still being friendly with her. You can't. For one thing it is dishonest and this alone should be sufficient reason against. For another, the odds are it won't work. I promise she will know ninety-nine out of a hundred times. It is not necessarily a bad thing for a girl to know that you have a crush on her, especially if she is mature enough to handle it and she is actively seeking to discern God's will. However, it can cause a lot of grief if you refuse to own up to it and just go on pretending like nothing is going on. She will know and your families will know, especially if it is mutual. The danger then arises that you will begin to be inconsistent and unpredictable, half of you wanting to reach out and pursue her, the other half of you knowing that it is not time yet. This will be confusing and frustrating, and ultimately unfair to her. It's a hard question, and I can't give you any rule on it. I would only offer this thought. The number one rule in man/woman relationships is honesty or integrity. The whole point of this attempt to guard her heart is to guard her from dishonesty, but not to guard her from responsibility. It is to keep yourself from the temptation to engage in passing, frivolous attachments that you have no intention of following through on, not to keep her from having to make a choice. Choice comes with being human, with being adult. If she is human and adult, and you are free to do so, then you might consider simply telling her the truth. If she is not both, then what on earth do you see in her?

If you find yourself consistently hiding the truth in the interests of "protecting" her, then you are not protecting her at all. You are babying her. This is not consistent with her dignity as an adult, as a human,

149

as a woman. At a certain point, to keep the truth from her out of fear becomes wrong. It is a refusal to trust her to be able to handle the truth, and discern God's will for herself in prayer. I will talk more about this later. This chapter is only meant to guard you, and her, from using each other as momentary entertainments. It is meant to guard your honesty, not compromise it.

Nor is it a foolproof thing. If you are reading this book at all I assume you are struggling to become the Image of Christ in this world, and that is a dangerous thing. Women are attracted to Jesus. The more you struggle to be transformed, the more danger there is that they will be attracted to you. Even if you consider yourself a million miles away from being remade in that Image, women see only the outside, which nearly always looks better than the inner reality. To make matters worse, most women have a natural tendency to believe the absolute best about the men they care about. This is a very beautiful and womanly trait, and it should inspire us to rise up to the level of their quiet trust in us, but it can also make them vulnerable to false assumptions. They see us as better than we really are, and they can fall for that image. Just as Jesus would never have allowed a woman to get false expectations about Him, neither should we. Our response should be to remember that it is not us, personally, that they ought to be attracted to, but rather Christ, to some imperfect extent made manifest in us. Point them to Him, and then take up your cross and keep your eyes on our Master.

"But above all, my brethren, do not swear, either by heaven or by earth or with any other oath, but let your yes be yes and your no be no, that you may not fall under condemnation." James 5:12

32. What to do with a Crush

At some point in every man's life it is all but inevitable that he will notice a girl and think to himself, "Wow!" He will most likely raise his eyebrows when he thinks that. If he doesn't raise them physically, he will raise them mentally. They will be rising on the inside of his head, and there, all in a moment, he will have experienced the beginnings of a crush. This thing will then try to grow from its initial molehill status to a mountain of fluttery, uncomfortable but strangely exciting emotions that want to take over your life. Actually, I can say in all honesty that that sort of crush has never happened to me. The "Wow!" moments never seem to translate into a crush in my personality. That sort of emotion is too flighty and easily stomped on to be very dangerous.

What has happened to me before is that I will meet a girl, and start talking to her and getting to know her and slowly but surely, over the course of a brief acquaintance, I will find myself becoming attracted to various qualities about her. It is slower, sneakier and a little harder to beat, because by the time you know you're in trouble it already has a foothold, and then you're in for a fight. However I have been successful in defeating that also, by the grace of God, in the vast majority of cases. I have not been one hundred percent successful, but overall surprisingly more successful than you would expect, given my age and some of the very wonderful young ladies it has been my good fortune to meet.

Yes, either way it tries to come about, I have always considered a crush, since the first moment I knew what the word meant, to be some sort of insidious invader to be resisted at every turn and shown no mercy whatsoever. I still think there is some truth in that. For a long time I knew that I was not ready to be involved with a woman. For a long time I didn't know whether or not God was calling me to a celibate life. Under those circumstances it would not have been honest, or wise, to encourage feelings that I wasn't yet ready to act on. Later on I'll discuss in what ways it is good to feel such things, but for now I want to concentrate on the practical aspects of crush crushing. (Sorry, couldn't resist).

I take it as a given that a man who is not free to be married for whatever reason (too young, still in school, too busy, committed to some other course for a time, not financially stable, or immature, to name a few possible reasons) is not free to be in any kind of romantic relationship whatsoever. Period. If you are not ready to commit, then you are not ready to enjoy. If you aren't ready to take on the responsibilities, then you are not ready for any of the privileges. This does not mean that your heart or your hormones (the two are very, very closely related) will always obey your head. In fact, if you spend an above average amount of time alone with a girl, and she is not completely unattractive, physically and personally, it's a safe bet you will develop feelings for her. Even if you don't spend a lot of time alone with girls, at some point you will develop feelings for someone anyway. The trouble with these feelings is that they are very powerful. I don't think any young man can ever really appreciate how powerful they are until he has felt them full force, and the first time that happens it can be very dangerous. You start out walking and talking, then walking a little closer, then holding hands, then not talking much at all, and things progress very rapidly from there. Physical affection belongs in its proper relationship. If you are not willing that a relationship should proceed, you had better not even hold her hand, because it will proceed from there willy-nilly. Think that isn't you? Still think girls are kind of weird and that's stupid mushy stuff that doesn't really appeal to a tough guy like you? Yeah. Me too. Until that right moment when someone small and soft gets under your skin and stands very close and then you spill your guts. Trust me, there is no idiocy too astonishing to be committed under such circumstances. I have seen it far too often. Sometimes it is good and innocent, and sometimes it is merely nauseating. That is why I say if you don't want to swim in the ocean, don't wade in a rip tide.

A rip tide is a powerful current that runs out into the ocean from the beach, caused by water from waves returning through a gap in the sand banks. It can grab swimmers and drag them under or haul them out to sea in the blink of an eye. On the surface all the water is moving into the shore, but if you wade into the rip tide you step into a river that is flowing very fast in the opposite direction. If you don't want to get swept out to sea, you have no business wading in the rip tide. So it is with this crush. That is what can happen if you let feelings run the show. That's not what feelings are meant to do. That is the job of your mind. It is up to your reason and conscience to drive your actions, and your mind is the first line of defense. First, it has to recognize the existence of a crush. Red lights, sirens, klaxons, the whole nine yards. Next it has to decide what the right thing to do is. Not what you want to do, and certainly not what you wish you could get up the nerve to do, but what is the right thing to do?

If you don't want to be in a romantic relationship, then stay away from this rip tide. Do not encourage it. If it is weak, don't pay too much attention to it, and it will dissipate in time. But what if it is not weak? What if this attraction is so strong that you can't get her out of your head, you can't think of anything else, you're absent minded, you stammer and shake whenever she is nearby, startle whenever someone mentions her name etc. etc. etc. It doesn't change anything. A strong feeling is still just a feeling, and no feeling, no matter how strong it may be, should ever trump your conscience. If it is not yet right for you to act on your feelings then how strong or weak they are is really inconsequential. It is irrelevant to that point. Sometimes a crush can be no laughing matter. They can last for years, as steady and consistent as the sunrise and sunset, and you may be tempted to ask after five or six years, "Isn't this love? I mean, it hasn't gone away in all this time, it must be love." Sorry. Nope. A feeling that hangs around for a while is still just a feeling. You cannot afford to make so monumental a choice based on something as ephemeral as a feeling, but rather by following the word of God above all else which will be "A lamp to my feet, and a light for my eyes," Psalm 119:105. In fact, I would go so far as to say that until you desire the Will of God more than you love a girl, you can't really love a girl.

So what do you do with something that strong and that long lasting? Use it. If you try your best to get rid of it and it won't be gotten rid of, then God has sent it to you for a reason. He is trying to teach you something. Of course it is possible that He might be pointing out the girl He wants you to marry, but that doesn't really change anything. If you are not ready for that relationship yet you still cannot act on it, even if that is what He is doing. You still have to stick it out patiently and silently until you are ready which will happen in His time, not yours. Or maybe God just wants you to learn a few other things before He lets that attachment die a natural, albeit seemingly belated death. So what use can you make of a crush?

1) Incentive to purity. If this girl that you have so much regard for is a woman of God, then she should be an inspiration to you. Think of her the next time some scantily clad female or girly magazine catches your eye. Let her outward modesty inspire true inward purity in you.

2) Learn to love. Whether or not you are in love is really not important at this stage in the game. It isn't important at all until you are ready to get married. Right now, attraction really only means that you are a reasonably healthy young man and she is a reasonably attractive young woman. What is incredibly important is whether or not you really love, for that is part of your character. Can you place her best interests ahead of your own desires? This is the crucial test of manhood that you must pass before you can even hope to be ready for all that being in love entails. This will mean things like not blurting out "You're the

most beautiful girl I've ever met." Of course if you're brave enough to say that, you are a braver man than I am, but regardless, think of what is best for her. Does she need to hear that from you? Are your motives pure in telling her so? Are you telling her that she is beautiful because it is true and she needs to know it, (which, under the right circumstances, can be a very valid and noble brotherly act of love), or because you want her to know how you feel which might well be merely self-serving? She doesn't need to know how you feel until you are ready to act on that feeling. That is one of the greatest sacrifices you can make for her. Even better, put your family first. Pay more attention to your family than to her. Take that desire to be all nice and attentive to her, and turn it towards your most annoying sibling. I am very serious about this, because this is how you learn to love. Right now you want to be nice to her because you have a crush on her, but you won't always have a crush on her. You will probably be desperately in love before you get married to your wife. You won't always feel that way, but you will have to act as if you did. You will have to love then whether you feel like it or not, and this habit of sacrifice cannot be learned too early. I firmly believe that when you are a young person looking at another young person with liquid shiny eyes, you should turn a slightly colder and more analytical glance to the way you treat your family. That relationship you have with your most annoying sibling, or with your slightly overbearing father, or slightly meddling mother is precisely the kind of relationship you will have with your wife after a year of marriage. 1 Corinthians 13:4-7, the famous passage on love, describes a list of actions, not feelings. Love is a discipline, not a high, and this is a God given opportunity to practice that discipline. Pay more attention to your family than you do to her, until she becomes family, should that be God's will for you.

3) Pray for her. You don't have to tell her you are praying, though it won't hurt to say so if she asks. Don't say too much to other humans. Do not breathe a word to her, although I do encourage you to confide in a trusted brother or a sister or cousin, or a mentor, or your parents. But in your prayer to God you can pour out your heart. Lay it all on the line. Speak every word that is there. Lay it all out before Him and let Him pick and choose what He wants you to keep. Ask Him to bless her. Ask Him to give her the greatest good (which He's already working on anyway). Then ask Him to keep you from doing or saying anything

that will distract her from His plan. Pray for her to do well in school. Pray for her job, pray for her family (very important, love her family). If she already has a boyfriend be sure to pray for him as well. This is exceptionally important, perhaps the most concrete example I know of an opportunity to pray for your enemy. Whatever is going on in her life, pray for her to live in God's will. In this way you will be training yourself to love, rather than merely to be in love, and you will be beginning a habit that will carry with you all your life and which will do more to keep your feelings in God's Will than any other thing you can do. Remember to pray for your family as often as you pray for her. This will do wonders for the sheer volume of your prayer life if nothing else. One more thing, and this is also very important. Continue to pray for your wife every single day. (You are praying for your future wife every day, aren't you?) Continue with that discipline separately from your prayers for your crush. The two are not the same people as far as you know yet. Do not confuse them!

4) Learn to think in a fog. When you have to be near her you're going to have to keep your wits about you. It's one thing to make resolutions to be strong and not let on what you feel to her, when you're praying about it alone at night. It is quite another matter entirely when she walks in the room unexpectedly and the floor comes up and smacks you in the chin. When floors do that they have a tendency to disorient you for a while. Practice praying in a crisis, and keeping your eyes on the goal, and then let go of it. Simply relax and trust in God to get you through this.

5) Start evaluating wife material. When we are all in a tizzy over some girl, we tend to miss things. The old saying that love is blind was definitely speaking about puppy love, which is all this really is. (Some puppies are bigger than others but they are still puppies.) You may not even notice that she has a tendency to dress immodestly, speak roughly, laugh at inappropriate jokes, stretch the truth or not keep her word in little things like appointments. These are important indicators. As a Christian man, you are not looking for a nice girl to marry, because you don't want to be a nice guy. You are striving for heroic sainthood, and as rough a time as you're having on your own in that quest (how did I know you were having a rough time, right?) it won't get any easier if she doesn't share that goal. Your wife will likely either make you or break you as a man, (although even the worst choice of mate can be redeemed by God's grace) so choose wisely, or better yet, let God choose

for you. You are not looking for someone who is mildly Christian, but with a healthy dose of worldliness. You are looking for a woman who is passionately in love with God, and continually striving to grow in His grace. You are looking for someone who is seeking His will, who is serving those around her, who is capable of maturity. Does she love children, or does she just get mushy around them and spoil them? Does she love her younger siblings, if she has any, or does she merely tolerate them? Do they love her? Does she go to church and read her Bible because her parents make her or because she suspects you would like that? Or does she do it because God is the center of her life? If this is not describing you, don't even think about approaching a woman yet. If this is not describing her, you would be setting yourself up for failure. What you are trying to do is train yourself to be picky. Literally. I'm not joking. Train yourself to fall in love only with the woman who is striving for holiness. Anyone else is probably going to get in your way later on. Any girl who distracts you or tries to discourage you from following the path that God has set you on is bad news. You can scratch her off the list immediately. The only woman worth marrying is the one who inspires, and positively encourages you to love God more than you love her. Only fall in love with the woman who draws you closer to God. You are looking for a sister in Christ before you are looking for a bride. If this girl you are crushing on does fit this bill, well then, you've found a treasure, and it doesn't change a thing. If you're not ready, you're not ready, no matter how perfect she is. Rough, I know, but that's how it goes. Until you are ready to commit, you are not ready to look around for someone to commit to. Trust in God that He will find your wife for you, and protect her until you get there, and let this one go free to do God's will for her. Maybe it includes you, and maybe it doesn't. It doesn't matter. It doesn't matter in the slightest whether you know what God has planned, just so long as God remains in charge.

6) Surrender. You must surrender that desire to God. It is absolutely critical. As soon as you find yourself falling for someone you must start taking that affection to God in prayer every day. It isn't necessary to ask anything from Him, though if you feel led to ask, do not be afraid to do so. There is no evil in honest desire. Just remember, the one thing needful is that you surrender it to Him. Say out loud and explicitly, "Lord, I surrender this affection to you. I want you to do with it whatever you want." If you remember nothing else in this

whole book, you can still get by with that one sentence. Say it every day, but only if you mean it. I promise you, if you do say it, God will do it. If you open yourself up and surrender to Him, and ask Him to do whatever He wants, He will do whatever He wants until you rebel and take back control. He might fulfill your wildest dreams. He might crush those dreams because He doesn't think they are wild enough and He wants to give you better ones. God is wild. No one can say what He will do when given free reign, only that He will do something and it will be good. It will be very good.

If it seems a bit odd that I consider it so necessary to temper so strong an emotion with reason, think of it this way. Right now, as a young man not ready to look for a wife, it is necessary to control your emotion in this way, trying not to act on a feeling that you have. Later on, as an older married man, I can almost guarantee there will come times when you will have to do the opposite, trying to act as you would if you did feel that overpowering emotion, even when you don't. Right now you can't show her you love her, even if you feel it. Later on you will have to show your wife you love her, even if you don't feel it. The irony is tragic and comical, but mostly comical. I am not talking about faking love for her, I mean that you will have to show the deepest and most sacrificial love when you are tired, grumpy, upset, hungry, sick, poor, stressed out and annoyed all at the same time. Right now you can only give little bits of yourself, to your friends, family, and neighbors. If you begrudge giving even those little bits, and spend your time chasing after emotional highs, how will you ever survive when the necessity is laid on you of giving, not just bits of yourself, but yourself away to your spouse? Best to be thankful for what God has given you now. It only gets more challenging from here on out. But the love of a man who has given himself for twenty, thirty or fifty years to his wife is a thing compared with which the teenage high is hardly even worth mentioning. This is the report brought back by those men who know. We who do not know would do well to listen to them.

"For I know the plans that I have for you, says the Lord. Plans for good and not for evil, to give you a future and a hope. Then you will call upon me and come and pray to me, and I will hear you. You will seek me and you will find me, when you seek me with all your heart." Jeremiah 29:11-13

157

33. Why God Sends a Crush

You know, there was a time when I wanted to go my whole life not having a crush on anyone, ever, until I found the girl I was going to marry. Then I would go ahead and fall in love with her (on purpose) and that would be that. To that end I ruthlessly and efficiently set out to kill every attraction I ever felt when I was a teenager, and in fact up until now, at the threshold of a quarter of a century old I have been mostly successful. I am really not as hard hearted as I sound. It didn't always work, and those singular and powerful failures led me to have to re-evaluate what to do with that unruly affection once it had taken root. What to do with it I have already written about in the previous chapter. Another question, however, more important though perhaps of less practical step by step value, began to trouble me. Why would God put me through that? Surely it was His will that I devote myself entirely to His will without distraction (as if that was really what I was doing. I was solitary all right, but in all honesty not really all that devoted to His will. That is a work in progress). According to that plan, whenever or if ever a wife became part of His will for me I would be ready, but until then I didn't need the distraction, I thought. God apparently has seen fit to disagree with me at least once. It wasn't until now that I began to get a clue as to the reason why, and it is beautiful. There is such magnificence in God's plan and what He has been doing for me. I can't tell all of it, but I'll try to make clear what I can.

All through my life, as far back as I can remember, I have been offering God all my worst. I have offered Him my laziness, my pride, my weakness, my vanity, my lust, everything that is ugly and evil in me, and rightly so. He came to take it all, and it is false humility that refuses to burden Him with it. He has already carried it; I insult Him if I do not surrender it all to Him. But what have I given Him that really cost me? If any of those vices cost me to give them up, that is to my shame and no more than I deserve for hanging onto them. They are soiled and foul things anyway, and I give them to Him to be destroyed. But what can I give Him that isn't corrupt? My time? It's all His time. My money? It came from Him, and I don't much care for it anyway. It's all collecting dust as far as I'm concerned. My will?

Yes, but I can only give my will in concrete actions, that is, in sacrifices. The greater the sacrifice, the greater the love, and this, I think, is the purpose of God allowing us to love (for it is a sort of love, after all) when we cannot honorably act on it. Maybe she already has a boyfriend. Maybe she is not suitable wife material. Maybe she is too young. Maybe you are committed to work that requires you to remain single for a time. I cannot act on every feeling I have. Feelings change with my digestion and the state of the air-conditioning in my apartment, but God's word remains year after year and outside of time, from all eternity. When we are led by the Spirit (Galatians 5:16-18) surrendering our natural desires, even the good natural desires, to the will of God, we are stepping outside of the temporality of desire. Then we can be free to love from the permanence of eternity, a love rooted in and nourished by God, ordained in His plan, growing in His time. God deliberately gives me good desires and innocent feelings which I cannot act on, so that I have something worthwhile to give Him. In surrendering it and laying it on the altar, I allow Him to resurrect it and give it back to me as He always intended it to be. It may look nothing like I wanted it to, but that is only because I was aching for a mirage, while He is offering me living waters.

A crush is a good thing, in and of itself. When the girl I have such regard for is a good and beautiful woman then I am admiring and appreciating that goodness and that beauty, and that appreciation of that beauty is a gift from God. The ability to see it is a gift from God. He has given me something that is pure, innocent and beautiful which has no other purpose than to be given back to Him. It is material for sacrifice. When God commanded a sacrifice from Abraham, the patriarch could give only something that God had given him. When God commanded a sacrifice of the Israelites He knew it was not going to be enough. It was not worthy. It was not until He Himself sent a Lamb, spotless and without blemish, that there could be a sacrifice worthy. So it is with all our sacrifices. We can sacrifice only what He has given us. The good news is that He has given us nothing we cannot sacrifice.

In sacrificing something that is good and pure right through from one side to the other I can finally give God a gift that is worth giving, one that need not be destroyed. It can be raised up on the last day, in the form that God always intended it to have. Every love that we will have in heaven, even the most casual affection, will be stronger, deeper and more perilous than the most majestic romance ever lived on earth, stronger as wine is stronger than water, as blood is stronger than wine and as love is stronger than any of them. We see now only symbols, sacraments and shadows, but then we shall possess and be possessed by the reality of Love Himself. Nothing can live that is not first sacrificed. When God sends us a crush or an affection we cannot act on, He is not teasing us. He is giving us a seed, which, if we plant it now, will blossom into something as yet unseen in eternity. The only way we can plant that seed, however, is to let it die and bury it. "Unless a grain of wheat falls to the ground and dies, it remains but a single grain of wheat." John 12:24

Of course it hurts, but the pain is a cleansing pain. It is a crucible. It burns, like a refiner's fire, but it burns the impurities out of us. The long trek through the desert of loneliness melts the fat and flab off of us, and leaves us better men, lean, tough and unafraid. Did you really think it could be any other way? Even a love that God destines to last a lifetime must be sacrificed, every day, in every way. Did you think that the love between husband and wife will require less sacrifice than a casual teenage infatuation? I tell you, it will require more, much more. An entire tree of seeds must die and be planted in a lifelong marriage, and that love too will be greater in heaven than anything we could dream of.

Do you really wish it could be any other way? Really? What can you know about yourself if you have never suffered? If you have never sacrificed, or fought some fight, or bled in some way, can you really hope ever to achieve true manhood? God gives us affections so that we can learn to die, to ourselves, to the world, to those we love even, and live only to Him. Once we have learned to do that we can be trusted to love. Once we lean on God, we will stand so firmly that all our loved ones will be able to lean on us at need, but we must give Him everything first. Can you really want to give God something that cost you nothing? If I have never looked on sweetness personified in human form, on bright, splendid stubbornness and fierce charity, on innocence and grace in the flesh, and known her for what she was, for what God made her, and turned away, can I ever really appreciate the greatness of God's gift? Unless I give her up, in whatever respect I have to, and go out into the dark and do my job, simply because that is what is required of me, could I even be worthy of her? And if I am not worthy of that gift, or at least willing to be made so, what good can hanging on with over eager hands do? I will only destroy that which I most love. I would a million times rather be worthy of love and not have it, than have love and not be worthy of it.

That is what it costs to be a Son of God. Not less than everything.

"For this slight momentary affliction is preparing for us an eternal weight of glory beyond all comparison, because we look not to the things that are seen but to the things that are unseen; for the things that are seen are transient, but the things that are unseen are eternal." 2 Corinthians 4:17-18

34. Our Ogre Who Art in Heaven

I'm sure few of my readers believe that God really is an ogre. Very few people who believe that God is an ogre will have read this book this far. However, something I've noticed about myself is that, although I believe that God is a loving Father, I sometimes find it very hard to pray that way. My training and temperament have created such an emphasis on doing the right thing, no matter how tough it may be, that I spend a good deal of time looking forward to challenges and trials, with eagerness even, and praying for the strength to deal with them. Perhaps there is a good bit of willingness to look for the worst case scenario. As Puddleglum would have it, I'm the sort of chap who likes to know the worst and put as good a face on it as I can.[13] In other words, I take myself too seriously.

Every once in a while I realize that God's will might just be, not only good and noble (which I never doubt) nor even fun (I can have fun doing almost anything), but perhaps it might even be pleasant. Perhaps it might be more pleasant than otherwise. Perhaps God's will might be gloriously, exquisitely happy. It is always a surprise to me when I come to that conclusion. It's as if I've been so intent on pushing through trials and temptations, that when there are none I'm not sure what to do with myself. And when God says to me, "Be happy," it's like He's speaking a foreign language. Happy? What do you mean, happy?

Not strong? Not courageous? Not vigilant? Not joyful in the midst of hardship? Not all of these things that I fail at so often and need so much practice at? Just happy? What, am I in pre-school?

And the answer comes back with a deep, rumbling laugh: "Yes."

"Rejoice in the Lord always. I will say it again: Rejoice!" Philippians 4:4.

"For the Lord God is a sun and a shield; He bestows glory and honor. No good thing does the Lord withhold from them that walk uprightly." Psalm 84:11

PART IV

35. The 'S' Word

If you live in the kind of society I do, the word "sensitive" has a lot of bad connotations. When a man says that another man is 'sensitive' he usually means that he's homosexual. When a woman says that a man is sensitive, she seems to mean that he does exactly the same thing that her girl friends would do in any given situation, or that he is a mind reader. No man wants to be either homosexual or someone's girl friend, so it's not hard to see why calling a dude 'sensitive' is rarely seen by the guy as a compliment. Maybe it's just an Army thing, but that's what I've seen. I have never in my life ever heard of a man complaining that another man was insensitive, except in a movie, and that character was homosexual. On the other hand, most of the women I have met have complained at one time or another about men not being sensitive enough, while many married men complain about their wives being too sensitive.

And yet, sensitivity in its right form is such a truly noble trait. It is a great shame that we have so perverted the word that it no longer points to a virtue. You can be sensitive, and you should be sensitive, without being effeminate and without being a mind reader.

Sensitivity is not about doing exactly what a girl would do or would want you to do. It is far deeper than that.

Sensitivity is really about a re-ordering or refocusing of priorities. A lot of men will accept that we need to be leaders and servants. We will accept that this means sacrificing, and paying attention to those we are to lead, listening to them, placing their needs above our own, but what we very often have trouble accepting, or sometimes don't even think about, is that this sort of servanthood is not just about doing the best good for our loved ones, but it has a simpler dimension as well. Most often it is simply about making people happy. Just happy. Simply happy. If all we ever do for those we love is worry about their needs we are still living at a basic, superficial level of service. If you are concerned only with what they need, it is too easy to translate that into concern only for what you have to do for them. This is a bare minimum level of concern, which is not love. Before we can grasp the full meaning of service, we have to move into asking what we can do for them. Love leaps to the service of the beloved, no matter how inconsequential the matter. Even if it is only getting someone a glass of water, real love rejoices to do it.[14] This is where sensitivity comes into its own. Sensitivity is the art of taking other people into account in order to make them happy. It is the epitome of courtesy, and make no mistake, it is an art, in every sense of the word. It is not a science, it cannot be solved with technology. It requires time and practice, for most of us. I suppose it comes naturally to some people, but for most men it requires effort. Most of us would do anything for those we love. We will solve any problem, make any sacrifice, fight any battle, if we see that it needs to be done for our loved ones, and that is all well and good, but not really the soul of love. We are in love with the idea of loving, not with the person, if we think only of the big things we can do for them. If all we ever think about in our pursuit of service is the grand sacrifices we can make for others, aren't we really still thinking about ourselves? We want to be servants, and we want to be known as servants, so we pursue visible acts of service. When we forget about ourselves, however, and think only of the beloved, it does not matter in the least how small or great the act of service is, only that "at last, here is something I can do for the beloved."

Sensitivity also looks to the desire of the beloved by trying to stop listening to our own desires. If you can't empty yourself of your own internal monologue, you will never be able to listen, and you will limit your ability to serve. You can see this in married couples. Marriage counseling books make a lot out of the claim that men are always trying to fix problems, while women just want them to listen, empathize and show support. This may be something of a cliché, but I've heard it from real married men too and seen it in other forms, so I am inclined to believe it. The sensitive man, being the student of the beloved, learns to keep his own desires in perspective against the desires of the beloved, and so he will be more concerned with how she wants to be helped than with how he wants to help her. This does not mean that we have to give up solving problems. That is what we were made to do and we cannot quit our vocation. However fixing problems is only the means to the end goal, which is helping people. The goal comes first. Comfort and encourage first, then get out the tools and attack the problem, but always keep the focus on the beloved, not on a project. We should leap to the service of the beloved, not to the solving of a puzzle.

Take a look at the story of the wedding at Cana, in John 2. The wine gave out and Mary pointed it out to Jesus. She didn't ask anything of Him, she just pointed it out. He asked, "What has this to do with me? My time has not yet come." Archbishop Fulton Sheen speculated that when He said this He was pointing out that this miracle, if He did it, would be the first step along the path that could end only on the cross. Whatever His intent, it is obvious He had a history at this point of serving others, since His mother knew He would help. She didn't even ask Him what he was going to do, and apparently she didn't know what He would do, since she told the servants, "Do whatever He tells you." She just knew He was going to do something, and that it was going to be good. She knew her Son, and that knowledge was based, no doubt, on countless tiny acts of love performed throughout their family life in Nazareth. Sure enough, Jesus acted. We all know the story, and if you don't I suggest you put this book down immediately, pick up your Bible and read it until you do know the story. Our Lord not only supplied their immediate need, He overflowed it. Six jars of twenty to thirty gallons apiece, filled to the brim, not with just any wine, but with the best wine. Jesus filled their needs, then filled their wants, and then gave more than they even knew enough to want. Not just enough, but more than enough, and an overabundance of the best, between a hundred and twenty and a hundred and eighty gallons of the best wine anyone had ever tasted! Though she had no clue what He would do when she brought the need to His attention, Mary knew her Son. He was all she needed to know.

I do not know whether she knew what she was asking, or whether she knew what the ultimate result of that miracle would be, but Jesus knew. John concludes the story by telling us that this was the first of Jesus' signs, and it manifested His glory. After that, there was no turning back. He started with a simple act of love, and ended shedding every drop of His blood, and at no point in between those two events did He ever change. Both acts equally flowed from who He was.

This is why I don't consider sensitivity, or courtesy, to be an extra as many do. It is not just icing on the cake, but rather the revelation of the innermost character. I say this knowing what my life reveals to those who are familiar with it, but there you have it. I am not the image of Jesus yet.

So what does this mean in the concrete? Well, I think there are two parts. You have to desire the best good of the beloved, and that is the easy part. That is a matter of decision. More difficult, especially for us men, is the second part, which is noticing. Women seem to have more of a knack for picking up on other people's needs. Notice that even though Jesus was the perfect man, it was still Mary who pointed out that they had no wine, (which is yet another courtesy of God, that He allows us to ask Him for the things we need, and thus take part in His love for others.) Paying attention to people seems to be a special genius of women. However, while I doubt many men will ever get as adept at noticing things like that as most women are, this does not give us an excuse to be oblivious. The reason I say this is because there is one phenomenon that proves that we are not hopeless. Take the most oblivious, head in the clouds and even self-centered youth you can imagine, and add one beautiful woman to his life, and suddenly he will become a student of her the like of which the world has never seen. He will know everything about her, her favorite movies, music and colors, what she likes to eat, who she hangs out with, everything. Nothing will be beneath his notice. He will hunt down details like a detective hunting for clues. Whether his motives are correct or not is a question I will save for a little bit later, but that he has the ability to pay attention to her slightest whim is not in doubt. Courtesy, or sensitivity, practices as a lifelong discipline what romantic interest inspires as a momentary means to an end.

Men will pay attention to detail in anything they are interested in, whether a car, hobby or job. Indeed, women often marvel at the sheer volume of information that we can remember without effort on anything that interests us (and we wonder the same thing about them).

Courtesy is the practice of putting that same effort into people that we put into our jobs and hobbies. By people I mean people in general, old women, young kids, annoying sisters, obnoxious brothers, everyone. One of the men I admire most in the world is an uncle of mine, who is the epitome of courtesy. He has a rare talent for bringing people together and conversing with them, regardless of their age, background, or level of sophistication, and it is entirely a result of his habit of deep, profound courtesy. He takes people seriously. No matter who you are or where you are from, if he is speaking with you, then you know that when he listens you have his entire focus, consistently and habitually. When he answers you have the full weight of his thought and attention. Courtesy has ceased to become a practiced lesson and has seeped right down to his bones until it is an inseparable part of who he is.

But of course, no discussion of sensitivity could be complete without a discussion of romantic relationships, though that is not because they are the point of courtesy. Everyone we meet, no matter how casually, is the point of this virtue. Rather, the husband/wife relationship is the deepest expression of this virtue. Ordinarily no one in our lives will be closer to us than our spouse, and this closeness, though boosted initially by the phenomenon of in-love-ness is not accidental. It doesn't just happen, but is the product of two people who are each dedicated to studying and learning the other.

I mentioned above that the teenage boy becomes a student of the girl he's crushing on, but there are a number of reasons why he might be doing this and not all of them are noble. Lots of girls have found themselves losing their hearts and bodies, and sometimes worse, to men who swept them away with attentiveness. These guys were definitely dedicated to studying the women they were interested in, but not out of love. They were studying like a predator studies his prey, searching out weaknesses, looking for buttons to push that would give them what they wanted. The lover, the one who loves, studies just as avidly but with a completely different motive. A lover studies the beloved in order to appreciate her beauty. Just knowing her is an end in itself, discovering little by little all the beauty that God put into her, but there are more pragmatic reasons as well. The lover is not only in love, he also loves, meaning he actively desires and pursues the good of the beloved, if anything more than he pursues the beloved herself. So not only will a lover know as much as a predator about her habits, likes, dislikes, values, beliefs, opinions, passions, and everything else, but the lover will know more for he will seek to know her. Not just things about her, but her, in herself. The person that God created and is creating is what interests the lover, not just the facts about her. He wants her to be happy. His knowledge of her is the material that his service can draw on to make her happy.

The further difference between the lover and the predator is in duration. The predator is focused only on himself, therefore as soon as he loses interest in the object of his obsession he cuts her loose. The lover is focused on the beloved, and therefore he doesn't lose interest in her. Even if the emotional attachment loses its first thrill, he is not committed to a thrill but rather to a person. He remains faithful and the habit and discipline of courtesy comes to the rescue. Decision, and the long established habit of consideration for others, is what takes a beautiful but frail emotion and establishes it on a foundation of rock. There, protected behind a shield of obedience to the will of God, this emotion can bloom again and again, each time more beautifully than before, because it is not being stepped on by the world and the devil. The devil hates love of all kinds, but no kind more viciously than true, deep romantic love. He attacks marriage with all his strength (as our society is dying proof) because marriage is a living sacrament of Christ and the Church (Ephesians 5:31-32). He does this primarily by introducing and encouraging selfishness, but sensitivity, the discipline of courtesy, is the habit of unselfishness in full combat mode. This is not an effeminate virtue. This virtue is a virtue of bright, burnished steel, made for the spiritual war. This is where the fight is.

Sensitivity is not an extra. It is God's way of taking a weak and self-centered boy and turning him into a man strong enough for others to depend on, no matter what. It is how we learn to be servants, and unless we can be servants we can never be leaders, and unless we are leaders we will forever fail our vocation as men. Our vocation is a vocation of love, regardless of what form it takes. Sensitivity is not for chick flicks. It is far too strong for that.

"A new command I give you: Love one another. As I have loved you, so you must love one another. By this all men will know that you are my disciples, if you love one another." John 13:34-35

36. And The Two Shall Become One

This is going to be the longest chapter in this book because in this chapter I am going to talk about one of the ugliest and nastiest battles that we men have to fight, one which all men have to fight at some point in their lives. This is the battle for personal purity, against pornography and masturbation. I do not intend to talk about detailed tactics, though. I have learned from my own experience that tactics are secondary to desire. All the best tactics in the world will not make a difference if your heart is not in the battle. On the other hand, when you really desire purity with all your heart, tactics will come very naturally to you. So my focus is more to present a positive vision of why to love purity than a negative plan for how to avoid lust.

Read this chapter slowly. I am going to skim across a lot of ground in a very short time, and this is very important stuff. The understanding of purity, what it is and where it comes from, is the understanding of our whole purpose as men, and also a key part of winning the struggle against lust. (The key, by the way, is nothing less than total trusting surrender to God. Just in case you were wondering.) Until we love purity, all the fighting in the world will not give us permanent victory. This does not mean that all that fighting is useless. Sometimes young men who grew up in good families, with good morals and good formation, are amazed and bewildered to find themselves struggling with this vice. They ask, "Why? I never wanted this struggle. I don't want this sin. Why can't God give me rest?"

Perhaps the answer lies in the very fact that we are given good formation and upbringing. Of course there is a lot to be said for testosterone. That is going to cause struggles, like it or not, but a lot of young men take the virtue of purity for granted, I think. This is especially true of homeschoolers, who are brought up outside of many of the influences of the world. I don't consider this to be a bad thing, up to a certain point. However, if you are given the gift of purity on a silver platter, just because you're too naïve to know any worse, there is the danger that you will never value it sufficiently. On the other hand, if you fight for it you will begin to cherish it as you ought, to resent and despise attacks against it, and really to be disgusted by offenses against purity. This is the gift that God gives by allowing us to be attacked, and this is the point of fighting. The goal of course is to be so transformed in our hearts that purity is our first, last and only instinct, but for most men that transformation happens slowly, over time and by means of much sweat and tears. Once that transformation is complete, we will not be conscious of fighting anymore, but the only way that transformation will ever occur is by fighting for it. When you've fought for something, in this case the virtue of purity, for years, against all odds, through thick and thin, you're going to love it. It will become a part of you. This transformation is brought about by the action of the Holy Spirit, to be sure, not by our own efforts, but it is our efforts that are the work of the Holy Spirit. The fact that we can fight shows that He is working in us, and the fact that we do fight is the mechanism by which we prepare ourselves to receive His cleansing grace. The fact that we struggle indicates we are not yet perfect, but at the same time, the very fact that we struggle also indicates that we are being perfected.

But there are those, well meaning "Christians" among them, who do not consider there to be anything wrong with these sins. They are "private" sins. They don't seem to hurt anyone. I have even heard "Christian" writers argue for masturbation as a legitimate way of "remaining pure until marriage"! To that I say, not just no, but Hell No! That is a damned lie in the most literal possible sense of the phrase. It comes straight from the depths of hell.

The only way anyone could possibly ever make such an error is by a deep and fundamental lack of understanding of what purity really is. Such misguided guides think of purity in such legalistic terms, as if it were the mere fact of not having had sex that renders you pure. If that were true, then everyone would immediately be impure as soon as they were married, and this is clearly not the case. That is a flat, legalistic, pre-grace way of thinking. Jesus made it clear that more was expected of us than mere obedience to external laws and standards. "But I tell you that anyone who looks at a woman lustfully has already committed adultery with her in his heart." Matthew 5:28. It is not the mere physical status of the body that Jesus is concerned with. He wants to claim the heart for purity, both before and after marriage.

In order to understand this, we have to go back to the beginning and understand the meaning of sexuality. I have already said in a previous chapter that the gift of sexuality, especially the giving of one's virginity, is a gift of self. If you've been paying attention you've probably noticed that the main theme of this whole book is self-gift. The heart and soul of manhood is to "give Himself up for her." This is manifest even from the book of Genesis, for in the beginning, God "Created Man in His own image, in the image of God He created him; Male and female He created them. And God Blessed them and God said to them, 'Be fruitful and multiply, and fill the earth and subdue it." Genesis 1:28.

This single verse tells us volumes, literally, about what it means to be both a human and a man. The human being is made in the Image of God, but that image is not simply in the individual human being. The sacred writer emphasizes that Image, because the whole point of being human is to be the image of God, to live out and fulfill that image. And what does that image consist of? "Male and Female He created them. And God Blessed them and said, 'Be fruitful'." You can continue on reading the rest of the commands and prohibitions to man in the light of these words. The Image of God is made complete in the fruitful union of man and woman, in their mutual gift of selves to each other.

Why is this so? Because God is a Trinity, ("Let us make man in our image, after our likeness.") God is an eternal, inseparable communion of Divine Persons, constantly giving and receiving love between each other. God is one, and thus each human being is the image of God. God is trinity, family, communion, and thus each human family is the Image of God, completed and perfected in the Holy Family, which was God's own human family on earth.

What does this have to do with anything, right? Aren't I getting a little sidetracked? I was going to talk about pornography and mastur-bation, and what does Theology of the Body have to do with them? Actually, the question is, what do those two evils have to do with the Theology of the Body? This theology explains what human sexuality is for, why it exists, how it is fulfilled and how it becomes the blessing it was meant to be. It explains what human beings are for. Once you know the truth, the goodness and the beauty of it, you can see why the perversions are perverted. "What have you to do with me, Satan?"

Human sexuality quite literally symbolizes God, both as He is in Himself and as He is in relation to the Church. The human race was created to share in the inner life of self-gift, the eternal communion of Persons, that is the Holy Trinity. In order for any creature to do that, God would have to give Himself to us in a way we could understand. We could never reach out to take Him, nor is there anything we could give to Him. He would have to create us able to receive Him, just as He created woman to receive man, and He would have to pursue us, and woo us, slowly and patiently, just as He created man to pursue woman and to woo her slowly and patiently. This correspondence between God's relationship with the Church and human sexuality is so close that if I ever write a book about romance, it will be a study of how a man ought to learn courtship from studying God's courtship of the Church.

Do you see what this means? Look at the second account of the Creation of man from Genesis 2. This account focuses even more strongly on the relationship between the man and woman.

"The Lord God said, "It is not good for the man to be alone. I will make a helper fit for him."

Now the Lord God had formed out of the ground all the beasts of the field and all the birds of the air. He brought them to the man to see what he would name them; and whatever the man called each living creature, that was its name. So the man gave names to all the cattle, the birds of the air and all the beasts of the field.

But for Adam no helper was found fit for him. So the Lord God caused the man to fall into a deep sleep; and while he was sleeping, He took one of the man's ribs and closed up the place with flesh. Then the Lord God made a woman from the rib He had taken out of the man, and He brought her to the man.

The man said,

"This is now bone of my bones
and flesh of my flesh;
she shall be called 'woman,'
for she was taken out of man."

For this reason a man will leave his father and mother and be united to his wife, and they will become one flesh.

The man and his wife were both naked, and they felt no shame."
Genesis 2:18-25

There is such a wealth of love revealed in this short passage that I can never hope even to scratch the surface in one short chapter. John Paul II preached a hundred and thirty or so homilies on these passages[15], interpreting them in the light of Christ's words in Matthew 5:28, Matthew 19:3-8, Paul's words in Ephesians 5 and the words of the Song of Songs. Taking them together and praying and meditating on them for decades he came closer, perhaps, to understanding the meaning of marriage and the family than anyone ever has before. I don't even know where to begin, but I must start somewhere, or I will never understand.

Why are pornography and masturbation so evil? "It is not good for the man to be alone." This is the indictment of God Himself against His own creation. In all of creation there was found only one thing that was not good, that was not complete and perfect. Man was alone. The body and vocation of manhood do not make sense in solitude. John Paul II wrote, in his pastoral letter Redemptor Hominis, (Redeemer of Men) "Man cannot live without love. He remains a being that is incomprehensible for himself, his life is senseless, if love is not revealed to him, if he does not encounter love, if he does not experience love and make it his own, if he does not participate intimately in it." (Redemptor Hominis 10). I literally cried when I read that passage for the first time. Man (human being) and man (masculine humans) were created with only one purpose, and that purpose is to enter into Love. This is done in two ways: first, we must receive Love. This is the purpose of solitude, the solitude imposed on Adam from the beginning, the solitude of the one person surrounded by beasts who could neither desire nor require love. Adam was called from among them, out of the sixth day, into the Sabbath rest, into a "unique, exclusive, and unrepeatable relationship with God Himself."[16] None of the beasts were suited to share this call. None of the beasts, and by extension, nothing in the created world, could satisfy the ineffable longing of Adam for union with his Creator. Only God Himself is enough for us, because He created us to be so.

But there is more to it than that, or else the story would end there, with Adam learning that this world simply wasn't enough. There were other longings, not separate, but different, created into Adam by God. Adam didn't long only to receive love. He needed to enter into love more deeply than that. He needed to make Love his own, by also giving love. This is the second meaning of Original Solitude, the loneliness of the man without the woman.

Before we go any further, there is something I want you to learn from this. God created man, male, first. He created Him alone. He created Him alone so that he could learn something. First and most basically of course that no creature can take the place of the Creator, and I talk a good deal about that aspect of solitude in other chapters, when I talk about seeking solitude before God and following Him before all else. But God did not create Adam to remain alone before Him forever. The relationship that we forge with God is not meant to be horded, "Freely you have received, freely give." Matthew 10:8. It is meant to be shared. In God's good plan, through the gift of solitude there always comes the call into love. This was true for Adam then, and it is true for every young man who walks this earth now, secretly longing, hoping, praying, wondering and struggling to place God first. This is what loneliness is! It is nothing less than the call to communion, the longing of the human heart for union with another heart, whether through marriage or through some other vocation. Out of every solitude must come the call into love, always. Always, or God is not God.

Therefore, God made a helper. He took from Adam a rib. Can you imagine if God asked you for a rib? Would you say, "Sure, Lord. You gave me this rib, I give it back to you freely?" Would I say that? What if the rib is a symbol of a deeper sacrifice? What if a rib is literally God asking us for our flesh and blood, our body and soul, our life, our works, our hopes, our desires, everything? Does that make me more afraid to surrender the rib? But if I hold back a rib, I will never meet Eve. There is great meaning here.

He formed from the rib a woman, and He brought her to Adam. I am reminded of the parable of the mustard seed in Matthew 13 (see also Matthew 17:20). Out of the smallest act of Faith, God can make the Kingdom of Heaven. All Adam did was surrender. God did all the work (Adam was asleep), but it hinged on Adam's surrender. And what a gift He gave! Adam awoke to behold the perfect woman, created especially for him, by God Himself, living proof that God is always more romantic than we are. Adam loved her. He would not do otherwise. He was created as a being perfectly free, and so his heart leapt in joy to love the good, the true and the beautiful. These three things that we have to struggle and fight to teach ourselves to love by pain and sweat, Adam saw standing before him in the flesh. He loved her at first sight, not compulsively but freely, not grudgingly but totally, with every fiber of his body and soul. Why?

He tells us why. "This at last is bone of my bone and flesh of my flesh." She came from him, she took her nature from him, and her nature was equal to his. Unlike the beasts, whom he could rule and play with but never love or share with, she was created to be loved and to love in return. It was through Eve that his vocation began to make sense. He was created to receive God's love, because he was human, but also to pour out his love, freely and prodigally. She was created to receive God's love also, because she was human as he was, but she was also created to receive the love of the man because she was woman.

Even their bodies proclaimed this, and Adam recognized this. She was built to receive him physically, and he to give himself physically. They saw this, they knew this, and it was very good. Their relationship was perfect, unmarred by any jealousy or domination. Adam knew his place and accepted it, for he named her: "She shall be called woman, for she was taken out of man." He shouldered his responsibility with the dignity of a king. Eve, for her part, accepted his authority gladly and without resenting it. She knew her vocation, her calling to be his queen, his love, the reason for which he worked and gave himself. She knew that she would take every blessing he could lavish on her, and she would make it better and give it back to him greater and more beautiful still, in daily life and most especially by turning the gift of his marital love for her into the gift of a new life. There was perfect harmony.

Therefore, a man shall leave his father and mother, and cleave unto his wife, and the two shall become one flesh. Thus it is, and thus it always shall be, God willing. That line was clearly written for the audience of the person writing, appealing to God's design in the beginning for an explanation of the way things are, and it still holds true. God's plan is not undone by centuries or millennia. These are nothing to Him. As Adam was called out of solitude into communion, so are we. Not all communion is in a marriage covenant, but communion we must have, or we will die.

They were both naked, and yet not ashamed. Why? And what does this have to do with the two sins I am supposed to be writing about?

Can you ask that? It should be obvious by now. It is not good that the man should be alone. Look at your body in a mirror sometime. If you are young and reasonably healthy, and have taken decent care of yourself, you will see more easily what the body always says, regardless of what sin and our fallen world have done to it. You will see shoulders, chest, back, arms, and legs, all designed to be strong and tough. You will see your loins, created to give life! However, even if you are not young and strong, even if your body is in shambles from age, sickness, injury or neglect, the meaning is still there. You are man! You are a man, an eternal soul with a body created to be the house, the expression, the visible sign of that spirit. Your body was created to be a temple of the Holy Spirit and a gift to everyone around you. Your body does not make sense alone, but that is precisely what all sexual sin does. It isolates. It perverts the meaning of the body. The body that was created to give, that was not meant to be alone or to horde gifts for its own selfish pleasure, is sinned against. These sins do not make man less alone. They do not bring him closer to the communion of persons. They contradict God's statement. The act of sexual sin says, "I want to be alone. I want to use these gifts for myself." It blasphemes the image of the Trinity that was meant to be formed by the communion of persons.

This is the root of every sexual sin. These two are not the worst. They are ugly, but they are the mildest of all sexual sins. This does not mean we should compromise with them, it means that this is where the battle should be fought, here, on this level. The devil may win his little skirmishes here, but he goes no further. After this the sin gets blacker and even more perverse. We move from merely using our own bodies and lusting after other bodies, to using other people, our sisters whom we were created to love and protect, for our pleasure. Beyond that there are deeper evils still. Contraception in marriages seeks to separate the joy of love from its fruitfulness, closing our hearts and our lives to God's greatest gifts. Broken faith, broken hearts and broken homes are caused by divorce and infidelity. Broken lives and broken bodies are caused when men descend to the deepest pits of all. Every act of rape begins with the habits formed in the heart by solitary sins of lust.

This is what is at stake, my brothers. That is what lies on one side. What lies on the other?

"Be fruitful and multiply." We create new lives, new souls that will exist forever in the Kingdom of Heaven. I have little patience with "population explosion" alarmists. For one thing, the birth rate in the west is not increasing, it is decreasing at an almost, and in some cases absolutely unrecoverable rate[17]. For another, the command to be fruitful really is not concerned with comfort in this world. It is Heaven we are populating. Each human soul is created to be an eternal glory before God, and these people will exist long after this earth burns to a cinder, taking with it the yachts we bought with the money that we saved by our sterile unions. Who cares if the road gets crowded? There's plenty of room where we're going.

"The Two shall become One." The human man and woman are One, imitating in their flesh and spirit the eternal unity of the Trinity. This is the fullest and deepest of all human relationships.

"Behold, you are all fair, my love, and there is no flaw in you." The lover sees with interior eyes to the unrepeatable beauty of the soul of a woman, that only gains in beauty, only grows richer and fuller, more loving and more lovable, even as the body stretches, sags and grays. The interior gaze can see beyond what sin has done to our bodies, and in the eyes of the beloved can catch a faint and far off glimpse of the resurrection promised us when all things, including our bodies, shall be made new.

"This is a profound mystery, and I speak of Christ and the Church." The loving couple gives themselves to each other, as Jesus gave Himself for the Church and to her, and the Church gives herself to and for Him.

In a word, love.

Love, my brothers. This is not the stuff of chick flicks. This is not sappy. This is perilous, this is drumming for the heart to march to war by, this is mighty adventure. Do you begin to see how much is at stake here?

It is true, masturbation is not the most serious sin. There are other sins, perhaps just as common, which are more evil by far, but that does not lessen the evil of this sin. It is grave and disordered, even if it is a disorder we all struggle with. Resist it. Fight with all your strength. Do not be discouraged by years of apparent failure. Think of it like trench warfare. The devil attacks this area in us hard and fast, right at the beginning of puberty because he wants a foothold. The human heart is vast and well defended by God, especially if you are close to Him. The devil cannot take over all at once. He needs a foothold and this is a good one. It is easy for him to take and hard for him to get pushed out of. It gets discouraging retaking the same three yards of trenchline over and over and over again for years on end, but this is where the battle must be fought. As we've already seen, this spot in the trenches may not be the biggest or most important in itself, but from there the devil will try to branch out, and slip into the rest of the trench network. This is both our greatest threat, and our greatest hope.

It is a threat because all virtues are connected. This virtue especially has a direct line right to the heart, and the devil will fight viciously for control of that line. He isn't interested in petty individual acts of lust or impure thoughts. Those can be forgiven and recovered from. He wants to encourage despair, or apathy, or a habit of using other people, either lustfully or through greed. This one foothold gives him options. It is tactically significant on a level we cannot understand, which is why it must be fought tooth and nail.

But this is also our greatest hope. Our hearts are bigger than this one vice. Our trench lines stretch far and wide, and there are places that he cannot touch yet. From these places, we can draw comfort and renewed strength, whenever we get beaten back. We can regroup here and charge back in with renewed determination. Pray for and cultivate Holy Stubbornness. As long as we never give up fighting, and never give up hope of victory, God cannot fail to rescue us in the end. When He comes, and He will come, He will find us at our posts, fighting like men, for ourselves, for our families, for our future wives, for our future children. When that return charge comes sweeping across the plain, we will be ready to join in and take the fight to the enemy.

We will be ready to love.

This is purity. To love as Christ loved the Church and gave Himself for her. I said towards the beginning of this chapter that whatever we fight for we will love. This is true on an even deeper level. It is only by fighting that we recognize how precious some things really are. The struggle for purity now is the struggle for love, most specifically the love you will one day be able to share with your future wife. This fight will teach you what her love is worth, namely, your life's blood. She is worth the struggle.

> "This day I call heaven and earth as witnesses against you that I have set before you life and death, blessings and curses. Now choose life, so that you and your children may live" Deuteronomy 30:19.

37. The Way of a Man with a Maiden

As will be clear by now, my romantic experience is unusually limited for a young man of twenty-five. This is by design, and by God's leading, but it is not necessarily a permanent thing. For nearly every man, there will come a time when he will look at himself and realize, "I could get married." It is a shocking thought, the first time it hits you. Whether it hits you all in a second or slowly grows over years of watching and praying, it is a shocking thought that I, me, this person here, who has been so single and solitary for so long, might not be that way forever. When you look that possibility squarely in the face, as it were, it changes you, or at least it ought to. You have to face the calling to cease to live by yourself, pursuing your own relationship with God, and to live with someone else, to form what literally amounts to a three way relationship: You, your wife and God, forming a union from which can come children, new human souls. The meditations on this profound mystery are beyond the scope of this book. This book stops with the simple thought, "I am ready to look for a wife."

That thought will come at different times for different men. For me it seems somewhat late; others may be able to say it honestly at twenty. It is a question that must be answered before God in each man's heart. Some men will never be called to marriage, and the possibility that God might be calling you to a life of celibacy for the kingdom is not to be taken lightly. Some men will feel the call to celibacy so strongly that it will overwhelm all else. Others will not feel it at all. Some men know what they are going to do by a sort of inborn certainty. My maternal grandfather told me that he never had the slightest question what his vocation was to be. He always knew, from when he was very young, that he would be a husband and father. I have never been gifted thus. I have walked in uncertainty my whole life, and in looking back I am astounded to see how in spite of this God has led me with perfect certainty and a simple elegance beyond all explanation. I suppose most men will experience at least some struggle in discerning, if they put any thought into it at all. Some will experience strong desires in both directions, and be forced to choose, others will feel desire pulling one way and a strong feeling of guilt pushing the other way. There is a lot of room for scrupulosity in this discernment, and also a need for trust and faith.

However his discernment process goes, each man must wrestle with this question, answering to God for his choice. Make no mistake, choose we must. Too many women complain, with good reason, about men who are in their thirties, otherwise good men, who are neither married nor pursuing a celibate vocation, but just drifting along, refusing to make a choice. Such passivity has no place in the character of the man of God.

But for most the answer will be that we are to be married. When that is made clear, things change. Everything I have written, how to get friend zoned, how to avoid leading women on, how to keep your mind focused on living the single life that God is calling you to in the moment, all of that goes out the window. Maybe not completely, but you will find yourself in a place where the exterior practices I put forth in previous chapters will cease to be relevant. You must search for the deeper root of all of those practices, since now you will be going in exactly the opposite direction.

This is in many ways the whole point of all my philosophizing about women and how to relate to them. I think and pray about how to protect myself and the women I know from inappropriate intimacy, not so that I can always be protecting, but so that someday I can fully experience total intimacy. The distance we maintain when we are single is not an end in itself but a means to the end of true Godly intimacy; perhaps with our wives if God means us to marry, but certainly with all of our sisters in the Kingdom of Heaven.

We, as men, must relate to women in integrity, in the "language of the Body, reread in truth."[18] The human body speaks a language, both in itself and in the use we make of it. In itself the body of a man reveals something about the purpose of manhood, about the vocation of manhood. That language remains constant no matter what we do. The masculine body, like all human bodies, reveals the presence of a soul, the existence of a being made in the image and likeness of God, endowed with free will. A man (human) is a being called into a "unique, exclusive, and unrepeatable relationship with God Himself."[19] However a man (male) is a unique manifestation of humanity, and God said, "It is not good for the man to be alone." Genesis 2:18. The male body reveals part of the purpose of this design, by which the human race is divided into male and female, masculine and feminine. The male body is designed to be tougher, stronger, more mobile, more dangerous on a physical level than the feminine body. Even the sexual design of the male body reveals the purpose of man. Man is designed to lead, to initiate, to reach out, to give of himself, and so, it is the man who is tasked with a special responsibility to initiate the relationship with the woman, and to guide and guard it, to till and defend it as it were.

The human body was designed to be a bridge between souls. Without our bodies, we would not be human. We could have no human contact with each other. We would not be able to shake hands, to hug, to kiss or to marry, anymore than we would be able to speak, or listen, or see, or look into someone's eyes. This is the language of the body that we speak by our actions, and, unlike the language of the body which is simply written into the body by God, this language can be a lie. It can be spoken in untruth. Whenever a man seduces a woman and uses her as a temporary entertainment, whether for passing emotional flutters or for sex, he is guilty of lying. I said in a previous chapter that if you do not intend for a relationship to proceed with a girl, you had better not even hold her hand, because it will proceed from there whether you like it or not. I did not say that because I have anything against holding hands, or physical affection in general or with relationships proceeding to the deepest levels of intimacy. All of these are goods and among God's greatest gifts. However, if you hold a girl's hand, or even flirt with her at a party and forget about her the next day, you have lied with your body. You have spoken a lie in the language of your body. It is not the flirting that is bad, anymore than the English language is bad simply because people use it to tell lies. Such language was created to speak the truth, and it is only when that purpose is perverted that it becomes evil. That is why there is a lot of flirting in healthy marriages I have seen. There is *a lot* of flirting in healthy courtships. When flirting is done truthfully, it is beautiful, even if it tends to embarrass cynical onlookers who take themselves too seriously. This principle of truth holds true from the lightest flirtation to the deepest physical intimacy. When a husband makes love to his wife, he speaks the truth with his body, telling her that he loves her, that he cherishes her and will protect her. The teenager who can't wait to get to that next level of physical intimacy, no matter how childish it might be, is lying, to himself and to her. So sick and ignorant is our society, that he may well not even know he is lying.

Now you see the apparent conundrum. When a man decides to pursue a woman he is caught in the gap, trying to move from the place where even a light kiss would be out of place, to the place where there is no barrier left between bodies or souls but "the two become one flesh." Between the one and the other, many Christians, in all good faith, fear only the temptation to sin. I think this is a tragedy. If you think of the courtship of a young woman by a young man, and all you see is opportunity for temptation, that in itself is an indication of how deeply the devil has wounded our ideas of what it is to love. That he will try to introduce temptation I have no doubt, but that is not the point. The deepest reality is that God has created us to love, and in opening ourselves up to love we are fulfilling His deepest will. Temptation is largely irrelevant to the truth.

This conundrum does, however, make us cautious in how we think of the whole art (for it is an art) of pursuing a woman's heart. If we are to love, and not grasp after, a woman, we must "reread the whole language of the body in the truth." Too many people, thinking of morality as a line to be walked on, but not crossed, ask in the dating phase the question, "How far is too far?" They isolate and dis-integrate physical affection, so that each particular display is "only" itself. It is only hand-holding, only a hug, only a kiss, only making out, only whatever. Once again this shows the tendency to define the virtue of purity in terms of what we are not doing. This is not the truth. Nothing is only itself, but each is a part of a whole continuum from brother and sister in Christ to husband and wife in Christ. Each type of physical affection says, in its own way, "I love you." If that is not true, if you do not love her in that way, and to that degree, then you ought not to say so by your actions. Each action slightly deepens the bond that you are forming, and it is in reference to this bond that each one is right or wrong. I said that if you don't intend for a relationship to proceed, then don't hold her hand. In exactly the same way, and for exactly the same reason, if you do intend for a relationship to proceed, do hold her hand. If your intention is not to follow through with God's leading in this relationship as far as He takes it then you have no business speaking that language with your body. If your intention is to follow Him wherever He leads, then by all means, say so, both with your words and with your body (obviously at the appropriate level for your current level of commitment).

People always ask, "How much is too much before marriage?" I challenge you to rethink the question. Form your conscience and your heart by practicing chastity in your own life and loving others that you aren't in love with, and then trust God to show you the right thing. Personally, I can't see myself kissing any woman who has not already agreed to marry me. This is not because I am afraid of being tempted, but because, to me, a kiss seems like the sort of thing that really ought to have a promise attached to it. I believe it should say more than, "I like you right now. Let's see how long we like each other." To me it seems it ought to say, "I love you, and I intend to go on loving you. I intend to love you even more, and to give myself to you, body and soul. That gift is not yet to be, but for now this kiss is a token of it."

But that is only my thought. Each man has to understand this for himself; it cannot be legislated. I wouldn't if I could. It would defeat the whole purpose of this book. I am not at all interested in a bunch of men who follow established rules. I want you to take responsibility and be a leader, which means I want you to seek out and follow God's will for yourself. I want you to understand this and to think deeply about it, to pray and to act on God's leading, both in your living of celibacy now, in your singleness if you are single, and later on in your courtship and marriage if that is what God has planned for you. Make it your own. Understand what you say with the body God has given you, so that you may keep yourself pure for your wife now, that you may seek her purely in God's time, and that you may love her purely when you have found her.

"There are three things that are too amazing for me,
four that I do not understand:
The way of an eagle in the sky,
the way of a snake on a rock,
the way of a ship on the high seas,
and the way of a man with a maiden." Proverbs 30:18-19

38. As Christ loved the Church

I said earlier that the point of all that resistance to romantic attachment I talked about was to protect integrity, to keep you from falling to the temptation to use the women around you for temporary amusement. Being used is not consistent with the dignity of a human person, but neither is being treated like a child, so there comes a point at which you have to stop working to maintain that friendly distance and put all your effort into drawing closer to her. At this point you must have an already firmly established habit of drawing closer to God, and so must she. If you and she are both drawing closer to God, He will have no trouble bringing you closer to each other if that is His will. If you are not, then no matter how close you get to each other, it will never be enough.

Once you believe that God's will is for you to pursue a particular woman, things change. Once you pass that point at which you can say, "I am ready to court her," you are no longer operating alone. From that time on, everything you do towards finding and pursuing a wife can be done only with her consent, and since it is the job of the man to lead, it is the man who should take the responsibility of stepping first into the gap between friendship and married life.

There is always risk involved in being a man. I spoke before about avoiding pointless, transient attachments, not seeing any benefit in putting your heart through needless pain. However, I don't want you to think that all the caution urged in those previous chapters is at all about avoiding pain. It isn't. Pain is a consequence of love in a fallen world, or rather, sacrifice is. There is no love without sacrifice, without self-gift. There never has been. Even when Adam and Eve lived in the garden of Eden they still sacrificed, it just wasn't painful. It was a delight to give of themselves. It still is for us, sometimes. Sometimes it is painful. There is no use avoiding that pain. Jesus did not avoid that pain but embraced it, accepting the agony of loneliness and rejection in the Garden of Gethsemane, the torture of scourging and mockery, the weight of carrying all of the sins and sufferings of His beloved Bride, and in the end, shedding every last drop of His blood for her. According to Saint Paul's magnificent passage in Ephesians 5 it is the husband's task to love his wife "As Christ loved the Church, and gave Himself up for her." (Ephesians 5:25) So it is the man's responsibility to face up to and accept whatever sacrifice comes in offering himself for his bride, as Jesus did. This begins long before marriage and is expressed in many ways outside of marriage, but it finds its usual and primary expression inside the covenant of marriage. I do not consider it only a husband/wife thing. Brothers live this responsibility to their sisters, as I have already argued in previous chapters, and that is how we ought to learn, but at some point most of us will move beyond that. We will single out one woman in particular, by God's grace, and determine to love her alone among all women and to be the image of Christ to her in a special way.

All of us should be single for a few years of manhood at least, I think. We should spend some time, whether long or short only God can say, focusing on our relationship with Him so that He can build us up into the Image of His Son. Until we are at least started on that path, we have nothing to offer a woman anyway. However, after a time there will come a point when that will change. We will have to take everything we have learned through those years, all the knowledge, skills, wisdom, character, and love, and all our material possessions, basically our whole lives, our whole selves, everything, and we will have to lay it all on the line for a woman. Remember though that ultimately we are laying it all at God's feet, placing it all in His hands. He may ask for a sacrifice, but He will never let it be wasted. This does not make it easier. It only makes it possible. We will have to offer ourselves to her, to accept or decline just as she pleases, knowing that she is completely free to do either. It's as if God says, "You have done well. You have turned your one talent into ten talents. Now take those ten talents that you have earned, and lay them all at her feet. Let her do as I lead her." And that's it. We work so hard to build this strength, only to be told that it isn't ours but is to be sacrificed for someone else, who may not even accept it. Do you begin to understand how rough manhood can be sometimes?

It is in this freely chosen vulnerability that we are called to an ever deeper imitation of Christ. Meditate on that for a few years and see what you come up with.

People will ask, "How do you know she's the right one? How do you know when to pursue her? How do you know what to say? How do you know what to ask?" Well, I'll tell you.

I don't know.

I have not yet entered that stage of the game. I am looking out on it and trying to pick out some landmarks, trying to go over the tools I've picked up in my previous years up until now. I don't have a plan. I am relying on the work God has done to form my character. He has taught me to trust Him, and He will teach me more deeply from now on. This is my only plan: to trust.

I can't tell you when you're ready. I can't tell you what to say. I can only tell you what I know, and that is:

1) God will lead you, if you ask Him.
2) Pain will be involved.
3) It is never wrong to love.

I have spoken before of God's leading, but this kind of leading is a little different. This is not a question of you kneeling in prayer, weighing the paths, judging your motives and making your choice. This decision is not yours alone. You are moving from the place where all decisions are made by you, on your own initiative, to the place where all decisions are made with someone else. In fact, you are not discerning God's will for yourself alone anymore. The two of you together are discerning God's will for two people, whether or not it is His Will that you marry. You cannot discern anything for her. She must do that on her own. You could say that when God leads a man to pursue a woman He gives him a question. He gives the answer to the woman. Only by working together, and listening to Him, can the two discern His will.

Sometimes the question may be one that the woman doesn't want to hear. Sometimes the answer may be one that the man doesn't want to hear. This is one way in which pain can be involved. God can lead you to ask a question to which the answer is "no," or to put it another way, just because He leads you to pursue a woman doesn't guarantee He will lead her to respond as you would like. Even if He does so lead her in time, before He does there can be days, weeks, months, and even years of misunderstanding, distance, uncertainty and loneliness. There are no guarantees in love, other than that God's will is perfect. Sometimes, however, it is not the same as ours, and then our will must be given up. This is one kind of pain. Other kinds of pain can come from the simple fact of loving. When you love, whatever hurts the one you love hurts you as well, so in seeking to unite with a woman for the rest of your life, you are accepting a share in her pains as well as her joys. At yet another level, whoever you love is a fallen human being, and whenever you are reminded of that, there is also pain, just as you will cause her pain because you are a fallen human being.

Why am I emphasizing the pain so much? It is not because I think that pain is the point of love. Joy is the point of love, pain is only the test. However, if you ask Jesus to teach you to love as He loved, (and if you haven't, then you aren't ready to be in love yet) He will do so. You will love with great joy and freedom, you will love from your heart, and in the last, you will love in Heaven with the Love of God Himself. But first there is Gethsemane and Golgotha. There is no Easter Sunday without Good Friday. There is no resurrection without crucifixion. This is very serious. I want you to know what you are asking for when you ask God to allow you to marry. You are asking for the right to give yourself up for your bride, as Jesus did. You are asking for His Will to be done. You are surrendering to Him and letting Him work His will in you. When you ask, "Father, may I court this woman?" you are standing at the foot of the cross. You are looking up at the man who hangs there naked and tortured, pouring out his last drop of blood for His Church, and you are asking, "Father, may I join Him on that cross?" Do not ask this lightly! I promise you, God will grant that request. There will be crucifixion, and there will be resurrection, Praised be He!

This leads me to an idea that I am not entirely sure of. It is very new to me, but there is a beauty about it that leads me to put it forth. It started when I began to question what I had said in previous chapters, that no one has to learn how to fall in love because it happens by itself. I still think that is true to some extent, so I'll let it stand. However, a new idea is growing in my mind. Maybe we fall in love by accident, but I wonder if, in all honesty, we really do naturally know how to be in love. What if we don't? Obviously we fall in love, and that does happen to us without our help or even consent sometimes, but on the other hand I've known many older men who are more in love with their wives now than they were when they married ten, or twenty, or fifty years ago. We younger men would do well to listen to the older men, and their testimony indicates to me that, although the beginning of being in love might be something we don't have to learn, the depths and heights of it take time and experience and maturity. Really to be in love might take more practice than I thought at first. In-love-ness ages, like wine, slowly over time. It is an art, only perfected after decades of practice. So in that sense, I guess we do have to learn how to be in love.

Once I started thinking about this, I began to think about how in-love-ness relates to the love that Jesus has for my future wife. Without facing up to the truth that Jesus loves her more than I ever will, I doubt if I could ever truly love her at all. I say I would live for her, but He already has. I say I would die for her, but He already has. I pray for her, but He has prayed and sweat blood, and given Himself, Body, Blood, Soul and Divinity for her. Try as I may, I will never be in love with her like He is, never desire her with the intensity that He does, nor seek her good as fervently. My love, no matter how strong it becomes, can never be anything but a pale shadow of His Love, a shallow, unsatisfying substitute. Unless...

Unless He gives me His love to give to her.

What if my love could be His love? What if I were surrendered so completely to Him that He could give me as a gift, when, how and to whom He pleased? What if my love was nothing but His love passing through me? Then, instead of competing with His eternal love, and feeling sorry for myself because I am not God, I could take my right place. I could let Him join me into His love, and be one of His gifts, be His love.

I wonder if all the things I ask for in prayer, all the good things, anyway, are not really just His way of leading me to join in and desire what He desires?

So pain might have a purpose that I had never thought of before. Every man knows, in his heart, that what comes easily is not as precious as what must be sacrificed for. We all laughed when we got out of basic training, and they gave us speeches about how we were members of a "brother-and-sister-hood" (forsooth!) that stretched back two-hundred years, blah, blah, blah. We didn't care. Basic wasn't all fun and games, but it was not too incredibly difficult either. The drill sergeants made sure we passed. All you had to do was not be incredibly stupid and not give up. Even if you did give up, they wouldn't let you go until you made yourself more trouble than it was worth to keep you. They weren't trying to weed us out, they were trying to assembly line us through, hoping that somehow we would pick up some good habits and a little discipline along the way. That is what political correctness did to basic training, and so we laughed when we graduated.

No one laughed when we came out of Selection. Each of us had stood there on the first day, one of a large crowd of soldier-athletes, tough, strong, focused, and all in the best shape of our lives, and let me tell you, overall it was a pretty studly group of guys. On the last day only a fraction of us remained, and we hobbled, moaned and stooped like old men from joint and back injuries, blisters, stress fractures, ketosis and sheer physical and mental exhaustion, but we were proud. Every one of us, once we finally had that Selection Memorandum in hand, felt like a conqueror. That victory cost something and so it was worth something. Not one of us will ever forget it.

So a romance that requires no sacrifice, no "sincere gift of self,"[20] is worthless compared to the love that has cost everything, and the cost begins the moment we begin to desire it. In this world the sacrificing must begin long before you ever meet the woman who will one day be your wife. The pain and loneliness now is part of the joy and intimacy then. God might well be saying to us, "You think you desire to love, but you know nothing. You want union and intimacy? You are a child. You don't know the first thing about union or intimacy. I want you to, though. I want you to know and desire as fervently as I do, and I will teach you. I will teach you to desire as I desire, if you only let me." God cares more about the strength of our romantic loves than we do.

Be careful, though, because we are not offering ourselves up on the altar of romantic love. That is idolatry. We are offering ourselves up at the foot of the cross and asking God to let us share in His saving love. Whether that sharing involves a wife or not is up to Him. If we want to love as Jesus loves, and I believe with all my heart He will teach us how if we ask Him, then we have to know what it is to give everything as He did. He is in love with His Church, and when we ask for the privilege of being a husband and father we are asking to imitate that love. We are asking Him to teach us the Love that was made manifest from Cana to Calvary. Therefore we surrender everything, every attraction, every wish, hope, dream and desire to Him. They are material for sacrifice, seeds to be sown, clay in the Potter's nail-scarred hands. May He shape us into the image of those Holy Wounds.

For this reason I say that it is never wrong to love. It is not wrong to want to bless a woman, to pray for her, to intercede for her. This is what Jesus does. He loves. He gives Himself freely and unstintingly, whether anyone returns that love or not. If and when God leads you to pursue a woman's heart, pray for Him to teach you, not only how to love her with the love of charity, but also how to be in love with her, purely, passionately, generously and constantly. He will teach you.

With this prayer you begin to leave singlehood and step out into courtship. I don't have much to say about courtship, mostly because I have never courted anyone. My only thought is that courtship must necessarily involve two parts, one of which will eventually become obsolete, while the other will be part of your life as long as you are married.

The first part is the mutual discernment of God's will as to whether or not you two ought to marry. Once you have received God's go ahead to pursue her, the decision ceases to be entirely your own and becomes one that you must work out together. The closer you get to marriage, the more mutual the decision will have to be. Of course, mutual discernment of God's will must become an integral part of your marriage, but at some point it will be made clear whether or not you are to marry and then this phase of courtship will be over. Actually, it technically ends on your wedding day. At that point the covenant is sealed and the relationship is established before God. There is no more question in that regard. His Will for you is quite simple, that you image the relationship between Him and the Church for the rest of your lives together, and all your mutual seeking of His will from that point on (jobs, children, parenting etc.) are within the framework of knowing that it is His will that you be married. Of course even though the question is still open right up until the moment the vows are spoken, most couples will be quite sure of His will long before that. The discernment of a vocation to marriage cannot last forever which leads me to the second part of courtship.

The second part continues on past the wedding and the honeymoon, past the children and the work years, past old age and the shadow of death. This part continues on as long as the marriage continues on. This is the constant pursuit of your wife's heart. It begins, well, I don't know when. At some point, God will lead you. He will let you know you have His permission to pursue her and that your decision is made. This decision, I suppose, could be expressed by saying, "As God wills, I will marry her, if she will have me." At that point it then becomes your task to convince her to have you, by wooing her heart and love. She may not agree. That is a distinct possibility. As I said, He gives you the question and He gives her the answer. There is no guarantee the answer will be yes, and so the question has to be asked in a way that takes that into account. The wooing must be at her pace, not yours, each successive stage requesting her permission and approval, and waiting patiently for as long as it takes before moving on. You must also bear in mind the fidelity you owe your future wife, and not give away that which belongs to her to someone who has not committed to going the whole way with you. This would do dishonor to you, to your girlfriend, to her future husband, and to your future wife.

No doubt about it, from where I sit now, it looks like a tangled mess, the very devil of a question. As I said, I have never done this, merely thought about it a lot. I'm very likely over thinking it. It is possible this whole last paragraph is just me blowing smoke in your ears. It is the best I can do for now, and so here I stop.

God will teach us, if we will learn.

"Show me your ways, O LORD, teach me your paths; Guide me in your truth and teach me, for you are God my Savior, and my hope is in you all the day long." Psalm 25:4-5

39. For the Sake of the Kingdom

This chapter may not make much sense to non-Catholics, since, to my understanding, there is not a widely recognized role for consecrated virginity outside of the Catholic tradition, but I still encourage you to read it if you are not Catholic, because this is the chapter about fatherhood. I speak about fatherhood and celibacy together because that helps me to understand both better. If you miss the true meaning of the call to fatherhood, you will forever miss what it means to be a man.

It first became clear to me about a year ago when I was praying. I have often prayed that God would someday allow me to be a father, without ever questioning why I was asking that. It just seemed like a natural thing to want. I have always liked kids, so much so that I regard dislike of children (in either men or women) as a serious indication of severe personality flaws. I like teaching kids, I like playing with them, I like reading to them and goofing around with them. All of that is pretty self-explanatory. Every guy I knew growing up was the same way. In fact it wasn't until I joined the army that I met guys who were not that thrilled about hanging out with kids.

However, because it was something I took for granted all my life, I never questioned why I should desire all this and it didn't open up to me until that time about a year ago, when I was praying about my vocation and I mentioned to God that I would like to be a father someday. And as I prayed it, the words came out of my mouth, "Because I want to be like you." I said it in exactly the same way I used to tell my dad, "I want to be a hardworking man when I grow up because I want to be just like you." (Yes, I really did say that when I was little. I didn't say farmer, I said "hardworking man". Then one day my mother told me, when I didn't want to do some chore, that being a hardworking man started with doing my chores and helping her. I never wanted to be a "hardworking man" again for the next ten years or so). It was precisely the same way when I prayed this. All at once I realized I had said something profound, quite by accident. Or, more accurately, God had shown me something profound, why I, or any man, would want to be a father. We desire to be like Him. We quite literally want to play God.

The more I think about it, the more I think this is colossal. We have been told to call God Father, but not, I think, because His Fatherhood is anything like ours. Rather we call our earthly fathers "father" because their fatherhood is a shadowy reflection of the true Fatherhood of God. To think the wrong way around has disastrous consequences, for it makes God a reflection of us. Essentially, He then becomes anything we want Him to be. If you grow up with a horrible, abusive, violent, or neglectful father, God becomes a tyrant or an absentee dad. But this is not so. The earthly father is so horrible precisely because he denied the reality of the Fatherhood of God, which he was called to image. Not that he fell short of it. Everyone falls short. The greatest father in the world has his flaws, makes his mistakes and commits his sins, but God is there to take up the slack. An evil father goes beyond falling short and actively denies and blasphemes the gift. It is not just cruelty or negligence, it is sacrilege. He is spitting on the image of God.

But that is not how it should be. The image of God is stamped into the very nature of man and of men. John Paul II said that Ephesians 5 could be seen as the centerpiece of the entire plan of salvation, and the more I think about, the more I think he was right, as usual. We men are meant to be symbols of Christ, to image God Himself by our lives, to give ourselves as Christ loved the Church and gave Himself for her. We are meant to give life, as God gave life to us. We are meant to give our strength, as God gives us His strength. In fact we could go so far as to say that we are meant to be channels through which God's strength passes to others. When a man gives life to a child in the womb of his wife he is giving God's life! And there are men who don't want to share this gift! We are meant to build others up, wisely and lovingly, as God builds us up. We are meant to raise children as God raises us.

On the one hand it is a calling so great, and a responsibility so terrible, that no man could dare to enter into it uninvited. On the other hand, the invitation is greater still, and we dare not refuse it. It is why I haven't got a lot of patience with fathers who think of fatherhood as just another thing they do, mashed in together with their jobs, hobbies and friendships. Fatherhood is not what we do, it is who we are when we are remade into the image of God.

This sheds light on the vocation of men in general, apart from the particular vocation of biological fatherhood. Whether or not fathering children physically is ever part of God's plan for any particular man is of less importance than this truth. It is in fatherhood, in giving of ourselves to bring life, to support life and to protect life, that we fulfill our vocation, of which biological fatherhood is the most common, natural and accessible symbol. Immediately the practice of calling priests "Father" comes to mind, as does Jesus' statement about those who made themselves eunuchs for the sake of the Kingdom, (Matthew 19:12). Saint Paul's numerous references to his spiritual children, (especially Titus and Timothy) but most especially Isaiah 54:1-5 indicate that biological fatherhood, far from being the end of our vocation to image God is only the beginning and a symbol of a reality which must then be lived.

This is why I say of my father that he was the image of God to me. It is also why I say the same of my parish priest who taught me when I was a child.

Bear in mind, when I speak of celibacy for the kingdom, I am not talking exclusively about the sacramental priesthood of the Catholic Church, but rather about Jesus' words in Matthew 19:12: "For there are eunuchs who have been so from birth, and there are eunuchs who have been made so by men, and there are eunuchs who have made themselves eunuchs for the sake of the Kingdom of heaven. He who is able to receive this, let him receive it."

Compare this to Paul's famous (or as some would say, infamous) passages concerning marriage and celibacy. Read 1 Corinthians 7 in its entirety sometime, and Paul's opinion of marriage will be made abundantly clear. It will be clear, I say, if you read the whole thing, and not just pick and choose. One verse, taken out of context can give the wrong impression. For instance "Now to the unmarried and the widows I say: It is good for them to stay unmarried, as I am. But if they cannot control themselves, they should marry, for it is better to marry than to burn with passion." 1 Corinthians 7:8-9.

If you read that by itself, it sounds like Paul is basically saying that marriage is for the weaklings who can't hack it on their own. It almost sounds as if he is saying the only reason for marriage is so that you can have sex and you won't be tempted to fornication. Yeah, you're one of those weaklings who can't control their sex drives, so you may as well get married.

195

This is not what he is saying. One need only read Ephesians 5:21-33 to understand that Paul's vision of marriage was deep, loving, Christ-centered and supernaturally beautiful. In fact, you can get some perspective if you just take the time to read 1 Corinthians 7:7: "I wish that all men were as I am. But each man has his own gift from God; one has this gift, another has that."

Paul makes no secret that celibacy for the Kingdom is the higher calling, but he does not denigrate marriage thereby, nor does he reduce it to a mere concession to human weakness. Marriage is the original calling, the original sacrament. It is the most basic calling of all humans, as it was in the beginning, and it was this calling, this union of men and women in the flesh that God blessed, saying "Be fruitful and multiply." God's plan did not change, marriage and sexuality did not suddenly become bad after the fall. That is never God's way. What He creates good stays good. When we do evil with His creation, He does not take that creation away, He redeems it. He makes possible something better.

You can see this pattern throughout salvation history. We took food and wine and made them idols, through gluttony and drunkenness. God took those idols and made them sacraments, first through the Passover and then definitively in the Eucharist. God gave us life. We brought death. God gave us resurrection. We were God's creatures. We rebelled and became His enemies. He sent His only begotten Son, that we might be adopted as His Children. There is no gift that we can spoil that He cannot redeem. He doesn't simply take things back to the way they were; He takes them to a whole new level.

So it was with sex and marriage. God created marriage, and we brought in divorce, prostitution, sterility, adultery, contraception and a host of other perversions. God did not simply take marriage back to its original state of innocence. Instead He redeemed it, first by revealing it as the definitive symbol of His union with the Church, and secondly by creating a new way in which the deep inner meaning of sexuality could be revealed, which we call celibacy for the Kingdom.

Sterility, throughout the Old Testament, was always identified as a reproach, a curse, a punishment, and in short, a result of Original Sin. Infertility is one of the tragic consequences of sin, whether through the decay of the human body in congenital defects or through the action of sinful men. Nowadays sterility is a commodity, so far have we fallen from God's vision for us. Whether as a result of deliberate actions, or as a result of harmful practices (i.e. pollution, drugs, environmental causes etc.) we human beings are rendering ourselves sterile all the time. Jesus addresses this in His statement, saying that some eunuchs are born that way and some are made so by men. In His day, male slaves were often castrated, especially those given charge over the king's harem (see Esther 2:15). This was done for all the same reasons one castrates a horse or an ox, so that they have less testosterone and hence are easier to work with. Jesus acknowledges both of these evils, but then places before the eyes of His apostles the redemption of them. He makes possible another route, that of those who "make themselves eunuchs" for the sake of the Kingdom. It is this that St. Paul argues so strongly for, presenting it to a culture that automatically assumed that if you were not married and having kids, there must be something wrong with you. This has broad applications to our culture, with its constant insistence that if you are not "in a relationship" or at least sleeping with as many women as you can, there must be something wrong with you, but I'll leave you to think that one through on your own.

In giving us this gift, Jesus fulfilled a prophecy:

"Let no foreigner who has bound himself to the Lord say, 'The Lord will surely exclude me from his people.' And let not any eunuch complain, 'I am only a dry tree.' For this is what the Lord says: 'To the eunuchs who keep my Sabbaths, who choose what pleases me and hold fast to my covenant- to them I will give within my temple and its walls a memorial and a name better than sons and daughters; I will give them an everlasting name that will not be cut off." Isaiah 56:4-5

God does not take away the evil of sterility. Instead He creates the possibility of something better. Because these men suffered so much in being denied fatherhood, they will be able to receive a gift greater than biological children. This is not a consolation prize. God is really electing them to a higher road, a better road, and giving them a greater gift than physical fatherhood. In this we should not hear an indictment against biological fatherhood. Rather, knowing how supernatural and precious is the gift of "natural" fatherhood we should be blown away that there could be something better! God created us as men with the ability to give life! We can cooperate with Him and with a woman to create a new human being, an immortal soul! What could be more glorious than that? And yet, God has promised that there is something more glorious. Incredible! Not only does He give this great gift to some, who have been denied the gift of fatherhood through the tragedy of Original Sin, He actually allows men to choose this gift for themselves. "Some make themselves eunuchs for the sake of the kingdom. Let those who are able to receive this receive it."

I am not going to lie to you. The idea of renouncing marriage and family is not attractive to me at all. It never has been, and yet, the possibility that God might call me to it has been present in my mind since I was seventeen. Reluctance, by itself, is no argument against. There is good precedent for reluctance being almost a prerequisite. Nearly all the prophets were reluctant. Very few who are called to the higher, harder road are thrilled about it from the start, but it is not within the scope of this chapter, or my ability, to tell anyone how to discern the answer to a question I have no certainty of myself.

Fatherhood, however, concerns us very closely. I said before that if we miss the calling of fatherhood, we miss the calling of manhood, and this is true, no matter how young you are or how uncertain is your vocation. In my family, all of us boys were taught to be fatherly as soon as we were not the youngest anymore. In a large family, that's the only way to get by. The older ones have to take care of the younger ones. My brothers and I were taught to be fatherly when we were taught how to change diapers and make bottles for the foster babies, when we were enlisted to babysit or watch the younger kids while playing outside. Did we complain at the time? Sometimes. But we were being taught. I am not in the least concerned with learning particular skills. Anyone can learn to change a diaper in the time it takes to change a diaper. By the time you've changed four or five, you're an expert. It's not that complicated. Skills don't make a man a father.

No matter what your age, fatherhood is an inescapable part of your calling. The eighteen year old boy who answers the call to be a youth pastor is living out this vocation, as is the young man who arrives at karate class an hour early every day, just so he can help teach the younger kids. The ten year old boy reading to his eight year old sister is living this vocation.

Fatherhood is not in the particulars, but in the essence which is self-gift. Catholics call their priests "Father" because their vocation is to give of themselves, to create, provide for and protect the spiritual life of their children. Freud would (and probably did) say that this was a sublimation or translation of the sexual drive. These poor celibate men;

they've got so much repression going on they can't handle a normal sexual relationship, so they have to invent all these ideas about "spiritual fatherhood" to make themselves feel better.

Actually, that is precisely backwards. The truth is the Fatherhood is in the nature of God. It is translated into the spiritual reality of the masculine soul of a man, and it is that masculine soul that informs and determines the body that God creates for it. Physical fatherhood is an expression of spiritual fatherhood, not the other way around. If you think about it, it's obvious even from what we admire in our sick culture that spiritual fatherhood is the more important. If it were not so, we would not see anything wrong with a man simply siring offspring and leaving. As it is, we all know that as an evil. We condemn those losers very loudly and praise as heroes those men who are "father figures" to children not their own. Our words indicate that we know what is right. Our actions as a society proclaim that we really don't care.

So it is this fatherly meaning of the masculine person, both in his body and in his soul, that allows him to enter into this new and deeper redeemed reality of celibate fatherhood. Of course those who are called to physical fatherhood are not released from the responsibility to be spiritual fathers as well, but there are those who are called to renounce physical fatherhood in order to enter more deeply and completely into this spiritual fatherhood, and, we are solemnly promised, the joys and rewards are greater. So, also, are the crosses. It truly is a higher calling. A priest once told me that he had meditated on the story of Abraham sacrificing Isaac when deciding to embrace the call to the priesthood. As Abraham was told to sacrifice his son, and responded without knowing how the story was going to end, so those who have chosen celibacy for the sake of the Kingdom have, in a very real sense, sacrificed their children. They lay them on the altar, not knowing what God will do. It is a real sacrifice, a terrible act of trust, to take God seriously when He tells us that He will be enough. If we are not called to it, that is no reason for shame. It is enough for us to understand and to appreciate those who have been called, and who have heard that call, and who have responded with generous hearts.

It would probably take a whole book to explore this subject thoroughly. This chapter is not meant to provide any arguments for or against, if you are currently discerning. It contains none of the arguments I have wrestled with. It contains no answers. It contains only the promise of life. The choice between Godly marriage (the Image of Christ and the Church) and celibacy for the Kingdom (the Image of the Kingdom where "they neither marry nor are given in marriage but are like the angels") is not a choice between good and evil. It is a choice between birth and rebirth, life and resurrection, natural and supernatural goods. Yet those who choose the natural goods will share in the resurrection no less than those who have lived it in their surrender of their natural sexual desires. And those who have chosen the supernatural path? Will they be repaid? Will they also experience the natural joys of their married brethren when they receive their reward?

I don't know. Part of me is tempted to affirm "Yes." The other part thinks the question is probably somewhat irrelevant, or at least, it doesn't mean as much as I think it does. All I can do is accept Christ's words at face value: "And everyone who has left houses or brothers or sisters or father or mother or children or fields for my sake will receive a hundred times as much and will inherit eternal life." Matthew 19:29

"Give, and it will be given to you. A good measure, pressed down, shaken together and running over, will be poured into your lap. For with the measure you use, it will be measured to you." Luke 6:38

"However, as it is written: 'No eye has seen, no ear has heard, no mind has conceived what God has prepared for those who love him'" 1 Corinthians 2:9

God can be trusted. He will ask nothing from you, except to make room for what He wants to give you, and whatever He gives may well include that which He asked you to sacrifice, in some way you cannot see right now. Whatever His plan, He can be trusted.

That's this chapter in a nutshell. Whatever vocation God calls, He is going to ask everything from you. He is going to call you to a total gift of self. The calling of marriage is no less a gift than is the calling to celibacy for the Kingdom, and it is that self-gift that is the soul of fatherhood, and thus of manhood. The difference is that in marriage the gift is to God through another person, while in the case of celibacy for the kingdom, it is to God directly.

I don't know your calling. I don't even know mine with any kind of deep gut level certainty, though like you I have my hopes and fears, my dreams and desires. All I can do is urge you to surrender yours, and work to surrender my own. No matter where you are or what you are doing, give God everything. Let everything belong so completely to

Him that no matter what He calls you to do, you will be His gift, to be given away freely to whomever He pleases, however He pleases.

Thus we grow up into the full stature of our calling into fatherhood, the very image of God.

"Sing, O barren woman,
you who never bore a child;
burst into song, shout for joy,
you who were never in labor;
because more are the children of the desolate woman
than of her who has a husband," says the Lord.

"Enlarge the place of your tent,
stretch your tent curtains wide,
do not hold back;
lengthen your cords,
strengthen your stakes.
For you will spread out to the right and to the left;
your descendants will dispossess nations
and settle in their desolate cities.

"Do not be afraid; you will not suffer shame.
Do not fear disgrace; you will not be humiliated.
You will forget the shame of your youth
and remember no more the reproach of your widowhood.
For your Maker is your husband—
the Lord Almighty is his name—
the Holy One of Israel is your Redeemer;
he is called the God of all the earth." Isaiah 54:1-5

40. Out from Sinai

It seems the more I pursue the question, the further I am from an answer. What does it mean to be a man?

Not that I am farther from the answer in actual fact. I just have a better idea of how far I have been all along. It's something like running up cannon hill outside Fort Riley. From the bottom you look up and see the gun at the top of the hill, and it looks so close you could throw a rock up there and hit it, but when you start running up the slope you find that it was a lot further than it looked, and it's going to take a lot longer than you thought. This book is exactly like that. Years ago I began thinking about what I had to do to be the man that God wanted me to be, and the more I think of it, the more I realize how far I fall short. This realization is only a good thing, however. Unless I am taught by God how far I fall short, I can never ask Him to lift me up, which is what must happen if I am ever to do what He has in store for me, or become that which He has created me to be.

Of course it is quite fair to ask why I am writing about it if I haven't gotten there yet. There are two answers to that. First, writing is how I sort out my thoughts. It helps me collect them and organize them and see how each one fits in with all the rest. Writing about things is the second best way I know of learning them. The best way of learning is by doing.

Secondly, I know that I never will arrive there in this life. Never will I ever reach a point in my life on earth when I can look at myself and say, "I am the perfect man." If I have to be perfect before I have anything useful to say, then I shall never have anything useful to say. This is why all men who wish to pursue manhood ought to read the Bible, by the way. That is the only place you will find the words, life and person of a Man who actually was perfect.

The essays in this book are not the answers. They are the questions. They are the first immature forms of lessons I will never complete in this world, but which may be of use to others starting out on the same lesson. They are the lecture notes of someone who has attended a similar class to the one you are attending. This book is just comparing notes.

To be honest, though, I do like to think it might have another purpose, not so much to teach, for who am I to teach, after all? But I can encourage. I admit, what I believe about manhood is a far cry from what I practice, but I am still practicing in the hope that I will master it someday. Not many of us are left who still keep practicing, no matter how many times we fail. Most of us have been conditioned by society to try something a few times, whether it be a sport, a subject in school or a job, and if we don't take to it right away like the proverbial duck to water, we are expected to quit. No one expects men to make great efforts any more, and everyone is ready to laugh at great failures. It can be discouraging when you are the only one who believes in something better than video games, booze and hot chicks. Even just one more guy who shares that belief would make a huge difference, would make all the difference, for "Two are better than one; because they have a good reward for their labor. For if they fall, the one will lift up his fellow; but woe to him that is alone when he falleth; for he hath not another to help him up." Ecclesiastes 4:9-10 But we are few and far between. If you are fighting alone, rather than be discouraged, look upon it as your testing in the desert. God tested Moses in the wilderness for forty years before He sent Him back to Egypt on His mission. The greater the desert, the greater the promised land. God sends us solitude to drive us to rely on Him alone, so that later others may rely on us, and we will not fail them.

You are never alone, brothers. We few, we band of brothers willing to stand up and be men, to try and fail and be laughed at for trying, and laughed at even harder for failing, and then pitied when we pick ourselves up to try again, we are truly brothers. And we are never alone, for Our Father is always with us, and Our Brother, Jesus Christ, has walked this road first. With such support, why should we shrink back? We can dare to be heroes. We can even dare to be men.

"Not that I have already obtained this or am already perfect; but I press on to make it my own, because Christ Jesus has made me His own. Brethren, I do not consider that I have made it my own, but one thing I do, forgetting what lies behind and straining forward to what lies ahead, I press on toward the goal for the prize of the upward calling of God in Christ Jesus. Let those of us who are mature be thus minded." Philippians 3:12-15

(p.12) [1] I highly recommend Christopher West's series of lectures entitled "Naked without Shame" available from The Gift Foundation, and his book "Theology of the Body for Beginners."

(p.15) [2] Quoted in Pavel Tsatsouline's book "Enter the Kettlebell" available from Dragon Door Publications Inc.

(p.18) [3] "The Church 'forcefully and specifically exhorts all the Christian faithful...to learn the surpassing knowledge of Jesus Christ, by frequent reading of the divine Scriptures. Ignorance of the Scriptures is ignorance of Christ.'" Catechism of the Catholic Church #133.

(p.30) [4] C.S. Lewis "*The Necessity of Chivalry*" published in his essay collection "*Present Concerns*".

(p.39) [5] http://uscg.mil/leadership/comp.asp under "Stewardship."
[6] The Saint Crispin's Day speech from Shakespeare's "*Henry V*". Seriously if you have never read that play, you need to square that deficiency away immediately. The Saint Crispin's day speech is one of the greatest treasures of the English language.

(p.41) [7] See Paul Cartledge, "*Thermopylae*", a historical account of one of the most important battles in history. I also highly recommend Steven Pressfield's "*Gates of Fire*" a highly researched and superbly crafted historical novel of the same battle.

(p.55) [8] For further reading on the origins and evolution of the concept of Chivalry I refer you to Brad Miner's "*The Compleat Gentleman: The Modern Man's Guide to Chivalry*."

(p.110) [9] C. S. Lewis, *The Last Battle*.

(p.116) [10] I usually let verses speak for themselves, but since this verse is so often misinterpreted, let me point a few things out. In this verse, Peter takes women from their previous status as property or subjects, and shows that they have the dignity of being fellow Children of God in their own right. Based on this he points out that the gift of superior strength is not meant to be a tool of domination, but rather a means of service. (p.120) [11] That's more or less the Theology of the Body in a nutshell. For a short, easy to read overview of TOB, see Jason Evert's "Theology of His Body/Theology of Her Body."

(p.147) [12] Mother Teresa, *"No Greater Love."*

(p.167) [13] If you don't know who Puddleglum is, you had better read C. S. Lewis's "The Chronicles of Narnia" at the earliest possible opportunity. Do not watch the movies. Read the books first.

(p.172) [14] See *A Severe Mercy*, by Sheldon Vanauken, one of the greatest (true) love stories ever written. Vanauken and his wife defined courtesy as a 'cup of water in the night' in one of the greatest explanations of courtesy I have ever read, in chapter two. I highly recommend the book to everyone.

(p.180) [15] These sermons collectively make up the foundation for Theology of the Body, and the current updated and definitive version of them is called, "Man and Woman He Created Them: A Theology of the Body", translated and with an introduction by Michael Waldstein. This volume is available from Pauline Books and Media.

(p.181) [16] John Paul II's "Man and Woman He Created Them: A Theology of the Body." 6:2.

(p.184) [17] Check out Steve Mosher's intro to the truth about the much hyped myth of Population Explosion at http://pop.org/20090122808/white-pestilence.

(p.188) [18] John Paul II's *"Man and Woman He Created Them: A theology of the Body."* 118:6

(p.188) [19] John Paul II, *"Man and Woman He Created Them: A theology of the Body."* 6:2

(p.196) [20] "Man is the only creature on earth which God willed for itself, [and he] cannot fully find himself except through a sincere gift of himself." (From the Vatican II document *Gaudium* et Spes 24)

My Dearest Sisters
Thoughts about modesty from your brother

By Ryan Kraeger

If you look around at the fashions in vogue today, it seems there is no such thing as modesty anymore. The secular world treats women as objects ... promoting styles of clothing that are increasingly revealing and demeaning. Segments of the Christian world, on the other hand, over-react, insisting on floor length skirts and knee high stockings as the minimum acceptable standard. Young girls and women are often caught in the middle, left feeling that either there is something wrong with their bodies, or all men are just hopelessly depraved ... and that it is all somehow their fault. In response, Ryan Kraeger, a young Catholic soldier, wrote this short book for his own sister and cousins, offering them his thoughts on this touchy subject. Drawing from his own experience as a man constantly struggling to remain pure in an impure world, and presenting insights from John Paul II's inspiring Theology of the Body, Ryan goes beyond the issues of clothing styles to the dignity of the person wearing them. In this book you will find an honest, straightforward, and loving account of what one young man values in a truly modest woman. It is a vision that has changed his life, and will be sure to give encouragement and hope to all women who know ... or want to know ... the true value of modesty.

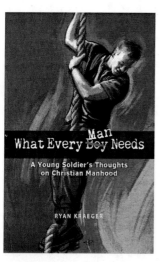

What Every Man Needs
A Young Soldier's Thoughts on Christian Manhood

By Ryan Kraeger

In our society manhood is under attack. Complex forces conspire to break down our idea of what it means to be a man. Men are the butt of jokes in sitcoms, movies, and commercials. The media present contradictory and unflattering images of men as self-centered jerks or witless wonders who simply can't make it in life without someone (usually a woman) to do their thinking for them. Manhood itself is treated as a joke, or ignored as something nonexistent. Boys growing up today too often do so in a vacuum of meaning, without a positive, clear, and convincing model of manhood.

In response, Ryan Kraeger offers the modern reader a thoughtful, challenging concept of manhood. Seen through the lens of his experiences in the testosterone charged world of the Army's combat arms, and balanced against his early faith formation and continuing study, he presents insightful musings about the pressing question of our generation: What does it mean to be a man?

Men of all ages will be challenged and encouraged by this unique look into one young soldier's inner journey ... into manhood.